GLOBAL NOMADS AND EXTREME MOBILITIES

Päivi Kannisto has written a cutting-edge book on modern mobilities. She sheds new light on the nature of the mobile risk society and what dwelling in mobility seriously means. This is a highly innovative book. It is well crafted, thought-provoking, and a pleasure for all those interested in mobility, modernity, and social change.

Sven Kesselring, Nürtingen-Geislingen University, Germany

T0270757

Studies in Migration and Diaspora

Series Editor:
Anne J. Kershen, Queen Mary University of London, UK

Studies in Migration and Diaspora is a series designed to showcase the interdisciplinary and multidisciplinary nature of research in this important field. Volumes in the series cover local, national and global issues and engage with both historical and contemporary events. The books will appeal to scholars, students and all those engaged in the study of migration and diaspora. Amongst the topics covered are minority ethnic relations, transnational movements and the cultural, social and political implications of moving from 'over there', to 'over here'.

Also in the series:

London the Promised Land Revisited
The Changing Face of the London Migrant Landscape in the Early 21st Century
Edited by Anne J. Kershen
ISBN 978-1-4724-4727-2

Migration Across Boundaries
Linking Research to Practice and Experience
Edited by Parvati Nair and Tendayi Bloom
ISBN 978-1-4724-4049-5

Human Exhibitions
Race, Gender and Sexuality in Ethnic Displays
Rikke Andreassen
ISBN 978-1-4724-2245-3

The Somatechnics of Whiteness and Race
Colonialism and Mestiza *Privilege*
Elaine Marie Carbonell Laforteza
ISBN 978-1-4724-5307-5

Secularism and Identity
Non-Islamiosity in the Iranian Diaspora
Reza Gholami
ISBN 978-1-4724-3010-6

Global Nomads and Extreme Mobilities

PÄIVI KANNISTO
Tilburg University, the Netherlands

LONDON AND NEW YORK

First published 2016 by Ashgate Publishing

2 Park Square, Milton Park, Abingdon, Oxfordshire OX14 4RN
52 Vanderbilt Avenue, New York, NY 10017

Routledge is an imprint of the Taylor & Francis Group, an informa business

First issued in paperback 2019

British Library Cataloguing in Publication Data
A catalogue record for this book is available from the British Library.

The Library of Congress has cataloged the printed edition as follows:
Names: Kannisto, Päivi, author.
Title: Global nomads and extreme mobilities / by Päivi Kannisto.
Description: Surrey, UK, England; Burlington, VT: Ashgate, [2016] | Series:
   Studies in migration and diaspora | Includes bibliographical references
   and index.
Identifiers: LCCN 2015028320| ISBN 9781472454997 (hardback: alk. paper) |
Subjects: LCSH: Nomads. | Stateless persons. | Statelessness.
Classification: LCC GN387 .K36 2016 | DDC 305.9/06918–dc23 LC record available at
http://lccn.loc.gov/2015028320

ISBN: 978-1-4724-5499-7 (hbk)
ISBN: 978-0-367-24656-3 (pbk)

Contents

Preface

One morning in Kuala Lumpur, Malaysia, while my husband and I were having breakfast in a local restaurant, a Canadian man joined us at our table and told us his life story. He had been travelling for 28 years and made his living repairing Ferrari cars and doing other odd jobs a few weeks out of every year. At the time, he was working as a doorman in a local brothel with plans to leave for West Siberia to see a friend.

This chance meeting occurred just as we were at the beginning of pursuing a similar path. We had left our country of origin, Finland, in 2004 to go travelling. We knew nothing about the lifestyle we had chosen or of the existence of any other global nomads. We were intoxicated with the feeling that anything was possible and wholeheartedly enjoyed our newfound lifestyle, thinking that perhaps we were the only ones who had solved the riddle of finding freedom in the modern world.

Our brief encounter with the Canadian haunted me for half a decade: how had he come to choose his lifestyle and what made him keep going after 28 years? In 2010, I decided I would try to gather together the pieces of the puzzle. I began to search for other global nomads to participate in research on location-independence.

I soon discovered that there were no books about this lifestyle other than those that individual travellers had written about their own adventures. Existing academic literature, on the other hand, focussed on people who travelled for reasons other than lifestyle – economic migrants who travel for work; lifestyle migrants for milder climates, cheaper prices, and better quality of life; refugees and exiles for political asylum; ethnic minorities such as the Roma people and Irish travellers to follow their century-old traditions; tourists for leisure.

Based on my own experiences, global nomads were on the move for the sake of travel rather than for wealth or a livelihood. These individuals were motivated by immaterial rewards such as interesting experiences, simpler lives, and a sense of excitement. They seemed to continuously be on the search for something new, not necessarily wanting to settle down anywhere. They were 'people of many places but of no one place in particular', to borrow the words of sociologist Zygmunt Bauman (2005, p. 67).

I started to call them global nomads, conscious of the controversial nature of the concept. 'Nomadism' has been used in romanticising interpretations when highlighting freedom from places, norms, and values. These interpretations have raised criticism about the elite nature of wandering (e.g. Cresswell, 2006, p. 54; Sheller, 2011, p. 2). The most commonly known nomads are the pastoralists and warriors of third world nations, whose wandering is an ancient phenomenon having evolved during the Neolithic revolution when livestock economy began to develop and people settled down in villages. Ever since, nomads have intrigued the settled.

I suspected that the modern-day nomads would rather travel alone or in pairs than with livestock and family, and instead of in the wilderness, they would be found in urban areas where services such as accommodation, restaurants, supermarkets, and internet connectivity were available. Consequently, a seeming discrepancy between the old and new nomads became evident, which raised questions of inequality, life choices, and agency. At the same time, these seemed to be some of the crucial topics to be addressed. Nomadism for pastoralists was a part of tradition that was handed down from one generation to the next, but for global nomads it seemed to be a cherished choice, a statement which they used to detach themselves from some of the ideals in Western societies. Therefore, 'nomad' with its ambiguous connotations evoked interesting questions for research: Why did global nomads decide to leave their former lives? Why do their lifestyles so captivate and disturb the settled? Where are their support groups and networks? Are they in or outside of societies?

I had a feeling that the wanderings of global nomads would provide us with a revealing mirror of the contemporary society and its contradictions. Through their frequent border crossings, global nomads make visible the power negotiations regarding mobilities – movement of people, ideas, and things. Therefore, this book is not only about the curiosity of a couple of globetrotting wanderers but about more general trends in society. I hope that it opens up fresh horizons for understanding ourselves – both in terms of what is going on in the world and how mobilities transform us.

Päivi Kannisto

Acknowledgements

I am proud to acknowledge the help, encouragement, and influence of Erik Cohen, Bertine Bargeman, Cassie deFilippo, Kevin Hannam, Molly Herrington, Petri Hottola, Mari Korpela, P.J. Martin, Hans Mommaas, Greg Richards, René van der Duim, T. Rowan, and Allan Williams in various phases of my work from PhD thesis to this book. My heartfelt thanks to all the global nomads who participated in the research, and my husband, Santeri.

Series Editor's Preface

The *Shorter Oxford English Dictionary* defines a nomad as 'a person who leads a roaming or wandering life'. It categorises a migrant as a person who 'moves from one country or place to another to settle'. In the context of this book it is 'settle' which is the operative word. As the author of *Global Nomads and Extreme Mobilities* explains, for the protagonists in this volume it is the ability to travel when and where they wish, free from the restraints of a rooted and regimented existence that is dominated by the demands of money and conformity, that motivates their lifestyle – one which some might consider consists of 'just drifting around the globe'. Significantly, this twenty-first-century nomadism is not carried out in the traditional group or tribal manner. The global nomads that are the subjects of this book travel singly or, as in the case of the author, together with a partner.

The book is rich in primary source material and introduces the reader to an array of nomads of varying ages, both genders and from all parts of the globe. However, it is not without a theoretical base. Päivi Kannisto ensures that the volume is theoretically grounded and explores a range of theories that might accommodate this newly recognised form of migration. She places the lifestyle of global mobility up against that of the more traditional mobilities such as economic migration, (holiday) travel, family reunification, and escape from persecution, in order to measure where, and if, conventional theorising can accommodate her drifters, or alternatively, whether there is a need for a new approach to analysis and theory which relates more directly to global nomadism. Whilst so doing she asks her readers to confront the issues that face those seeking to individualise their lives in order to live away from the mainstream, and by so doing, in an unwritten subtext, questions whether this is really a viable choice for the long term.

This volume pulls no punches about the hardships and issues faced by global nomads. The eschewing of the everyday and mundane may seem romantic but there is another side to it, as a number of those interviewed by the author – either face to face or via the internet – reveal. Unlike their pastoral counterparts, global nomads rarely, if ever, travel with families or become integral members of a community. For some, even travelling with a partner can prove stressful. As sociologists Ulrich Beck and Elisabeth Beck-Gernsheim have noted, 'Each partner wants his or her freedom and at the same time to be chained in the hands of the beloved'. Thus, the global nomad faces a dilemma: whether to travel totally alone or with a partner. For, whilst being unchained can seem highly desirable, this has to be weighed against the loneliness and isolation of the life of the individual location-independent traveller. Another problematic for the wanderer is that of nationality – is this something to be cast aside or maintained, even whilst traversing the globe? And, even if the former is the option, in reality can the baggage of a home nation and culture be simply left behind, or is it forever an unwanted travelling companion? For, as the author illustrates in this book, the inured culture of home frequently creates cultural confusion for the traveller abroad. Finally, when considering the pros and cons of global nomadism, it must be recognised that at some point there will arise a need to return to a settled life. Whether the decision is prompted by desire or necessity, re-immersion re-introduces the wanderer to all he/she sought to leave behind. How this is accepted will doubtless depend on the experience of life as a global nomad.

In presenting this new aspect of the movement of people, the author asks her readers to cast aside preconceptions about those who seek to be twenty-first-century global nomads and evaluate what this means in the lives of the men and women to whom we are introduced. With the benefit of the book's theoretical foundation and a fascinating cast of players, we come to recognise that a wanderer's life is not quite as simple and unproblematic as they, and indeed, the reader, envisage. This volume opens our eyes to what it means to be an individual wandering alone in the modern world. It is a life which is at the same time fascinating and daunting, satisfying and confusing. For all those engaged in the study of the diverse manifestations of migrants and migration this book is a must read.

Anne J. Kershen
Queen Mary University of London
Summer 2015

Chapter 1

Escaping Societies

Have you ever wondered what perpetual travel would be like? How it would feel just wandering around and seeing the world without planning too far ahead, without a home, a permanent job, and the proximity of your friends and family? Would you enjoy the experience, or would you consider it a futile and unproductive waste of time, or long for the security of home? For the global nomads in this book, this is business as usual. They are homeless, or – depending on your point of view – at home wherever they happen to be. They have left their countries of origin behind and have no ties to any geographic place, therefore being location-independent. They may remain in their chosen destinations for some days, weeks, or months, but in the end they always move on, belonging nowhere in particular.

Global nomads live in the margins of societies. Like other migrants and multi-mobile people who reside and work in various places, they question the conventional divisions between home and abroad, settled and mobile, work and leisure. Many of them have given up a regular income and the associated work ethic based on the moral virtues of toil and diligence, instead searching for alternative ways of supporting themselves. They have neither health care nor private insurance but try to function without these support structures.

The tensions between global nomads and societies become evident in the definition of the 'nomad' I have chosen for this book, with a few critical reservations. The definition derives from cultural theorist Caren Kaplan (1996), who argues that '[a] nomad is a person who has the ability to track a path through a seemingly illogical space without succumbing to nation-state and/or bourgeois organisation and mastery' (p. 66. See also Braidotti, 1994, p. 24). While the definition has glamorising tendencies – as implied in the word 'ability' and the idea that nomads' bobbing and weaving is successful – I leave the outcome open until there is enough evidence.

It is also questionable whether global nomads' lives are as antithetical to societies' conventions as the definition suggests. Individualisation of cultures, the rise of diverse lifestyles, and increasing mobilities also shape and challenge contemporary societies. People value their independence and mastery of their own lives. Many aim to gain, for instance, a healthier work–life balance by doing part-time work and downshifting rather than tying themselves down to mortgages and long working hours. Some push themselves into entirely new fields, while others engage in alternative lifestyles or search for the meaning of life outside traditional career paths (e.g. Bauman, 2005; Greenblatt, 2002; Rosanvallon, 2008). As extreme representatives of these trends, global nomads offer an interesting alternative environment for research. Through them, we can sketch what life could be like if it were less tied to territorial, structural, and financial attachments, and identify the obstacles to a freer existence.

From Traditions to Choices

To date, location-independence remains under-explored while interest in lifestyle mobilities has increased. Lifestyle mobilities cover a wide array of voluntary relocation to places that promise an enhanced, or at least a different lifestyle (McIntyre, 2013). This can be achieved, for instance, through cheaper living costs, better weather, or a more relaxed lifestyle. Pensioners might move from the north to the south and working people might reject their former careers in order to build new lives in another country. Some people zigzag between two places aiming to take the best out of both, while others simply visit (see O'Reilly, 2003, pp. 301–2, 305, 2007). As a result, lifestyle mobilities may involve the ownership of multiple homes, feelings of belonging to several places, and sustained mobility throughout the life course (Cohen, Duncan, and Thulemark, 2013). These mobilities illustrate that people do not necessarily belong in one place only. Several places, or movement itself, shapes their lifestyles.

Lifestyle mobilities are examined in tourism, leisure, migration, and mobilities studies that have largely remained discrete areas of research (see Williams and Hall, 2000, p. 7). To date, little convergence has taken place, although boundaries between the groups are artificial and blurred. This also applies to location-independence. Global nomads share many features with the other groups, and therefore research on lifestyle mobilities offers valuable comparative material.

This book, however, approaches the subject with a slight change of emphasis. While previous studies tend to be predicated on travel, mobilities, cultures, practices, and identities through ethnographic, practice, or system approaches, I hope to make a contribution by bringing these discussions into a broader context. My focus is on the classic dilemma of the relationship between individuals and society, which draws attention to power issues. Mobilities, in the contemporary society, are one of the central vehicles of power through which social organisation, norms, values, and ideals are discussed.

In this introductory chapter, I examine the theoretical and societal contexts where lifestyle mobilities studies have arisen, and their implications for the study on global nomads. I begin by analysing the two components of the concept, 'lifestyle' and 'mobility', in order to build a framework for understanding location-independence. I approach 'lifestyle' through the theories of second modernity that address one of the key topics related to location-independence: the erosion of traditions and individualisation (e.g. Giddens, 1991; Beck and Grande, 2010; Beck and Beck-Gernsheim, 2002). The notion of 'mobility', on the other hand, is explored through the mobilities paradigm that investigates different movements, their meanings, and implications.

Lifestyles

'Lifestyle', in contemporary societies, is often thought of superficially in terms of brands, products and marketing only (see Giddens, 1991, p. 81). However, the concept draws from more nuanced sources. It figured already in Max Weber's *Economy and Society* (1978), where Weber spoke of status groups that are based on honour and a distinctive 'style of life' (pp. 305–7). Social status, Weber suggested, was not reducible to economic and material resources only, as Marxist theories had proposed, but depended also on education and occupation. These involved agency and will, which are of particular interest for this study. Global nomads have broken with some of the traditions and norms of their respective societies, and so their acts need to be considered as individual lifestyle choices rather than simple derivatives of class or other signs of socio-economic status.

Weber's ideas were revived in the 1980s (Veal, 2001, p. 360), and since then, lifestyles have been discussed in a diverse set of literature. The notion has gained several meanings. In sociological research, it has been used to replace 'class' (e.g. Beck, Bonß, and Lau, 2003; Dunn, 2008, p. 14. See also Atkinson, 2007, 2010a), while leisure studies has associated it with subcultures (e.g. Veal, 2001, pp. 367–8). The most important strands of this wide-ranging literature, from the perspective of this book, are the theories of second modernity by sociologists Anthony Giddens, Ulrich Beck, Scott Lash, and Zygmunt Bauman. Their discussions on agency, freedom, and choice directly relate to global nomads' existence.

Giddens (1991), who has most thoroughly theorised lifestyles among second modernists, argues that they have become more important because of the erosion of traditions. As our lives are no longer decidedly structured in advance by social hierarchies and traditional authorities, we need to choose between various lifestyles. In this context everything has become a matter of options and choices, including habits of dressing and eating – and travelling, as lifestyle mobilities suggest. These practices do not necessarily fulfil utilitarian needs. They sustain a feeling of ontological security by creating continuity and order, and they may reduce anxieties over doubt, worries, and conflicts (ibid., pp. 81–2).

While Giddens's argumentation seems to aptly describe what is happening in the world, it is not unproblematic. It presumes an active and rational individual who, amid a puzzling number of options, knows what she is doing and why. Individuals, Giddens argues, reflexively monitor and assess all aspects of their life. According to critics, however, Giddens overplays individual agency and the possibilities for self-making, and they are not entirely wrong (e.g. Alexander, 1996, p. 135; Heaphy, 2007, p. 94). Giddens's outlook on individuals is excessively optimistic, while his own work contains a number of contradictions that question such a rationale.

When Giddens, for instance, identifies lifestyles and the resulting self-identity as a life-long 'project', he seems to imply that this project is overseen by a determined and centred individual. Yet, this individual is chronically uncertain about what to be and how to be – in search of herself, as sociologist Matthew

Adams has pointed out (2003, p. 224). The individual tries and rejects lifestyles in order to adopt new ones, and in this process various contingencies may become deciding factors instead of rational reflection.

Lifestyles may not represent individual freedom either. While individuals do have a choice, there is no option not to choose. Giddens stated that '… we all not only follow lifestyles, but in an important sense are forced to do so …' (1991, p. 81). This dilemma between option and obligation may be 'agonising' (Bauman, 2000, p. 61), rather than a manifestation of self-mastery, as Giddens seems to imply, as the number of choices available does not necessarily equal freedom, nor does it guarantee individual happiness.

Similar contradictions are characteristic of all theories of second modernity, including Beck's thesis on individualisation of cultures (see Beck, 1992; Beck and Beck-Gernsheim, 2002; Beck and Grande, 2010). As individualisation is an important prerequisite for the emergence of lifestyles, a few words on Beck's thesis are pertinent.

Like Giddens, Beck associated individualisation and the rise of various lifestyles with the breakdown of traditions, which enabled individuals to design their own lives free from predetermined identities (Beck and Grande, 2010, p. 420). This includes a high level of risk; life becomes an experiment for which individuals carry full responsibility – and also full blame if they fail (Beck, 2009, p. 7).

Risks arise, Beck argued, due to the unanticipated side effects of globalisation, increasing mobilities, erosion of safety nets such as the welfare state, employment security, and the nuclear family (Beck, Bonß, and Lau, 2003, pp. 1–5; Beck and Grande, 2010). They lead to the constant revision, transformation and uncertainty that are viewed to be characteristic of the contemporary society and personal life (e.g. Giddens, 1991, pp. 17–20; Heaphy, 2007, p. 170). While global nomads have voluntarily taken charge of their own lives – or so it appears when no further analysis has yet been conducted – Beck views that people leading more settled lifestyles also need to face the same challenge whether they want to or not, because risk is inherent in contemporary, post-traditional societies. There is no way out for anyone.

As can be expected, Beck's ideas have been met with controversy. Some critics have expressed doubt whether such individualisation exists at all, or what individualisation means in the first place (e.g. Atkinson, 2007b, pp. 356–7; Archer, 2007, p. 35; Chan and Goldthorpe, 2010, p. 7; Latour, 2003. See also Beck, 2007). He has also been accused of universalising the experiences of a select few while ignoring difference, inequality, and economic exclusion (e.g. Elliott, 2002; Bottero, 2005; Heaphy, 2007, p. 4; Mythen, 2005). However, Beck's individualisation thesis has also been influential. It has become 'so commonly accepted in social sciences that it is neither tested nor operationalised', as Julia Brannen and Ann Nilsen argued (2005, p. 413).

Although the existence of individualisation is difficult to evidence, Beck's thesis seems to express the spirit of the time. It 'chimes with our shared intuition' of what is happening in the world, as sociologist Gabriel Mythen argued (2005, p. 143). The rhetoric of individualisation and choice particularly appeal to young people, as the few empirical studies conducted in the field have demonstrated (Brannen and Nilsen, 2005; du Bois-Reymond, 1998), and if global nomads' examples can provide us with any further evidence, the appeal could be even broader. It may have relevance for all people whose social background and education allow them to think that they can create their own destinies (see Brannen and Nilsen, 2005, p. 423).

Therefore, instead of just adopting Beck and Giddens's theories or rejecting them, as has been a common strategy (e.g. Mythen, 2005; Atkinson, 2007. Cf. Curran, 2013; Elliott, 2002), these studies merit further analysis. The major themes that they discuss – lifestyles and individualisation – are central to understanding the societal context which has made global nomads' lifestyles possible. Note, however, that the notions of second and first modernity underlying these discussions are mere interpretations, as philosopher Bruno Latour (2003) has maintained, or descriptions of zeitgeist. Second modernity is not a radical rupture that would lead us to live more consciously. It is rather a subtle shift from traditions to lifestyles, from musts to choices, and from structure to agency – a question of shades of grey.

Mobilities

The changes associated with second modernity have increased not only the importance of individualisation but also mobilities, whether movement of people or things, corporeal or virtual, migration or commuting. Mobilities now represent central forces in social divisions, cultural difference, and political power defining our everyday lives. By studying mobilities, we will make the necessary preparations for understanding the relationship between location-independent lifestyles and societies, giving perspective for the various dimensions that they include. Alternative life choices are never isolated phenomena nor unproblematic; they have an influence on the society as a whole. I begin this section – just like the previous one – by analysing the notion of 'mobilities' and the theoretical and societal contexts where it has been employed. The aim is to understand different movements and their meanings, assessments, and implications.

Traditionally, 'mobility' was used in a rather limited sense in social sciences. It had nothing to do with physical movement. It was a synonym for 'social mobility' and referred to an individual's movement up or down in the social hierarchy (e.g. Byrne, 2005, pp. 133–42; Hirsch, 2005, p. 80). It was not until the turn of the millennium that the concept gained a significantly broader meaning. Researchers across different disciplines started to investigate various types of movements and their implications forming a loose mobilities paradigm that will be of interest for this study.

The mobilities paradigm emerged as a critique of sedentarism that was viewed to prevail in social sciences (Cresswell, 2011a, p. 648; Urry, 2001, p. 18). In the mobilities manifesto, *Sociology beyond Society* (2001), John Urry argued that people create meanings through networks where ideas, things and people are moving, rather than by inhabiting a shared sedentary space such as a nation-state (p. 210. See also Cresswell, 2010, p. 551; Cohen and Cohen, 2012, p. 2,181).

Mobilities, therefore, were introduced as a core academic and public issue that challenged the dominating dogma of methodological nationalism.

Research on mobilities and second modernity share many important features. Both describe changes that are taking place in societies seeking viable options for fixed categories such as class, citizenship, gender, and state. This shift from societies to individuals is important, although I will later also point out some of its weaknesses. Another similarity is that mobility, just like any other lifestyle, provides important biographical material for people. The tourist experience, for instance, organises people's knowledge of themselves and the world, as well as their aesthetic appreciation of nature, townscapes, and other societies (e.g. Lash and Urry, 1994, p. 256, 2002a; Lash, 1993, p. 19). Such transformations can act as motors of change in societies.

There are also differences in research. While second modernists examined trends and shifts within societies explaining what society is, how it functions, and how it should be reorganised, the mobilities paradigm focussed on cross-boundary movements (Urry, 2001, p. 19). Another difference lies in the outlook on human beings. As discussed, second modernists and particularly Giddens have overemphasised rationality and cognition, whereas mobilities research has revived an interest in aesthetics (e.g. Urry, 2002b), reminding us of other dimensions of human existence.

Aesthetics, in this context, does not necessarily have anything to do with art or style but with the individual's relation to self (see Foucault, 1997a, p. 131). When there are no longer any givens or anchors because of the diminished importance of traditions, people must decide by themselves how to live under the conditions of relative ethical freedom. They have to figure out how to answer to questions regarding who they are and how they should live.

In some interpretations, however, 'aesthetics' has been reduced to features of stylising and calculating hedonism, or attempts to stand out from the mass by employing a distinctive, sometimes shocking style (Featherstone, 1987, pp. 55, 59, 2007, p. 81; Lash and Urry, 1994, p. 54). Studies on lifestyle migration offer examples of both types of aesthetics. Some of the Western citizens, who move to other countries in order to find a better quality of life, actively transform themselves by seeking detachment from their past and defining their own values (e.g. Benson, 2009, 2011a; Korpela, 2009; D'Andrea, 2006; Bousiou, 2008; O'Reilly, 2002, 2007). They view their identity as shifting and evolving: 'Yesterday I was into rave, today I am into Wicca, tomorrow I may try Zen' (D'Andrea, 2006, p. 225. See also Bousiou, 2008, pp. 101, 130). Those prone to calculating hedonism, on the other hand, may turn such mundane practices as a breakfast into elements of style (Bousiou, 2008. See also D'Andrea, 2006). In this project, life itself becomes stylised (Dunn, 2008, p. 125; Featherstone, 2007, p. 81. See also Foucault, 1997b, p. 271).

The examples of lifestyle migrants indicate that mobility can act as an important means of transformation. Change of scenery and detachment from familiar norms, values, and social relations offers individuals fresh opportunities. In this context, it is perhaps not surprising that mobility has been hyped and used as an evocative keyword for understanding various contemporary phenomena (e.g. Ateljevic and Hannam, 2008, p. 253; Cresswell, 2010, p. 555; Frello, 2008, p. 29. Cf. Giddens, 1991, p. 16; D'Andrea, Ciolfi, and Gray, 2011, p. 150). It has been praised as generating 'new social relations, new ways of living, new ties to space, new places, new forms of consumption and leisure, and new aesthetic sensibilities', by tourist researchers Adrian Franklin and Mike Crang (2001, p. 12).

The excitement around mobilities is understandable. As a phenomenon, however, it is not as novel and unforeseen as visionaries lead us to understand, nor is it unprecedented in speed and scale (e.g. Euben, 2006, p. 174; Cresswell, 2010, p. 555, 2011a, p. 646. Cf. Rojek, 2005, p. 1; Sheller, 2011, p. 1). Even though global nomads, for instance, seem to represent completely new and radical forms of mobility, they in fact reproduce age-old formulas modelling themselves after explorers, philosophers, poets, gypsies, hobos and other itinerants, as I will show in the following chapters.

Furthermore, while mobilities are widespread, the whole world is not now on the move (Sheller, 2011, p. 2. Cf. Urry, 2002b, p. 3; Hannam, Sheller, and Urry, 2006), nor is mobility always desired. In the economic, social, and political context in which this book was written, the American and European financial crisis that began in 2008 prompted the media to represent very different images of mobilities. The crisis, which resulted in cuts across public and private sectors, forced many people to give up their houses and familiar living surroundings because they had become, almost overnight, too expensive for them. TV cameras showed villages of tents where people lived trying to transform their identities to better suit their new mobile and transient circumstances (Chernoff, 2011).

Judging from the desperate images that the media created about the mobility of the age, people hardly yearned for fluidity in their lives but rather for stable coordinates – whether in a form of a house, a job, or a localised circle of friends. These material and social anchors are still one of the most important means for gaining access, belonging, inclusion, and power in societies (DePastino, 2003, p. 271. See also Arnold, 2004, p. 164). This is particularly interesting in the case of global nomads who are homeless, and in this sense, outcasts (e.g. Cloke, May, and Johnsen, 2010). Whether their kinds of mobilities are wanted and encouraged, or rather the opposite, remains to be investigated.

Mobilities abound, and they refer to different things, gaining meaning within societies, cultures and politics (see Adey, 2006, p. 83). Therefore, they also need to be analysed in these specific contexts. All mobilities are distributed unevenly, and some mobilities may be coerced. Mobilities and their causes may include wars, illegal mobility, forced migration, and statelessness (Sheller, 2011, p. 2. See also Franklin and Crang, 2001, p. 11). One-sided celebration, where mobility is associated with travel, imagination, curiosity, knowledge and reflexive self-understanding only, does not accurately reflect this diversity of movements (see Euben, 2006, p. 29; Cohen and Gössling, 2015; Cresswell, 2011a, p. 648; Franquesa, 2011, pp. 1,019–20; Frello, 2008, p. 46). It merely implies there are inequalities that need to be discussed, and brings into question the norms and values that dominate in societies and in research.

Outside the Norm, amidst Power Negotiations

The theories of second modernity and the mobilities paradigm offer timely concepts and perspectives for examining location-independence. However, these concepts need to be assessed and employed critically in order to avoid theoretical biases. Although the notions of 'lifestyle' and 'mobility', for instance, seem to promise individuals freedom of choice, this freedom is limited by various factors. All these conditions imply discussions where individuals and societies negotiate desirable forms of being and moving. However, as long as the dominant models of the good life, as defined in each society and social circle, are followed and taken for granted, these negotiations remain under the surface. In order to question them and the purposes they serve, the lens of alternative lifestyles is needed.

Global nomads and other long-term travellers offer just this sort of lens, as their lifestyles appear to have a correlation with marginality (see Adler and Adler, 1999, pp. 43–4; O'Reilly, 2006; Cohen, 2010a, p. 298). They are away from work for long stretches of time, or they do not work at all, which suggests that for them, work is not a primary and leisure a secondary activity. This division between work and leisure has been one of the central structural pillars in developed societies: free choice and leisure activities have been expected to further work-related aims (Rojek, 2010, p. 2; Urry, 2002b, p. 2), although times of massive unemployment have undermined the ideals.

Global nomads, by contrast, are travelling neither for work nor for leisure. They may work during their journey but this is not always the case, and although they have a lot of free time which could be considered leisure (see Rojek, 2010, p. 19), travelling also contains work-like routines such as planning, long periods of waiting and long and dull passages on buses, planes and trains (see Edensor, 2001, p. 60). As global nomads are not necessarily returning to their country of origin either, they may also oppose territorial belonging and the familiar division between home and abroad.

Such alternative travel cultures are not a widely researched subject, although the theme was recognised in early tourism research. In the 1970s, Erik Cohen drafted an extreme traveller type, the drifter, based on a meeting he had with a German traveller in South America. The drifter became something of a mythical figure in tourism studies. Cohen described him (the drifter was always presumably a male) as a self-reliant individual who wanted to preserve the freshness and spontaneity of his experience. He travelled without an itinerary, timetable, destination, or well-defined purpose (Cohen, 1972, 1973, 2004).

The drifter ventured furthest away from the beaten track living with local people and avoiding contact with the tourism industry. While the mass tourist looked for familiarity, prior planning, safety, dependency and minimal choices, the drifter valued novelty, spontaneity, risk, independence, and having a multitude of options (see Vogt, 1976, p. 27). His journey was countercultural by character.

> The loosening of ties and obligations, the abandonment of accepted standards and conventional ways of life, the voluntary abnegation of the comforts of modern technological society, and the search for sensual and emotional experiences are some of the distinguishing characteristics of a counter-culture in its various forms, which motivate the young to escape their homeland, and to travel and live among different and more 'primitive' surroundings. (Cohen, 1973, p. 93)

Among travellers, drifting largely remained an unattainable ideal. Cohen later lamented that most young travellers would not qualify even as part-time drifters (1982, p. 221; 2004, p. 51). He admitted that long-term travel seemed to take much more competence, resourcefulness, and endurance than he had originally assumed (2004, p. 45). For a long time, the countercultural features of long-term travellers were not discussed. On the contrary, while Cohen relished the rebellious aspects of the drifter culture, associating it with bumming and substance abuse (1973, p. 94), his followers tried to clean up travellers' reputation by emphasising the educational aims of their travels, as well as their unwavering intentions to return home and become respectable members of society (e.g. Vogt, 1976; Riley, 1988).

These attempts at image improvement turned out to be in vain, however, and the dubious nature of long-term travel persisted, having been associated with irresponsible, anti-social, or even dangerous behaviour. Only more recent writing has suggested that the Cohen typology of the drifter overlooked the fluidity of practices and motivations: individuals can combine elements of drifter and mass tourism in a single trip or between different trips; they are not separate phenomena (e.g. Cohen, 2010b; Jarvis and Peel, 2010, p. 24).

The various meanings of full-time travel – just like mobilities in general – are part of an ongoing negotiation in which different lifestyles are being evaluated. Research is not spared from these negotiations either. On the contrary, it actively participates for various reasons – in order to mythicise, attract attention, pursue ideological aims, or clear the researchers' consciousness if they are part of the cultures they are studying. Societies, on the other hand, concentrate on regulatory issues determining who can be let out, when, why, and what is expected from them in return. These questions play a major role in labelling travellers, deciding what constitutes good and beneficial travel, and what kind of travel should be discouraged.

Some mobilities do indeed seem more desirable than others. This conclusion can also be drawn from a simple analysis of the notion of 'travel'. It relates journeying to home (as opposed to being away), and to leisure activity (as opposed to work). Home, therefore, is an irreplaceable reference point. When conventional tourists travel, they depart, enjoy leisure time in their chosen destinations and return back home (e.g. Cohen, 1979; Urry, 2002b, pp. 2–3; Van Den Abbeele, 1992, pp. xvii–xviii). Because of their location-independence, global nomads and many other multi-mobile people question this binary opposition (see Williams and Hall, 2000, pp. 6, 21). For them, home and travel can be intertwined. By thus questioning the relatively stable coordinates that form the basis for the settled life, their lifestyles have interesting implications for the wider society. It is here that power becomes a central concern.

Agents and Pawns

Alternative lifestyles have been studied as acts of domination and acts of resistance, which seems to implicate that they involve a high degree of agency and power (see Giddens, 1984, p. 9). This approach is dominant, for instance, in lifestyle migration studies where 'agency' has become a central concept (e.g. Korpela, 2009, p. 22; D'Andrea, 2006, p. 189; Benson and O'Reilly, 2009, p. 613; Ackers and Dwyer, 2004, pp. 469, 473; Bousiou, 2008, e.g. pp. 20–21). The underlying idea is that societies restrict personal choice and pursuit of happiness, and the individual is better off without them (e.g. MacBeth, 2000, p. 28; Benson, 2011b, p. 224; Korpela, 2009, p. 22).

When lifestyle migrants, and presumably also global nomads, reinvent themselves and their living conditions, they may be viewed as resisting 'push and pull factors', which academia has used to explain why some people move abroad (e.g. Casado-Diaz, Kaiser, and Warnes, 2004; Iso-Ahola, 1982, p. 258; Dann, 1999, p. 186). While pull factors are supposed to make one country appear more tempting than another, push factors are considered negative. They may include financial crises, unemployment, discrimination, and lawsuits, which leave the person no other option but to go.

Although often used, the push and pull model has been largely discredited (Papastergiadis, 2000, p. 31. See also Nudrali and O'Reilly, 2009, p. 141). It presumes that all people have roots from which they are suddenly cut off due to unfortunate circumstances and thus doomed to live the life of an immigrant, exile, or refugee (e.g. Worsley, 1990, p. 87). The model is also predicated by the state and its interests, with migrants perceived as passive and merely reacting to external stimuli (see Papastergiadis, 2000, p. 35). Lifestyle mobilities in particular show that leaving can also be a choice, or at least it may be represented that way. Migrants abandon their country in order to construct their own spaces, communities, and identities. Many of them dislike being recognised by their past, because they feel past was imposed on them rather than chosen (D'Andrea, 2006, p. 189).

The same may be said to apply to global nomads. For them, location-independence seems to be not only a cherished choice but almost a declaration of independence, with which they try to detach themselves from the norms and values of their respective countries. Here, however, I will apply a slightly different approach. Instead of presuming that location-independence is always and in all situations preferred, the focus will be on the interplay between agency and structure.

I will approach this topic with Giddens's structuration theory and Foucauldian theories of subjectivity and power. With structuration theory, I aim to expand the horizons for envisioning the crucial relationship between the individual and society. 'Society' does not refer here to any bounded system such as a nation-state, rather it is understood as social association in general, which can be organised in many ways (see Giddens, 1984, p. xxvi). With Foucauldian theories, on the other hand, I will broaden Giddens's rather static approaches and analyse the dynamics of power relationships. Power is central in this work because of the alternative features of location-independence, and as such, I will lean more on Foucauldian theories, which I now briefly present in order to ground the two central concepts I will be using throughout this book: biopower and subjectivity.

The first central concept of 'biopower', or subtle forms of power as it is understood here, is the form in which power is now increasingly practised. Rather than by laws, most conduct is guided by norms, values, ideals, peer pressure, status anxiety, alluring lifestyles, or emotions. To this list, welfare such as education, health care, and social security can be added (see Foucault, 2002a, p. 344). As global nomads want to reject these forms of power in their lives, biopower offers one of the key perspectives for understanding the facilitating and constraining factors in their lifestyles. My aim here is to study how other people and societies use power over them, how they themselves facilitate and use power, and how power is constitutive of their lifestyles and subjectivities.

Issues of identity and the self are central to this approach. Instead of 'identity', however, I adopt the concept of 'subjectivity' as the second central concept I will be using in order to better indicate differences within the 'self'. Subjectivity is a work in progress which is formed in different contexts, sometimes in contradictory terms (e.g. Hall, 1990, p. 222; Hall, 1996; Bauman, 2001a, p. 129, 2001b. Cf. Giddens, 1991).

I approach global nomads' subjectivities through two assumptions. The first assumption is that they construct their subjectivities in relation to the settled. Being sedentary, in the contemporary society, is the norm from which the location-independent deviate, and to which they are therefore tied in many ways. Note, however, that the term 'settled' is best thought of as in brackets to remind us that the lives of the settled are also fluid, changing, and mobile. The second assumption is that by analysing global nomads' subjectivities, I can also analyse power struggles in which people and societies organise between themselves discussing preferred forms of dwelling, living, and moving. Subjectivities do not exist in a vacuum; they are a part of wider economic, social, political, and cultural contexts.

The theories of Giddens and Foucault I have chosen are not coherent. Therefore, rather than present an interpretation of the 'original' meaning of these theories, I will need to develop and detail their concepts and ideas raised within this analysis. Foucault openly occupied several positions in his work (see 1969, pp. 26, 149, 1997a, p. 131) and, as a consequence, his theories were in perpetual motion. I will purposefully refer to both approaches in the plural in order to make their heterogeneity visible. I suggest viewing them as a set of approaches rather than as an overall explanation. Particularly in qualitative studies such as this, the theories need to be developed in relation to the research material, as they are based on a dialogue between theory, methodology, and the research object. This can be viewed as both a weakness and a strength: all research results must have evidence and support for an argument in a singular research material.

Approaches

The task of finding global nomads in order to collect the research material proved to be a challenging one which, in all fairness, I knew it would be beforehand. Chance encounters such as ours with the Canadian Ferrari repairman in Kuala Lumpur were rare because of the small number of global nomads and the large territory they cover. To reach the participants, I used both traditional and innovative methodologies, which are detailed in this section. I also discuss ethical concerns, particularly the challenges that my double role as a researcher and a global nomad posed to the research.

Alternative Ethnography

When searching for participants in 2010, originally for my second PhD thesis, my criteria were that they had been on the road continuously for at least three years without a home and a permanent job. I got leads for many interesting people but most of them had travelled only a year or two. Although people on a sabbatical also have an extensive travel experience, they are not location-independent. They usually return to familiar circumstances, having a home, a job, and perhaps even a partner waiting for them upon return. For the location-independent, on the other hand, travelling has changed their lives and living conditions dramatically. Their life is in a suitcase, backpack, trailer, trunk, or a cabin – wherever they happen to be.

My goal was to capture responses from people representing various walks of life, different age groups, nationalities, and different travel styles, and to examine how these factors affect participants' lifestyles, social relationships, and societal views. For this aim, I chose purposive sampling that maintains plurality. Therefore the sample cannot be put forward as representative.

When doing the sampling, I included a couple of restrictions. I limited the number of American participants given my observation that there seems to be more American global nomads than other nationalities, perhaps because of the country's large population compared to European countries (although Europe as a whole has more than double the US population). Another reason was that some of the prospective Americans had never travelled outside the United States, whereas the theme of this research required travellers who wander in countries and cultures other than their own so that border crossings, rootlessness, culture confusion, and adaptation could be discussed. I also limited the number of cyclists. Cycling seems to be popular among global nomads, or perhaps it appears so since my experience is that cyclists are more easily reached than other groups because of their mutual networks and strong presence in social media. Therefore, I limited the number of cyclists so they were not over-represented in the sample group.

Based on my criteria, I chose 30 global nomads for interviews. I found most of the participants through a hospitality exchange organisation (hospex) called CouchSurfing, which offers a tool and a network for people to connect with each other. The host offers accommodation, and guests can participate, for example, by cooking, buying ingredients, and washing dishes, or by telling stories in the manner of hobos and tramps of old entertaining the host with their travel accounts. I had been a member in the organisation, and my husband founded a discussion group there for long-term travellers to exchange experiences and trade tips. A similar method had been employed successfully in previous research on independent travellers (e.g. Richards and Wilson, 2004b; O'Reilly, 2006, p. 1,002). In this study, however, other search methods were also needed, as most of the group members failed to meet the research criteria of homeless long-term travel; rather, many were dreaming about it but had not yet realised their dream.

The rest of the participants were found through social networking sites on the internet, and by spreading the word through networks. This kind of snowball method is commonly used when surveying members of a rare population because it ensures that a diverse range of information-rich cases will be reached. However, these chosen contact methods had significant restrictions. The fact that I contacted the prospects by email and interviewed them through video conferencing meant that those who did not use the internet remained beyond the reach of this study.

During the course of the research, I accumulated a body of approximately one hundred prospective participants, and based on this, the current number of global nomads can probably be counted in the hundreds, and it is likely to remain under one thousand (cf. MacBeth, 2000, p. 25). Nobody knows the exact figure as the location-independent are beyond the reach of statistical surveys and censuses.

Interviews

The main research material was collected in in-depth interviews in order to explore various aspects of location-independence. As the participants were scattered around the world from Alaska to Fiji, meeting everyone in person posed major logistical and financial problems; therefore, video conferencing was chosen instead (see Pereiro, 2010, p. 183). The interviews probed a wide variety of topics: the participants' daily life, motivations, decision-making processes, directions, schedules, livelihood, relationships, and their encounters with societies.

In 2012, a short follow-up was conducted using chat and email. The purpose was to provide a temporal aspect to the research; therefore, the main issues addressed were about changes in the participants' lives. Through the analysis of these conversations, the fluid nature of location-independent lifestyles became clear. While the first interviews had sometimes given me a rosier picture of the participants' lives, some of the follow-ups were simply stunning as the participants seemed to have altered their views completely. These changes demonstrated that analytical methods which are able to maintain plurality and discrepancies, including longitudinal data gathering, were clearly applicable here.

Instant ethnography

Traditional participant observation methods were out of the question in this research because of the high mobility of global nomads. I could not live with the participants for months or years observing their habits in one site. Nor could I travel with them for long periods of time given their preference to move alone or in pairs, without planning their travels too far ahead, avoiding commitments. Under the circumstances, instant ethnography seemed the most viable option.

Instant ethnography is an emerging methodological area which has been used in similar situations that guide researchers to use multiple-site data gathering (see Marcus, 1995; D'Andrea, 2006; Söderström, Randeria, Ruedin, D'Amato, and Panese, 2013). It offers a quick but insightful dip into the participants' lives. This move towards new methods is paralleled by social and physical changes (Law and Urry, 2003, p. 1; Büscher, Urry, and Witchger, 2011). When people's lives are ever more transient, single-site ethnographies are bound to become rarer (see Falzon, 2009).

I met 14 out of 30 participants in Italy, Greece, Malaysia, China, Australia, Thailand, India, Turkey, Argentina, and China. During the observation period, I was hosting the participant or the other way around, we were both hosted by the same hospex member, or we both stayed in the same hotel or hostel. Living together for a couple of days offered the most favourable circumstances for observation. The situations were not constrained by appointments and the venues were relaxed, allowing everybody to go about their daily lives. Even those participants who had been shy in video conferencing became more open, and therefore the observations offered valuable complementary material.

Observations during this time particularly broadened the views I had formed based on the static Skype interviews, the format of which was inherently rather contrary to global nomads' lifestyles (see Büscher and Urry, 2009, pp. 103–4; Benson, 2011b, p. 222): the interviewees had to sit still and comply with a fixed time and date, and discuss their lifestyles according to a semi-structured list of questions. Participant observation, on the other hand, allowed me an immersion into the participants' lives. The time we spent together included everyday practices such as walking, sitting, talking, cooking, watching films, and exploring the surroundings.

Virtual ethnography

After the interviews and meetings, I followed the participants' paths on Facebook, hospitality exchange websites, blogs, and by email, dwelling permanently in the loose-knit community of global nomads that formed around my research. As is typical for virtual communication, these encounters involved a combination of proximity and distance, nearness and farness (see Hine, 2000). As most of the global nomads' relationships are maintained online, virtual ethnography became a revealing part of their lives. The participants share many intimate things to their networks in social media, and this material enriched the interviews particularly in the case of those global nomads who could not be reached for participant observation.

Personal Involvement

My next challenge in the research process was to make my own stance clear, and detail the challenges that my double role as a researcher and a global nomad created (see de Laine, 2000, p. 17). Researchers are always an important part of their own study, even if they try to stay in the background in the name of objectivity, which is not the case here.

Lack of transparency is the most common critique against any qualitative research (Chambers, 2007, p. 114; Franklin and Crang, 2001, p. 6; McCabe, 2005, p. 95). A considerable amount of self-reflection is required of the researcher so that the paradigmatic assumptions and mechanisms of the research are recognised. These assumptions and mechanisms influence the researcher to pose research questions in a particular way, which can obviously greatly influence the results.

For my part, I have written this book from a non-institutionalised position. I have not accepted any financial support for the research, authorship, and publication of this book. I have, therefore, minimal ties and agendas to declare besides theoretical and my aim to make location-independence, as well as its prerequisites and implications, known. My focus is on global nomads' voluntary detachment from societies. In contrast, a study made from an institutional point of view would have been quite different, focussing for instance, on global nomads' involuntary social exclusion. Such a study might have included normative aspects stressing global nomads' indebtedness to their society of origin, and suggestions of measures with which they could be reintegrated into society.

My lifestyle has both benefited and restricted research. If I were not a global nomad myself, I doubt that I would have been aware of the existence of the lifestyle or would have been able to find the participants. Being a global nomad also helped in that I was aware of the challenges faced by global nomads, was able to gain the participants' trust and address crucial topics. On the other hand, approaching the research from this position of familiarity might have restricted the amount of information obtained if participants left some topics unmentioned because they thought them to be too commonplace in a discussion between two colleagues. An outsider might have received more detailed answers, perhaps directing the research to areas that are now ignored.

Inevitably, some aspects of my person also influenced the interviews and observation situations. Someone else – of different age, gender, nationality, marital status, profession, and lifestyle – would likely have received different answers. This was most clearly seen in answers to questions about relationships. The participants knew that I am married, which seemed to affect some of them. A few of the solo travellers had a defensive attitude when I asked why they were travelling alone. I will explain these and other possible influences of my person in more detail in the analysis.

As many of my discussions with global nomads touched on intimate topics, the question of privacy is relevant, particularly because most participants appear in the research using their own names (e.g. Israel and Hay, 2006, p. 110), per their own decision. Many of the participants are public figures in the sense that they write blogs, newspaper stories and books about their life, and so there was no serious concern about violating anyone's privacy, although what they publish is naturally selective. The participants talk relatively freely about their health, relationships, sex, and other events in their life on the internet, and they were not necessarily shy in presenting these matters in the interviews either. Although I never asked the participants' sexual orientation, for example, in some cases it came out naturally as part of the conversation. A few of the participants opted to use a pseudonym, and their names have been altered to protect their privacy. In one case, the nationality was changed per the participant's request.

Ultimately, no matter how tight security measures researchers take, there is never complete privacy when using the internet for interviewing, communication, and data storage. This was proven by the US National Security Agency scandal, where Skype collected video calls with the help of Microsoft. Even the most private information can be accessed and handed over to governments and companies (Greenwald, McAskill, Poitras, Ackerman, and Rushe, 2013; Rushe, 2013). The only means to prevent this risk would be to use traditional face-to-face interviews without recording or storing any data in computers connected to the internet. Although this approach is in many ways preferable, it was not possible in this research. Because of the high mobility of the participants, the only means to contact them was through the internet. This raises the question of whether this research should have been left undone. I made the choice to take the risk.

Overview

This book is located within the field of lifestyle mobilities, focussing on the under-examined phenomenon of location-independence through a world-wide empirical research of 30 'global nomads'. The chosen theoretical framework, which is built on Foucault's, Giddens's, and second modernists' works, guides the analysis to the relationship between global nomads and societies. Location-independence is not only an individual lifestyle choice but a societal phenomenon that reveals important norms, values, and ideals in societies. Therefore, it also needs to be analysed in this broader economic, political, social, and cultural context.

Besides this introductory chapter, the book is composed of six chapters structured according to themes that correspond to the analytic layers of the research. I start by examining the practices global nomads have created and adopted, proceed to challenges that they encounter in their relations, gradually broadening the discussions from personal to societal and finally to a global level. Each chapter adds a new dimension as well as new theoretical viewpoints to deepen the discussion. Chapters also feature some of the global nomads' stories in more detail.

Chapter 2, titled 'Privileged Elite?', presents global nomads' lifestyles through the perspectives of money, time, and place. The focus is on their everyday practices with which they distance themselves from the norms and values of their respective country of origin. Attention is drawn to striking dilemmas in their lifestyles: between their modest and non-materialistic ways of life and the elite character associated with multi-mobility; their idleness and their simultaneous will to achieve and perform; and their high mobility and indifference to places. These paradoxes open up the discussion on the effects of power in their lives. On the theoretical side, the usefulness of the structuration theory is assessed from the point of view of structure and agency. The aim is to understand the contradictory forces in global nomads' lives.

Chapter 3 is titled 'Two Faces'. It examines two opposing discourses with which global nomads and outsiders alike represent location-independence. The discrepancy between the discourses is used to highlight the ongoing power struggle in which the role of mobilities in contemporary societies is discussed. While some mobilities are encouraged, others are suppressed, and this research examines where the fine line between the two is drawn. Theoretically, the chapter discusses how Foucauldian discourse theory and methodologies can help us in examining these power negotiations.

Chapter 4, titled 'Adrift', examines global nomads' personal relationships, which are among the most critical factors that may make them reconsider their lifestyles. Because of the two-year time span of the research, the chapter is able to investigate transformations in which global nomads search for a balance between their will to travel and their need for intimate relationships – for which, in most cases, a prerequisite seems to be being settled. The chapter's theoretical focus is on subjectivities, their changing character, and the ways in which they function as vehicles of power.

Chapter 5 is titled 'In or Out' and it examines global nomads' nationalistic and political attachments, which facilitate and constrain their location-independence. The focus is on how different forms of power affect global nomads' lives ranging from sovereign power practised by states through rules and regulations to subtle measures of biopower that are visible in norms and values that are woven into daily life. At the end of the chapter, the prevailing dogma of methodological nationalism and its emerging alternatives, that give more allowance to mobilities, are examined.

Chapter 6 is titled 'A Sisyphean Task?'. It deals with global nomads' laborious efforts to get to know local people and cultures in their destinations. Various forms of discrimination and culture confusion are examined, and particular attention is paid to the ways in which global nomads tackle these problems. The chapter continues the discussion on subjectivity by broadening it to include the dynamics of social interaction. The focus is on power asymmetries, which make people seek status thereby producing inequality.

Chapter 7, titled 'Alternatives', concludes the research results and reflects on their societal and academic impacts. The trends that the location-independent represent and their desirability for individuals and societies are discussed. These trends are encapsulated under the headings of individualisation and social exclusion. They challenge the states to take differences and mobilities increasingly into account in their policies. In regard to academic implications, the chosen framework, methods and the goal of the research are contemplated in order to assess the book's added value for studies on lifestyle mobilities and to social sciences more generally. Power theories are shown to be essential for understanding the relationship between the individual and society so that simple binary oppositions and interpretations of winners and losers are avoided.

Chapter 2
Privileged Elite?

A mutual friend introduced me to 47-year-old Michel, who calls himself 'Nomad'. He left France in 2007 when Nicholas Sarkozy was elected president, because of his differing political views. 'I'm planning to travel until 2012. Then I will vote for Sarkozy in the next election so that I can travel five more years', Michel jokes and adds that he would gladly change his French nationality to world citizenship if such a thing were available. However, he is not fighting to abolish borders and visas, as open-minded as it would be. 'We are almost there', he says, 'McDonald's is everywhere and diversity is killed like currencies in Europe'.

Michel started travelling young. When he was 14, he joined the navy, he says, where he had the opportunity to sail around Africa. Ultimately, he chose not to pursue military career, and started doing odd jobs, mainly producing videos and managing websites while living in various parts of France and in the French island of Martinique in the Caribbean. He never considered money important, but he felt he was almost obliged to adopt material values. 'Too many people complain but they don't do anything. If there's something wrong, you have to change it. It's a big reason why I'm nomadic. I don't complain, I just move out'.

Currently Michel earns his living by web hosting. He prefers to work as little as possible so he can enjoy his freedom. His budget is 21 dollars a day: seven dollars for transportation, seven dollars for eating, and seven dollars for everything else such as entrance fees, if he happens to visit a tourist site, and doctors.

When I originally interviewed Michel in 2010, he had no budget for accommodation because he was touring Europe and stayed with hospex members nine nights out of ten. He is exceedingly active member in the organisation and volunteers as a nomadic ambassador. For him hospex is, bluntly put, a free bed. He knows that many members have more sublime motives for participating in the system, but for him accommodation is enough. In his view, if there happens to be cultural exchange as well, it is a plus but not a must. Michel related me how he first heard about hospex, which then changed his travel style completely:

> When I started travelling in 2007, I didn't know about hospitality exchange. I did voluntary work. Then my mother, who is seventy-four, read a review about it and said to me, ironically: 'Look at this Michel, with this service you can be homeless for the rest of your life'. I joined right away. (MICHEL, 47)

Michel travels alone, although he often has temporary company. He knows that his style causes strong reactions in people and not everybody agrees with his opinions. Undiplomatic and without taboos, he can be a tough cookie. Some people find him rude. Michel explains his philosophy: 'People play too easily with life. We need a license to drive, we need a license to go fishing, but for creating life we don't need any license. The most dangerous and stupid people can procreate'. He believes that the earth would do just fine without us. For him, the greenest act would be to kill ourselves. Many think Michel's ideas are gloomy and pessimistic but he disagrees. He says it is just that he is not afraid of death.

Michel's story introduces themes that are common to all the global nomads in this book. They value mastery of their own lives more than money and status, and they seem to be privileged in the sense that they can afford to do so. It might be that their lifestyles are a silent protest against dominant values, norms, or politics in their countries of origin, from which they seek detachment. Often their one-time journey spontaneously develops into a long-term wandering lifestyle, which includes different phases. Many of them are solo travellers, and often wish they had someone to share their life with.

By exploring these themes of self-ownership, detachment from dominant norms and values and the different phases of global nomads' lifestyles, I aim to draw a rounded picture of the participants. In particular, I pay attention to their adopted practices that characterise their lifestyles and world views in a concrete and detailed manner. A topic that always excites people's curiosity and seems to give global nomads the appearance of a privileged status – money – is central to the analysis. Theoretically, the chapter focusses on the dynamics between the musts and the choices in global nomads' lives that draw attention to structure and agency.

Demographics

As described in the Introduction, the global nomads represent people of different ages, educational and occupational backgrounds, career stages, and nationalities. Their travel styles and experiences also vary. For most, travelling was already an important part of their lives before they left, and it gradually occupied a larger and larger part of their life. Many described travelling as a long-time dream, although in some cases the will to see the world arose from contradictory circumstances. In cases where there were no possibilities to travel as a child, the drive found its outlet later.

The participants started to roam the world at different stages in life. Some dropped out of school, a few, like Michel, as early as at the age of 14, while some middle-aged or elder men and women first had a family and only began to travel after their children left home. Table 2.1 shows the participants' basic coordinates.

The participants' backgrounds could be described as privileged in light of prevailing trends in social sciences that emphasise inequality between the citizens of the West and the rest. The majority of the participants carry passports that allow them to travel in most parts of the world. Many also have a higher education such as a master's degree, often from economics or engineering sciences that promise a well-paid job, and all have means to travel full-time for years and support themselves on the road. However, none of these factors automatically grant them a privileged status. Even among Western passport holders, rights vary, as the West is not homogeneous (see also Euben, 2006, p. 3). Nor do global nomads necessarily exploit all of their resources, particularly those related to education and work, whether by choice or as a result of their inability to find suitable employment.

Most global nomads earn their living by working, but their jobs and spending patterns differ. To give a rough idea of the spectrum, I have categorised global nomads into three groups. The first group consists of global nomads who consider their lifestyles as a temporary phase in life. They have usually saved for their journey, and when they run out of money, they will work, usually taking any odd jobs available (see also Cohen, 2011, pp. 1,546–7; Uriely, 2001, pp. 6–7). The participants have worked, for example, at construction sites, hostels and restaurants, and as guides, cooks, or bus drivers.

The second group of global nomads have portable jobs and work more or less regularly. The most popular professions are IT related. Global nomads work as consultants, programmers, or website designers, or they sell web hosting services or advertisements to travel websites. Other popular professions include artisan work such as massage or jewellery, writing books or newspaper stories, or teaching, for example, English or yoga. Most are freelancers or entrepreneurs, which means that their income flows fluctuate, and they take entrepreneurial risks.

The third group live on more steady ground enjoying a pension or utilising their long-time savings. They may have a house or an apartment for rent in their country of origin, which guarantees them a fairly steady income. These global nomads are usually more well off than the two other groups, and also spend more money. Some of them prefer to have their own vehicle, boat or motor home, which offers them accommodation and privacy on the road.

For the majority, location-independent lifestyle is not luxurious. Although the participants sleep in hotels and hostels as do more conventional tourists, more than half seek free accommodation from hospex organisations (e.g. BeWelcome, CouchSurfing, Hospitality Club, Servas, and cyclists' Warm Shower's List). Many also carry a tent with them, and when necessary, they sleep wherever: in airports, squats, schools, stations, temples, beaches, forests, park benches, on the street, in gasoline stations, or in ATM cabins (see also Cohen, 1972, p. 176).

The contrast between global nomads' backgrounds and their travel practices raises interesting questions for research, which has often emphasised either the privileged or involuntary nature of mobilities (e.g. Sheller, 2011; Massey, 1993; Birtchnell and Caletrío, 2014; Urry, 2007, pp. 51–2). By letting go of some of their privileges, and by borrowing from the forced practices of the homeless and their poorer namesakes, the pastoral nomads, global nomads expose themselves to criticism: by being able to afford to let their privileges go, they ignore the asymmetrical power relations at play, consciously forgetting that not everyone can do the same (see Ahmed, 1999). There are structural inequalities that set limits on choice and agency creating situations in which some are freer to act than others (Bottero, 2005, p. 56).

Table 2.1 Demographic data of the participants

Name or pseudonym	Sex	Age	Nationality	Education/profession	Interview location	Travel experience	Travel style
Guillermo*	M	42	Spain	PhD (biology)	Italy	10 years	Bicycle
Jukka	M	27	Finland	Student (geography)	Finland	4 years	Bicycle
Andy	M	54	US	Real estate agent	Dominican Republic	12 years	PT
Rita	F	72	US	Author	US	20 years	PT
George*	M	31	US	Student (international relations)	US	6 years	PT, bicycle
Tor	M	61	US	Captain	Grenada	30 years	Sailboat
Elisa*	F	54	US	Press officer	Costa Rica	7 years	PT
Claude	M	50	Switzerland	Social worker	Switzerland	15 years	Bicycle
Jens	M	30	Germany	Student	Ireland	4 years	PT
Phoenix	M	49	US	English/Yoga teacher	US	15 years	PT, van
Stefan	M	47	Austria	Radio broadcasting	Costa Rica	6 years	PT, sailboat
Glen	F	53	UK	Entrepreneur	UK	13 years	PT, RV
Max	M	39	US	IT entrepreneur	Brazil	7 years	PT
Jérémy	M	26	France	Student (hospitality)	Belize	3 years	Hitch-hiking
Ludovic	M	32	France	Business consultant	France	5 years	Hitch-hiking

Michel	M	47	France	Video producer / entrepreneur	France	3 years	PT, budget flights
Ingo	M	36	Germany	IT entrepreneur	Germany	15 years	PT
Jeff	M	25	US	Various	Indonesia	7 years	PT
Noam*	M	32	Israel	Musician	Peru	11 years	PT
Ciro	M	29	Portugal	Business consultant	Japan	3 years	PT
Barbara	F	52	US-Canada	Various	Canada	8 years	PT, car
Anthony	M	35	Belgium	Business manager	Italy	8 years	PT
Anick	F	29	Canada	Student (biophysics)	France	8 years	PT, hitch-hiking
Gustavo*	M	51	Argentina*	Business consultant	Greece	30 years	PT, bicycle
Taro	M	27	Japan	Office worker	Japan	4 years	PT, bicycle
Alberto	M	39	Mexico	Gardener	New Zealand	8 years	PT
Ajay	M	24	Russia	Student (software engineering) / DJ	Indonesia	3 years	PT
Maria	F	32	Russia	Web designer	Indonesia	3 years	PT
Scott	M	33	US	Kindergarten teacher	Australia	12 years	PT, hitch-hiking
Cindie	F	51	American	Geologist	India	9 years	Bicycle

Notes: * Pseudonym and/or country of origin changed. PT is Public transport.

Even some global nomads resent this kind of slumming as superficial and elitist. They sympathise with the less fortunate, either frowning upon such arrogance or by willingly admitting their privileged position like Claude (50): 'Traditional nomads had a hard life. They had family and animals, and they died young. It was not a choice for them. They were just following their parents. I chose this, I'm a luxury nomad'.

The criticism concerning global nomads' privileges goes to the heart of the sociological dilemma: are individuals' acts determined by life chances and societal structures, or are they agents who decide their own lives? This dilemma has puzzled social theorists since Marx and Weber. Most often, theorists have emphasised one of the two extremes, neither of which is better than the other: either individuals are viewed as able to have little or no influence at all on things that are going on around them, or their agency is inflated.

The latter option has gained currency among second modernists who tend to belittle the influence of structure in people's lives. Beck and Beck-Gernsheim (2002) have argued that second modernity is rather characterised by 'the *lack* of social structures' (p. 51). Although Giddens has also advocated individual agency and choice over predetermined factors, he has elaborated on the notion of 'structure' thoroughly in his early works. Particularly notable in this respect is *The Constitution of Society* (1984), where Giddens tried to transcend the dualism. As he is one of the rare contemporary sociologists who has taken on such an extensive task, his works are of particular interest for the following discussion (see also Thompson, 1989, p. 76). In order to understand the alternative features of global nomads' lifestyles, we need to know to what extent they are able to be the creators of their own life.

Giddens approached the problem of structure and agency by reconceptualising it. While 'structure' has usually been understood in terms of a valued resource that is most important in determining individuals' life chances, such as money, property, and means of production (Bottero, 2005, pp. 6–7), Giddens defined it as 'rules and resources' (1984, pp. 16–25, 1979, p. 64). These include, he enumerated, traditions, institutions, moral codes, and dominant ways of doing things that give form and shape to social life. Structure can be discursive, tacit, informal, or sanctioned, and it has no physical existence. It exists only in and through the activities of individuals.

The production of structure involves those capable and conscious individuals who are familiar from Giddens's theories as discussed in Chapter 1 (e.g. 1979, pp. 56–8, 1984, p. 25). They enter into a dual relationship with structure: structure shapes their conduct, but at the same time it is their conduct alone that makes structure possible (1981, p. 19, 1984, p. 25. See also Berger and Luckmann, 1966, p. 78). In other words, the two need each other, which seems to imply that absolute agency is not possible as structure always intervenes in our lives.

However, Giddens's theory includes a number of unsettling incoherences (see also Meštrović, 1998, pp. 78, 83, 89), which do not fully explain how this interaction works. While he argues, for instance, that structure is produced by subjects, at the same time structure is also marked by an absence of the subject because it is beyond the control of any individual actors (1993, pp. 4–5). This sounds rather mystical, but Giddens explains it with a simple comparison to language – not because society is like a language, he clarifies – but because language is central to social life and in some respects exemplifies the duality of social processes (1993, p. 8). When producing grammatical statements, we draw upon the same syntactical rules as those that our statements help us to produce (1984, p. 24. Cf. Archer, 2010, p. 230). In a similar way, we draw upon structural rules and resources, and meanwhile reproduce structure.

This seems fine so far; there are many things that science cannot fully explain although they seem to work in a particular manner, languages being a primary example. But structuration theory leaves perhaps a bit too many questions open. For instance, the crucial question of how individuals internalise the rules and resources is left unaddressed. Some critics have also questioned whether such a structure exists at all (Urry, 1982) – at least Giddens has provided no evidence of it other than stating that structure is virtual 'save in its instantiations and coordination as memory traces' (Giddens, 1984, pp. 17, 25). These are valid criticisms and cannot be ignored, but again, rather than rejecting structuration theory or regarding it as a panacea that solves everything, I suggest using it as an insightful metaphor, which effectively draws attention to the most central relation in sociology and also in this research: people and societies.

To address this relation, Giddens's practice approach, with which he explains how structure is present in our everyday lives, offers further material (cf. Gregson, 1989, pp. 236, 246). Simply by going about the routines of our daily lives, we create structure and at the same time social distance and inequality (see Bottero, 2005, p. 175). While these everyday practices for the settled might include choices of friendship networks and sociability, neighbourhood, and use of culture (ibid., p. 164), for global nomads they are related to mobility.

From a Foucauldian point of view, such notion of 'practice' could be considered obsolete or at least a tautology, because Foucault defined discourses as practices, as will be detailed in the next chapter (1969, pp. 66–7). However, the purpose of adopting this 'tautology' is to enrich analytical perspectives. In the course of the research process, I found that I could better illuminate global nomads' everyday lives and actions through its use, as well as approach the shared features of their lifestyles. When people reproduce structure by drawing from rules and resources, they end up adopting similar practices in their lives. We will see whether these practices also unite global nomads despite their demographic disparateness.

My assumption is that practices will offer an insight into the fascinating paradoxes in global nomads' lives in a way that a mere demographic view cannot. While their lifestyles seem to epitomise individual agency and mastery of their own life, we do not yet know how structural factors, such as financial resources, work/life balance, and social relations have influenced their decision to leave. These dialectics between mobilities and moorings – factors that influence people to stay put – is the subject of the next section. After all, mobilities cannot be described without attention to the necessary infrastructural, institutional and spatial factors that configure and enable them (see Hannam, Sheller, and Urry, 2006, pp. 2–3).

Money, Time, Place

I begin the empirical analysis by outlining the upsides that global nomads appreciate in their lifestyles, and then proceed to the practices they have adopted and created. Global nomads' practices often oppose some of the dominant models of the good life in their respective country of origin, and although these practices serve global nomads in shedding their cultural baggage, they also limit their choices. All of the conditions that guide global nomads' practices are important indicators of structure, and are therefore to be noted. They show those instances in which global nomads have to negotiate their choices with other people, social norms, or state regulations. Global nomads make an ideal object for this analysis, because the division between structure and agency only arises when people do not behave as expected (Bottero, 2005, p. 55). Exceptional cases, individuals who break the norms, are needed.

I have chosen three perspectives that seem to offer most insight into global nomads' habits and routines: money, time, and place (see also Giddens, 1991, p. 2). I investigate how these practices and mobilities shape each other structuring global nomads' leisure and work, how global nomads create and maintain their practices, and how their practices might fade away and be replaced with other practices.

Minimising Life

One of the most intriguing issues for outsiders is money – how big the global nomads' budget is and what they spend their mobility dollars on. A common misperception is that wealth enables their lifestyles. From the perspective of Western societies that value work, a high standard of living and the accumulation of wealth, it is hard to believe that travelling and leading a leisurely lifestyle could be desirable, or even possible, with bare means. When Finnish newspapers and magazines have published stories about my husband's and my lifestyle, some journalists have fabricated stories of an enormous fortune that makes our lifestyle possible, as if to convince the readers that long-term mobility is only meant for the chosen few (e.g. Malmberg, 2011; Riiali, 2014). The global nomads' stories, however, seem to indicate something different, which could be called the downshifting turn in travel. To elaborate on what I mean by this, I now examine two practices that global nomads have adopted in order to lower their travel costs: voluntary simplicity and alternative forms of exchange.

Voluntary simplicity is a way of life that rejects high consumption and materialistic lifestyles. Downshifters aim to simplify their expectations and commitments, especially in terms of the number of hours spent working, in order to live more modestly. Global nomads have assumed these principles rather literally. They work very little or not at all, they can fit their belongings in one backpack that they are able to carry themselves, and they only use a small amount of money.

In 2010, global nomads' spending varied between 210 and 2,100 US dollars a month, while the majority spent between 420 and 840 US dollars a month, including all costs from travel tickets to medical services. This is less than the average backpacker budget (1,850 US dollars per month according to WYSE Travel Confederation, 2013), and it is also below the poverty line in many Western countries. In the UK, for instance, low-income threshold in money terms (meaning disposable income after deducting housing costs) was around 690 US dollars a month for a single adult in 2012–2013 (Department for Work and Pensions, 2014). While these figures are relative, because they do not acknowledge purchasing power parity, they are illustrative of global nomads' low level of consumption.

On a global scale, global nomads are still advantaged as more than one billion people in the world – and also one-fifth of people in the developed world – live on less than one dollar a day (UN Millennium Project, 2006; The World Bank, 2014). Furthermore, some of them have reserves to draw on to deal with particular events or crises and to secure their later lives. Those who do not have reserves live from hand to mouth without envisioning the future. They live day by day trusting their abilities to subsist for themselves (cf. Warnes, King, Williams, and Patterson, 1999, p. 737).

Global nomads' will to live modestly is guided by their work ethic. They would rather consume less than earn more money and tie themselves down to mortgages and property. However, in some cases this non-Protestant work ethic has not originated as a result of their own choice; rather, it has been the result of their unemployment. Global nomads are not an exception among people; structural conditions play a role in their lives.

> After being a year bitter and depressed and another year freelancing and struggling to make my mortgage, I said: fuck it. Excuse my French. I'm not going to sit here and beg to get some work. I sold everything, I sold my house, my car, my furniture, my clothes and two hundred pairs of shoes. I packed my backpack and headed to Australia without thinking it through that much. (ELISA, 54)

Regardless of the reason why global nomads have ended up downshifting, the majority eagerly criticise work-oriented and materialistic values in their respective home countries. The more stressful or frustrating their experiences of working life have been, the more they want to liberate themselves from it. 'I want to enjoy my life. Most Japanese only think about work and business. They are in such a hurry that they don't even have time to live their lives', Taro (27) says.

Global nomads believe that money, possessions, and high status, or the lack thereof, do not limit their freedom in any way, nor do they believe that freedom has anything to do with material things. It is freedom to go wherever, whenever.

> Travelling has taught me that everything I need is right here with me [taps his chest], that really I don't need anything to be happy. I can be happier with one backpack on my back and everything that I own in that backpack than living in a house full of crap. (PHOENIX, 49)

Global nomads' refusal to communicate their lifestyles through material objects seems to call into question the theories that relate lifestyles primarily to products and brands (e.g. Dunn, 2008; Shields, 1992). Global nomads are content with fewer material goods than most of their compatriots, and even fewer goods than some homeless persons who try to keep furniture, pictures, and other valuables as signs of hope that they will once again join the ranks of the settled in the future (see Arnold, 2004, p. 66). If viewed from a Foucauldian perspective, global nomads aim to empower themselves by withdrawing from relations that construe people as consumers. They choose to choose less (Shankar, Cherrier, and Canniford, 2006).

However, global nomads are not hard-core ascetics. They carry with them laptops, tablets, mobile phones, and cameras; they fly often, buy other travel-related products and services, consume places, and crave the comfort foods and products they were accustomed to buying in their home countries. When one of the participants came to Hong Kong, where my spouse and I were hosting him, he had just finished spending a year in the Chinese countryside and found the product offerings of the half-Western city irresistible, hoarding cheese and deodorant bottles to our great amusement. We ourselves had experienced a similar buying frenzy when first arriving from the mainland.

Even though global nomads criticise the consumer society, they are themselves its products (see also Holt, 2002; Kozinets, 2002, p. 36). Downshifting does not necessarily mean that global nomads are free from the power of money either, although they have managed to reduce its hold. In some cases, living sparingly can paradoxically lead to an even stronger attachment to money. Cindie (51) describes this as one of the reasons that drove her and her husband apart on the road: 'He was all about living on the cheap and I was about finding meaning in what we were doing so the two really clashed quite a bit'.

Consumption and the act of not consuming bring people closer together or distance them from each other (Corrigan, 1997, p. 32; Douglas and Isherwood, 2002, 49). This occurs also among the settled as many downshifters have likely noticed. In particular, not participating in common small talk about brands and desirable products can isolate individuals from some of their former social circles.

Although downshifting and alternative forms of exchange are not necessarily aims per se for global nomads, they support their lifestyles, and therefore have an important function in sustaining their travels. Regarded by global nomads as antithetical to the dominant values in their respective societies, alternative forms of exchange include giving, sharing and serving other people, and do not require the exchange of money. 'I grew up in a society where the goal is to earn as much money as you can, to get as much social status and power as you can by any means necessary, but I think the true goal, the true meaning of life, is to give as much as you can to other people', Phoenix (49) explains.

While this can be interpreted as a criticism of capitalism and greed (see Kozinets, 2002, p. 34), alternative forms of exchange also have a specific function in global nomads' travels: they involve personal contacts that can help global nomads to get to know locals and local life. Global nomads' travels might also be directly dependent on other people, if they are for example asking for accommodation, a glass of water, directions, or a ride.

The most common form of exchange among global nomads is hospex, and some global nomads also work for food and accommodation in hostels or farms, or they volunteer. As the term 'exchange' implies, even when money is not involved, there are other media of exchange with which people must negotiate the fear of loss related to such transactions.

Global nomads actively search out alternative forms of exchange, and they cherish the relations thereby formed. 'The best is when I do find a shelter from the storm, when I find people who open their doors and hearts. I think that travelling really shows our need to be open to other people. I believe we are all interconnected. We do rely on each other', muses Barbara (52).

Global nomads seem to prove to themselves, and perhaps also to others, that it is possible to connect with people without the intervention of states and corporations. Money is a metonymy for the two. It is a territorial monopoly of the state used for funding government and war, and as a medium of exchange for buying goods that have use-value (Schlichter, 2014). Global nomads' attitudes towards money range from slightly oblivious to fanatical. Some merely minimise their consumption, while for others, avoiding money is a value in itself, because money complicates social relationships. It depersonalises them and increases the number of dependencies, as sociologist Georg Simmel already noted (2004, pp. 296–8). If a transaction is unbalanced, it positions the other person as a debtor or as an object of charity. Overcoming these barriers of communication is important for global nomads, as I will later discuss in Chapter 6.

Just like downshifting, alternative forms of exchange have become more popular also among the settled. This is an unintended effect of capitalism, as sociologist Helmuth Berking has argued in his article 'Solitary Individualism' (as cited in Urry, 2001, p. 146. See also Firat and Venkatesh, 1995, pp. 245, 255; Kozinets, 2002, p. 21). When abstract systems, such as capitalism and global economy, penetrate into daily life, everybody's life is affected. Alternative practices seem to offer a way to cope with the risks and downsides that this invasion entails, and create meaningful social bonds instead (Giddens, 1991, pp. 136, 193).

With money being the prevailing medium of exchange in the contemporary world – we will see in Chapter 5 that it is also the measure for citizenship – downshifting and alternative forms of exchange are not necessarily well regarded in all contexts. From societies' point of view, moneyless transactions do not embellish the figures that are used to describe income and wealth in societies (see also Byrne, 2005, p. 86). At an individual level, alternative practices may provoke the fear of exploitation. Non-monetary exchanges require a high level of trust because they are not necessarily directly reciprocated, particularly when involving highly mobile people such as global nomads (see Douglas and Isherwood, 2002, p. xxv; Hirsch, 2005, p. 80).

Abstract systems, however, are also based on trust, money included, although this is not widely advertised. The current paper money is a mere book entry that is not backed by anything. It works as a medium of exchange only as long as people accept it and trust it (e.g. Schlichter, 2014, p. 77). The only major difference between money and other forms of exchange is that money extends human cooperation beyond direct contacts, whereas alternative forms are usually tied to one's immediate environment. With their practices, global nomads favour the personal and the intimate, trying to overcome the downsides of depersonalisation and alienation that are associated with second modernity.

Seizing the Moment

Economic perspectives are often used to discuss inequality and privileges, but as the previous analysis showed, they do not illuminate the case of global nomads. Their privileges have to be sought out elsewhere: in their relation to time.

As global nomads' work ethic already implied, they consciously avoid toil and diligence. In this respect, they resemble the former leisure class that Thorstein Veblen criticised in *The Theory of the Leisure Class* (2014); instead of 'conspicuous consumption', global nomads enjoy conspicuous leisure. Note, however, that global nomads are not uniform in this respect. While most of them enjoy being idle, refusing to fill up their calendar, some keep themselves busy by working or engaging in work-like activities. Furthermore, the follow-up to my original study revealed that their time concepts are changing, just like other features of their lifestyles. The following analysis focusses on these changes, therefore broadening the discussion to processes by which practices are adopted, formed, and sustained at an individual level.

To give a rough idea of different attitudes among global nomads, I have divided the nomads into two main categories. These categories are not binding; more likely, they represent different phases in their travels. The first category consists of the so called idlers who are likely to enjoy the present moment. They have an indefinite travel time ahead of them, and no need to worry about their income, either because they have the necessary material resources available or because they trust their abilities to earn their living and survive in the times of crises.

The idlers enjoy life slowly. They follow their inner rhythm, eating when they are hungry and going to bed when they feel sleepy; or they live in the rhythm of nature getting up with the sun and retiring with the sun, thereby detaching themselves from civilisations that proudly demonstrate their potency by turning the laws of nature upside down. When travelling, the idlers choose the slowest vehicles possible because they dislike arriving too quickly at their next destination.

> When you have a lot of time, how do you travel? I didn't want it to be as fast as flying. Sailing is an ancient thing. It is very different to approach the country on the boat. You have to be aware, you have to look out, you have to be alert: where's the entrance, where's the port. In the train you relax, but on the boat you run around, you make yourself ready. (STEFAN, 47)

The idlers slow down in order to experience more of their environment here and now. This experience provides them with the opportunity to appreciate the abundance of stimuli that surrounds them: colours, smells, sounds, and the hustle and bustle of cities, strange faces, and the way people dress, act, and run their everyday errands. Immersing into this sensual regime can produce a heightened sense of reality. The present moment is so full of new experiences that it completely immerses and occupies them.

In the second category we find those who consider their location-independence as a temporary phase of life, or those who work regularly. The 'temporary' global nomads are mostly young in their twenties. They resemble backpackers on a rite of passage, growing into adult responsibilities, except that unlike backpackers, they do not have a fixed return date and their travels are longer than the usual 2.5 to 18 months of backpackers (see Sørensen, 2003). These temporary nomads' plans concerning their return are also uncertain and can be interpreted in various ways. Many started their journey viewing it as a temporary phase in their lives, but had later changed their minds. Those global nomads who work, on the other hand, usually have no plans to return, but the same uncertainty surrounds their trajectories. Although working global nomads are able to earn their living while travelling, some other factors, particularly social, may later change their mind – as will be discussed in Chapter 4. Defining 'permanence' in either of these cases is problematic, given the changing character of global nomads' lifestyles and contemporary lives in general (see also Williams and Hall, 2000, p. 6).

This second group of global nomads, the temporary and workers, seek the heightened sense of reality differently than the first group, the idlers. Their schedules are often tight and filled with activities, supported by the Western conception that metaphorically associates time with money (see Urry, 2001, p. 113).

> I did many things. I was staying with members of hospitality exchange, gave lectures, and shared my life on a daily basis with kids suffering from cancer in a hospital in Strasbourg. I sent them emails and photos of kangaroos and other animals, and sometimes we had web cam discussions. I also organised NGO discussion days in San Salvador, Jakarta, and New Delhi. At other times I was reading, visiting historical sites, and relaxing. (LUDOVIC, 32)

By undertaking various activities, busy global nomads want to experience as much as possible, and thereby justify their time off from conventional life (see also Richards and Wilson, 2004c, pp. 25, 27). Similar motivations also seem to drive round-the-world travellers whose itineraries are about timing. They regard the world as a product that can be bought and consumed with time (Molz, 2010, p. 338). Sociologists argue that such a time concept has a much more wide-spread appeal. In the contemporary world, individuals must continually strive to be 'more efficient, faster, leaner, inventive and self-actualising than they were previously – not sporadically, but day-in day-out' (Elliott and Lemert, 2006, p. 3. See also Bauman, 2007, p. 94).

The downside of a busy schedule is that it can make global nomads' journey as tedious as a nine-to-five job. If this interpretation holds, various mishaps such as getting lost along the way can lead to frustration, and sleeping in late might make them feel guilty. The travellers' perspective is in terms of future objectives which are expected to make the sacrifices made today worth the trouble. This delaying of the fulfilment of needs forms the basic idea of the Protestant work ethic, which is a form of biopower exercised through ideals and related sanctions (Weber, 2005; Foucault, 2002c, pp. 332–3). The downside of this ethic is that the future-oriented traveller cannot enjoy the present moment and therefore the travel itself. It becomes a means to an end.

As these examples show, integrating hedonic and utilitarian purposes is challenging. This is particularly true for working global nomads, although they rarely mention work as a constraint but rather highlight its virtues. Claude (50), who cycles and writes travelogues about his adventures, explains:

> I'm living out of my passion. I'm not an artist but that's the closest I can think of. A painter will paint even if he breaks his arm, because painting is his life. For me, it's the same. If I couldn't ride any more, I would be deeply unlucky. I don't earn much, but I'm independent. I don't have a boss. On my tax report, I'm a cyclonaute and a globetrotter. That's my official status. (CLAUDE, 50)

Another question is whether paid work can be considered leisure even when it is enjoyed. The critics point out that this merely threatens to empty the concept of 'work' of meaning, and make it an irrelevant subject for analysis (Gershuny and Fisher, 2014, p. 30). However, leisure and work are continually contested and transformed, and in this process the conventional boundaries have become more permeable (Edensor, 2001, p. 60; Boon, 2006, p. 595; Fincham, 2008, p. 619). Academia has begun to discuss a leisure-oriented lifestyle where work and leisure operate as 'allies' adding to the subjectivities travellers can have on the road (Boon, 2006, pp. 594–5. See also Edensor, 2001, p. 60; Fincham, 2008, p. 619; Cohen, 2011, p. 1,547). This offers interesting perspectives for understanding both the working nomads and the idlers: a close analysis shows that even the most easy-going lifestyles are not necessarily free from work-like routines.

Although travel is often described in terms of ultimate freedom, it includes unavoidable routines. On the road, next destinations must be pondered, tickets have to be bought, accommodation searched for, and friends and family kept informed about one's whereabouts. Those travelling with their own vehicle also need to spend some time in repair and maintenance. As Tor (61) remarks: 'Sailing around in a boat is not just sipping piña coladas at sunset but a tremendous amount of work, almost a full-time job'.

To say that the participants have no routines and plans at all is therefore misleading; rather, it seems that global nomads prefer to create their own routines and avoid those that are forced upon them such as regular working hours and sitting in the office. In fact, most participants believe that routines are necessary because they facilitate adaptation to a new environment. 'When you hit a new country, there's an inevitable period, about five to six weeks, where your mind sort of doesn't have familiarity and it freaks out a little bit. You haven't developed a social circle thinking why did I bother to go from the old place to the new place', Max (39) describes. Routines, therefore, seem to sustain a sense of 'ontological security', which is one of their most important functions according to Giddens (1984, pp. xxiii, 282, 1991, p. 167).

The two different time concepts, easy-going vs. active, found among global nomads do not relate to their personality but represent different phases in their lives. As a rule of thumb, the longer their journeys are, the slower they go, and the less structuring of time they need. However, a contrary development is also possible, particularly for those who are working. What started as a passion and from global nomads' own agency, may eventually become enslaving, which is perhaps not an uncommon event for settled entrepreneurs either.

One example of this trajectory is described by Anthony (35), the founder and CEO of a non-profit organisation that promotes tolerance among school children around the world. His calendar looks like that of a busy businessman's. 'We [Anthony and his partner] can only stay one or two days and then we're off to the next destination. I am not able to stay longer even if I wanted to, because that would ruin our schedule, flights, visas, everything', Anthony explains. I found it easy to relate to Anthony's story. When engaging in this research, my leisurely lifestyle soon changed into a busy working schedule with deadlines, milestones and to-do lists.

Idleness is obviously not an inherent feature of global nomads' lifestyles but a result of a long process of unlearning, a process which might not ever be accomplished. Any transformation of subjectivities is bound to be slow and tedious, particularly if it involves detachment from dominant discourses and related ideals. Time related values are taught at a young age, and they are hard to forget given they also change the person's subjectivities. Biopower, and the dominant discourses through which it works, have made global nomads who they are. Therefore, seeking freedom from these discourses would also alter their subjectivities in a radical manner.

As a result, the location-independent lifestyle can be made as stressful, busy, and enslaving – or as rewarding, depending on your point of view – as a regular job. However, after adopting the lifestyle, most global nomads seem to live more in the present moment than they did in their previous settled lives that required more planning and timing. They act more spontaneously and give in to the circumstances, and are therefore able to reject some of the Western societies' most cherished values, efficiency included. As Simmel (2004) observed, freedom is never absolute. Even 'a change in obligations is often experienced as freedom' (p. 299).

Searching for Novelty

Global nomads' desire to live in the present moment, enjoying new stimuli and excitement, implies that they are driven by the same hunger for experiences that is considered typical of the contemporary society (e.g. Bauman, 2000, p. 62;

Richards and Wilson, 2004a, p. 5; Beck and Beck-Gernsheim, 2002, p. 38); they just satisfy their hunger differently. While the settled pack everything possible to their holidays, global nomads have made the search for novelty a continuous lifestyle, consuming places one after another.

For global nomads, the quest for novelty seems to require constant movement, although novelty could also be sought out when being settled, even from an armchair. Whenever the places visited feel increasingly like home, they direct their quest further (see also de Botton, 2002; Richards and Wilson, 2004a, p. 4). They might stay one day, two days, weeks, sometimes months, but in the end they always move on.

> I need the daily rush of entering the ring of the city. It's a euphoric feeling of trying to learn about the city, all the changes. I am a person that needs something very different every day. When I am here [in the Dominican Republic] for about – I don't know – two months, I know I'll be bored and the routine will set in I and I'll start looking down the road somewhere. (ANDY, 54)

Global nomads' movements are greatly facilitated by their practice of living and travelling light. They have no mortgages, long leases, or jobs that require being in one place, and they might not bother to unload their backpacks even when staying in one place for some time. They are ready to go at any time. 'I can be off in five minutes, my bag is unpacked', Stefan (47) says. Global nomads feel their life is in a constant transition where inner movements are accompanied by physical ones. In this context, the packed backpack is a sign of freedom, both negative freedom from constraints of places and obligations, and positive freedom to decide about their own lives (see Berlin, 2002, pp. 30–54. See also Urry, 2003, p. 112).

To keep up their eternal search, global nomads prefer to travel one-way seeking new routes and avoiding long stops. Andy (54), who calls himself a hobo despite not bumming rides on the rails but flying, feels he has the luxury that nobody else on the planet has: he can 'enter a culture' and he can 'leave a culture'.

> If I didn't like this place [the Dominican Republic], I could be on the plane tomorrow. When I was in St. Martin in the Caribbean one time, I got up in the morning and said: I can't take it any more. By one o'clock I was on the plane flying to Guatemala. I try not to enter countries when I am in a bad mood [laughs]. (ANDY, 54)

While anthropologists would probably disagree – entering a culture is not a superficial game but takes a considerable amount of time – it is indisputable that compared to conventional tourists, Andy and the other global nomads have a greater degree of choice. They are not caught up in the often repetitive products offered by the travel industry (see also Maoz, 2006, p. 221).

What do global nomads do with this freedom – where do they go? If asked about their destination decision criteria, they tend to be evasive, emphasising the spontaneous nature of their travels. 'It's just coming back and forth and going to all directions. It's not organised, trying to cover certain areas. It just happens', Anick (29) says, shrugging her shoulders.

If examined from the point of view of rational choice, global nomads seem unwilling to consider that their decision-making could imply an existence of latent motivations that are just not expressed, for one reason or another. Global nomads might, for instance, want to make their journeys appear more interesting and free. As mentioned in Chapter 1, it is fairly typical that participants play down some of the activities, which might not fit the way they want to present themselves. This influences the participants' answers which, therefore, poses a major constraint on interview and observation situations.

If this interpretation holds, global nomads would consciously build a romantic image of their lifestyles by taking pride in their capriciousness and spontaneity. Some of the global nomads' stories seem to imply this might be the case. Consider the example of Elisa (54), who was in Israel and had trouble deciding where to go next. A friend of hers helped by putting an Atlas in front of her.

> He said, 'Hey, look at the Atlas, figure out what makes the most sense in terms of travelling'. I decided to go to Morocco but I couldn't find a reasonable flight so I flew to Spain thinking that I was going to take the boat back to Morocco but once I got to Spain, I was contacted by some friends in India who were all living in Pisa, and so we were all living in a squat in Pisa. I just follow my gut. (ELISA, 54)

The quotation pays attention to choice: practically the whole world is on global nomads' plate. As the quotation also indicates, however, global nomads have constraints such as the availability of budget flights and travel companions. Roads define where they are able to travel comfortably, and lack of internet might be an obstacle when considering travelling to undeveloped and rural areas, at least for those who need an internet connection for their work (see also Urry, 2001, pp. 12, 35). These constraints could be regarded as an antithesis of freedom: they decide *for* global nomads where to go, thereby illustrating the role of structure in their lives. If viewed from this perspective, the global nomads' world is not the world as we know it. The areas that are usually, although not always, excluded comprise isolated natural areas such as Arctic zones, large deserts and many of the Pacific islands, expensive countries such as Bhutan, or closed societies such as North Korea. As later discussed in Chapter 5, global nomads might also avoid war zones or areas infected with disease and crime, which further shrinks their world.

Global nomads' destinations may not always be their most preferred places, but as a trade-off they offer convenience, ease of travel, and cost savings. Some studies suggest that such limitations are not necessarily negative. They might lead to more satisfactory results from the individual's point of view, because more choice can be demotivating, and can lead to less comfort and satisfaction with one's choices (Carmon, Wertenbroch, and Zeelenberg, 2003; Iyengar and Lepper, 2000; Mick, Broniarczyk, and Haidt, 2004, p. 208; Schwartz, Ward, Monterosso, Lyubomirsky, White, and Lehman, 2002; Shankar, Cherrier, and Canniford, 2006).

In this complex interplay between structure and agency and their attendant enabling and limiting qualities, destinations become, if not altogether irrelevant, at least less important. Max (39) describes how his attitude has changed during the years: 'I've realised that everywhere is a little bit the same – depending on what you make of it – but transitions can be interesting and entertaining'. As the word 'transition' indicates, it is not, strictly speaking, novelty that attracts global nomads but change and contrasts. This is increasingly true for those who have already toured around the world many times. The repetitive features of places fade into the background when the contrast from one place to the next is great enough. Sometimes global nomads jump from one continent to another to increase that experience. Such travels for them represent both ultimate freedom and ultimate constraint: whenever the novelty value wears off, they *have to* go.

Whenever places themselves are no longer considered the primary object of interest, they gain meaning through their relationship to other places. This idea is familiar from Ferdinand de Saussure's (1990) theory of language, where each word gains meaning in relation to another. We can understand the meaning of 'day' only when contrasted to 'night' (pp. 100–102, 166), and therefore the meaning is postponed, arising from the interplay the two words, thereby leaving the words themselves without extrinsic meaning (Derrida, 1982, pp. 3–6). Similarly, places for global nomads gain meaning in relation to other places or people they meet, or they become a complex part of who they are (see also Urry and Sheller, 2004, pp. 1, 6; Cuthill, 2004, p. 57; Frello, 2008, p. 26; Hannam, Sheller, and Urry, 2006, 13; Butcher, 2010, p. 24; Massey, 1993, pp. 67–9). Jeff (25) describes: 'I cannot have a discussion without referencing a place I was before'.

When places are viewed as internally referential phenomena, global nomads themselves become the 'terrains' to be 'traversed'. This is how literary scholar John S. Thompson (2007) described the travelling Romantics of the seventeenth and eighteenth centuries. On their journeys, they searched for a revelatory moment that would rejuvenate their creativity in a conjunction of external and internal stimuli (pp. 194, 209). While the Romantics preferred beautiful natural landscapes, global nomads' revelations – whatever they are – can take place anywhere, even in a filthy slum. Places for them are mere platforms for their projects of the self, and if they do not like where they are, they will move on. Consequently, global nomads also experience fewer disappointments than more conventional tourists; after all, they have not constructed a norm to which their actual travel experiences would have to be compared.

Global nomads' travel style has interesting implications for the way in which travel is conceived, because places are usually viewed as the magnets that draw people. When conventional tourists travel, they create expectations and daydream about their destinations (Urry, 2002b, p. 3). Even global nomads' namesakes, pastoral nomads, were not oblivious to places, as philosophers Gilles Deleuze and Félipe Guattari (1987) argued in their rather romanticising account of nomadism. Pastoralists followed customary paths conscious of various points such as water, dwelling, and assembly points, although these had an instrumental value only. The nomads reached water points in order to leave them behind (p. 380), which implies that motion, for them too, mattered over destination. It was the in-between, the travel itself, which had autonomy and a direction of its own.

For research, such location-independence poses several challenges. Starting with practical questions, there seems to be no means to predict global nomads' routes. Most of the models used in migration studies assume that the place itself is the primary unit of analysis, while the perspective of the moving subjects is disregarded as expressed in the push and pull model discussed in Chapter 1 (see also Kalir, 2013, p. 325). In tourism studies, on the other hand, the available models suffer from the same methodological assumption as second modernist theories: they are based on the idea of rational choice and linear progression, as the travel career model shows. The model suggests that people's motivations change with their travel experience. In the beginning, they choose easier destinations, gradually proceeding to more challenging ones. The model suggests that people systematically move through such a series of stages, or at least they have predictable motivational patterns (Pearce and Lee, 2005, p. 227).

In order to switch the viewpoint to the mobile without exaggerating individual agency and cognition, I have suggested the concept of 'location-independence'. It represents a detachment from the magic of 'places' and recognises their relative significance. Places are treated, rather than as interests per se, as systems of meaning with which individuals build their lifestyles and subjectivities. Instead, attention is paid to differences, contrasts, and transitions, as is typical in the search for novelty. And if carefully considered, it would be an oxymoron to analyse location-independence through the significance of places (cf. Cresswell, 2010, p. 552).

'Location-independence' does not assume a belonging either, which would require individuals to split themselves between different places, for example between different states as in 'migration'. Although 'cosmopolitanism' also describes some degree of placelessness, it still assumes an attachment. Its advocates argue that people belong to a range of polities of which nation-states are only one (e.g. Calhoun, 2002, p. 877; Beck, 2002, p. 20). While this may sound accurate enough, the location-independent show that there are people who do not necessarily want to belong anywhere in particular. They refuse to be structured by places (see also Massey, 1994, p. 137. Cf. Hoey, 2010, p. 238).

'Location-independence' highlights the role of mobilities but avoids hyping them. Constant movement is not a nonstop holiday but includes many problems as the examples in this chapter have shown (cf. Snedden, 2013), nor is location-independence mere movement. For global nomads, it is a prerequisite for seeking the other detachments that they want in their life such as detachment from money and high-pressured working cultures. Notice the word 'seek', which reminds us that this process is never complete. Individuals are inextricably tied to structure from which they try to detach themselves; the act of opposing structure merely emphasises this relation. The result of global nomads' attempts to oppose the structure, is the topic of the next section.

Class and Structure

For the purpose of this analysis, I contend that it is more accurate to include a range of location-independent lifestyles in the discussion, rather than a particular lifestyle or a homogeneous social group. As such, the term 'global nomad' serves as a heuristic concept with which location-independence can be analysed, rather than as a definitive category. It is important to note here that location-independence can be realised in many ways, and the global nomads in this book are not an exhaustive sample.

To say, however, that global nomads are completely disparate would be misleading. They share a set of practices that structure their daily life and travels such as the previously discussed downshifting, employing alternative forms of exchange, slowing down the pace of life, and living and travelling light. If we agree with Pierre Bourdieu's (1984) argument that people living the same cultural lifestyles and similar tastes occupy the same social space (pp. 56, 60), then these shared practices seem to unite global nomads. But how useful is the concept of 'practice' when examining the role of structure and the inequalities that global nomads' lifestyles create? Remember that according to practice approach, people create structure, social distance, and unequal relations simply by going about their daily lives.

The conclusion that global nomads' practices create inequalities that put them in a privileged class is not a straightforward one. Global nomads' practices almost deliberately oppose the dominant discourses in the Western world, and therefore also the dominant ideals and norms. They enjoy, for instance, conspicuous leisure in a world where leisure is no longer a badge of honour but instead symbolises uselessness and unemployment. This is due to the so called substitution effect: higher wages make leisure more expensive in the sense that if people take time off, they give up more money. This has changed the status of leisure, and the most leisure-rich people now find themselves at the bottom of the socio-economic ladder.

However, global nomads themselves value their practices even though other people may not. According to Beck, this is an effect of individualisation. When people make decisions regarding their own lives, the social perception of what constitutes privilege changes. In some cases, less income and status, if they go hand in hand with the opportunity for more self-development and the ability to control things personally, may be perceived as an advantage (Beck and Beck-Gernsheim, 2002, p. 162). While social sciences have historically studied inequality in conjunction with class analysis, Beck believed that such analysis could no longer work because the meaning of life chances and status has become subjective. He called social class 'a zombie category' that is dead yet lives on (Beck and Beck-Gernsheim, 2002, p. 27. Cf. Elliott, 2002, p. 304).

The example of the location-independent seems to confirm these arguments, or at the very least serves to create a significant challenge to place these individuals in any class category, since traditional class divisions are based on income and property, which are not important for global nomads. They do not strive for better pay but rather lower their status. The closest to a social class global nomads can be said to represent is that of the precariat that lives with insecurity and, similar to global nomads, nurtures minimal trust relationships with capital and the state (see Standing, 2011, p. 8). However, rather than being a single social class, the precariat is a multi-class phenomenon (Ross, 2009, p. 6. Cf. Standing, 2011, p. 8). It now describes a great mass of Western people due to labour insecurity and collapsing welfare states that have left an increasing number of individuals at the margins of societies, to live the life of a modern vagrant (see Bauman, 1993, p. 240). The precariat is, fundamentally, 'we' rather than a stratifying class. It offers people a particular sense of the self that is linked to a claim of 'ordinariness' (see Bottero, 2005, p. 141), which appears to dissolve difference and inequality.

The usefulness of the distinction of 'social class' has been fiercely debated in recent sociological discussions (e.g. Atkinson, 2007a, 2007b, 2008, 2010b; Beck, 2007; Beck and Beck-Gernsheim, 2002; Bottero, 2005; Brannen and Nilsen, 2005; Curran, 2013; Esping-Andersen, 1993a, 1993b; Goldthorpe, 1996; Goldthorpe and Marshall, 1992; Pakulski and Waters, 1996; Wright, 1989). Regardless which side of the debate is chosen, inequalities do not vanish, but it is indisputable that they are harder to grasp with quantitative methods and static categorisations based on income and wealth (see also Atkinson, 2010a, p. 12). Global nomads are primary examples of this, as their wealth seems to be located elsewhere.

When the dilemma of inequality is approached with structuration theory, agency seems to be the key. Whenever individuals are able to 'do otherwise', Giddens argued, they have agency and choice (1984, p. 15). This implies transformative power and fewer structural limits. By contrast, whenever individuals are more 'structured' (see Bauman, 1989, p. 46), their actions are limited (Giddens, 1989, p. 258).

Agency and structure are not mutually exclusive, however. While it is true that global nomads are able to exercise transformative power by virtue of having choice, as the analysis showed, they still have many constraints that influence these choices. Of those constraints, the greatest is their criticism towards dominant discourses. By opposing dominant discourses, global nomads inextricably bind themselves to them, although in a modified form (see also Thompson, 1989, pp. 58, 71–2). This seems to suggest that structural features are still there; they have just become naturalised and thereby have become invisible.

Viewed from a Foucauldian perspective, naturalisation is an effect of power, which makes constraining factors appear normal and desired. Although individuals reproduce structure, they strongly believe in their own agency and individuality. The analysis showed, for instance, that when global nomads present the logic of their travels, they consciously ignore the constraints focussing instead on their own will. Research has shown that lifestyle migrants explain their acts similarly, although their acts are not always a matter of choice (Benson, 2010, p. 52; Korpela, 2009, pp. 19, 188).

If measured by choice, global nomads' privileges are therefore limited, and it is relevant to ask whether the notion of privileges helps us to understand their lifestyles in any way. Their elitism seems to derive mainly from the fact that they deviate from the norm, and basically everything that is somehow different can be considered either privileged or disadvantaged and therefore marginalised (see Warnes and Williams, 2006, p. 1,275). When the majority of people in the world stay in their country of origin – in 2013, just 3 per cent of the world's population were residing outside their country of birth (United Nations, 2013) – location-independence is an unusual phenomenon. However, this statistic reveals little about the status of the location-independent. Rather, it suggests that perhaps such value-laden arguments should be avoided in research.

While claims of elitism are usually intended to be critical, highlighting researchers' awareness of inequalities, the problem is that they paradoxically end up glamorising the rejected forms of travel. What also needs to be remembered is that deviance is always relative. Many of the global nomads' practices described in this chapter are also increasing in popularity among the settled, particularly the practices of downshifting and alternative forms of exchange. In the USA, one-fifth of the work force have voluntarily switched to a lower paying job and reduced the amount of working hours, and in Australia 23 per cent of people aged between 30 and 60 have done the same (Hamilton, 2003, p. 206. See also Ravenscroft and Gilchrist, 2009). The numbers are considerable, particularly considering that the research was done before the 2008 financial downturn. Since then, the figures have most likely gone up, although these people have not necessarily experienced downshifting as a lifestyle choice.

Global nomads also pioneer emerging leisure and work-related trends. While these are not as clear as downshifting – there have been, for instance, been many contradicting and failed predictions about the rise of leisure (e.g. Keynes, 1963) – various forms of slowing down and taking more time off from work have become more common. These trends affect travel as well. Instead of choosing aeroplanes and other forms of motorised transportation, people might opt for slower means of travel, favouring sailing, walking, and cycling (e.g. Molz, 2009, p. 277; Cresswell, 2008a, p. 14). Workplaces, on the other hand, are becoming more boundaryless allowing new forms of telework that can be performed from abroad or even on the road, as global nomads demonstrate. All these examples show that marginal lifestyles offer important indicators of where the world is going and how we should prepare ourselves for the upcoming changes.

Rather than ostentation, global nomads seem to represent emerging trends, at least on the grounds of money, time and place as discussed in this chapter. Even though global nomads themselves appreciate their practices, from the point of view of dominant discourses they are considered status lowering. The argument of elitism should not be dismissed, however. It shows that extreme mobilities – and alternative lifestyles in general – raise strong reactions both in the general public and among researchers. It encapsulates important power struggles revealing what people and societies consider to be good and beneficial travel, and what kind of travel they want to discourage. This is my next subject, which I examine through the image of location-independence.

For this task, Giddens's structuration theory no longer offers the best tools, as Giddens largely bypassed questions of power that are inherent in such discussions. This strikes me as slightly odd since Giddens regarded power to be essential in all structuration processes and even identified it as one of his own preoccupations (e.g. Giddens, 1979, pp. 54, 91, 1981, pp. 3, 28–9, 51, 1984, p. 31. See also Giddens, 1981, p. 3; McLennan, 1984, p. 128; Thompson, 1989, p. 75). Giddens, however, viewed power through two distinct lenses: that of individuals' sovereign ability to make a change (1979, pp. 56, 93, 1984, pp. 4, 14), and that of domination, particularly in terms of state power, both of which I will discuss later in Chapter 5. Foucault, on the other hand, offered a more balanced approach by theorising power in everyday life as both enabling and constraining, which I will adopt in the next chapter when analysing power issues related to location-independence. I will begin, in a now familiar manner, by presenting a story of one of the study participants, and will follow by detailing Foucault's discourse theory, the framework through which I will approach the subject.

Chapter 3
Two Faces

The decision to hit the road was not easy for all global nomads. Cindie (51) hesitated for a couple of years before she gave in to her then-husband's persuasion. He was an eager cyclist, even competitive, and wanted to extend the couple's bicycle tours outside their home country, the US. At the time, Cindie was quite happy with her life. She had a job as a geologist that she enjoyed, a house, a car, and a loving family. Then her husband wanted to start roaming about the world on a daily budget of US$20 a day, with no certainty about tomorrow.

'… it was really his dream, and he kept pushing and pushing and I was not interested. I was working and doing my thing and I really didn't have any plans on changing that', Cindie recounts. What eventually changed her mind was a sudden realisation of the absurdity of the American middle-class lifestyle. 'I started to look around at my boss at the time. He didn't have any children, he made a lot of money, he had a bigger house, a couple of extra cars, and a Harley-Davidson. One day I took a hard look at it and said, is that what I get for working for the next fifteen years, is a bigger house and a bunch of cars'.

As soon as it dawned on Cindie that she had no reason to buy a bigger house than she already had, and that she felt she already had everything she needed materially, there was no reason to stay and continue to put all her energy into acquiring more things. 'When this adventure was put before me, I finally said why not, we can always turn around'.

Listening to Cindie, I was amazed. For me, like for so many other global nomads I had interviewed, travelling had been a childhood dream. I would have up and left any time, had someone proposed to go round the world with me. Or would I have? The thought of living on modest or even bare means did not yet attract me in my twenties. I was ambitious. I had just received my doctorate and I wanted a job in business with a high salary. Although travel was my passion, at that time I would have considered plans to leave everything behind as frivolous and naïve.

With the virtue of hindsight, I see that I had been tied to the sense of security that everyday routines and a clear career path had provided – and to other people's expectations. This contradiction between what we want and what other people want from us often slows us down or even causes us to entirely abandon the pursuit of our dreams. Global nomads are no different in this respect, but over the course of time they detach themselves from these constraints. This change is, of course, most intriguing. What are the reasons that make global nomads choose to leave, and why have they chosen mobility instead of merely changing their lives in their country of origin? There are many, even more radical alternatives available within societies, for example living off the grid or becoming an activist. What is so great about travel that it makes global nomads quit their relatively comfortable lives?

Rather than explore individual travel motivations, on which there is already an abundance of literature (e.g. Cohen, 2010a, 2011; Hannam and Ateljevic, 2008; O'Reilly, 2000; Benson and O'Reilly, 2009; Richards and Wilson, 2004b), I examine the way in which global nomads represent their lifestyles. My specific focus is on global nomads' power negotiations with the settled: the factors that the settled find so unsettling about extreme mobilities, and the preferred modes of travel in the contemporary society.

Discourse analysis, an approach within the field of social construction that examines how meaning is created, offers the means to accomplish this. Note that although discourse analysis involves working with language, it is neither linguistic nor narrative research. Rather the use of language is viewed as a form of social practice that is socially conditioned and has social effects (Fairclough, 1989, p. 20).

I define discourses as 'practices that systematically form the objects of which they speak', to follow one of the Foucauldian formulations (1969, pp. 66–7). Applying this to global nomads, this means that discourses are vehicles of thought and action with which they, and outsiders alike, represent location-independence. Global nomads might employ such metaphors as nomadism or hoboing, or they might speak about their lifestyles in terms of freedom. All these meanings build them particular subject positions which have actual implications for their everyday lives, influencing how they travel, structure time, make decisions about their next destinations, and organise their consumption to support their lifestyles.

Discourses differ over time, with the kinds of institutions and social practices in which they take shape, and with the positions of speakers and their audience (Foucault, 1978; Macdonell, 1986, p. 1). Because of the high number of possible variables, discourse analysis is always contextual, taking into account the constraints of production and reception. These constraints explain what manner of information can be represented in a given context.

Contextual analysis reveals that different discourses compete for the dominant position. Those discourses that lose their contingent nature become dominant and are then treated as the truth. As such, they influence social conventions, mentalities, feelings, actions, and behaviours, and in this sense, they become 'real'. In the following analysis, I examine two discourses, one dominant and one opposing. The choice was made in the name of analytical efficiency, as two discourses are enough to show that there are tensions and struggle regarding location-independence. Remember, however, that there are more discourses than just these two, and even fractions of discourse can play alternating roles (see also Dews, 1979, p. 156). Therefore, this division is for analytical purposes only.

The tools I use are a combination of Michel Foucault's, Norman Fairclough's (1989), and Teun A. van Dijk's (2006, 2008) theories on discourses. While Foucault developed his ideas early on in his career in *The Archaeology of Knowledge* (1969), in the first wave of the so-called discursive turn in the social sciences, Fairclough and van Dijk represent a newer version of the methodology, the so-called critical discourse analysis. The task is to create a general methodological view, with the main division of labour, so to speak, being between Foucauldian approaches and the more practically oriented methods of the latter two, but without assuming their sometimes simplifying views on power as repression.

Discourses

In order to identify discourses, the interviews first need to be dismantled. The elements under scrutiny in the following analysis include structure and argumentation such as agency, degrees of precision and vagueness, choice of words, their etymology and connotations, and rhetorical devices such as synonyms, metaphors, metonymies, binary oppositions, causal relationships, and means of legitimisation (van Dijk, 2008; Fairclough, 1989). After this processing is complete, the analysis can be broadened to a contextual level with the focus on the conditions that prompt global nomads to produce the two particular discourses, and on their practical implications.

Adventurers

When talking about their lifestyles, global nomads focus on the upsides of travel, which serves to create a strong sense of agency for themselves. Living on the road for them is voluntary and sought out as is typical for leisure (see Rojek, 2010). The majority regard their lifestyle as a fulfilment of a long-time dream. It is a constant, exciting adventure.

> I guess I especially love the feeling of having backpack on my back, guitar by my side, my thumb out. When it starts getting dark, I go out in the woods with my sleeping bag and go to sleep under the stars. When I wake up in the morning, I never know where I'm going to be the next day. I love sleeping on the ground, under the stars, and I love new languages, I love new cultures, I love meeting people. But above all, I love the adventure. (PHOENIX, 49)

'Adventure' best describes also the dominant discourse among global nomads. The word comes from Latin *adventura*, which implies something that is about to happen (Online Etymology Dictionary, 2010). It can refer to an exciting experience or an undertaking that may involve discomfort, danger, and unknown risks. In this discourse, global nomads are free to go anywhere they want, anytime they want. They have no one – a boss, a partner, or a government – to tell them what to do. Being both flexible and able to support themselves with their talents, they care little about the constraints associated with a settled life, such as money (see also Rickly-Boyd, 2013). When asked how much the travelling lifestyle costs, Barbara (52) answers laughing, 'I have no idea. I don't even know if I have any money in my wallet now ... My usual style is to drive until I run out of gas'.

In everyday life, the discourse of 'adventuring' translates into risk-taking. One aspect is that global nomads might live like locals, often ascetically, because they travel in low income countries. This gives them an aura of endurance, courage, and resourcefulness. The discourse of adventuring is in many ways glamorising, emphasising those features that global nomads appreciate, regardless of the perceived status of these features in dominant discourses.

Despite their different ideals, global nomads are not detached from dominant discourses, however; they are bound to them through their criticism. When global nomads describe their own lifestyles in terms of freedom, courage, and spontaneity, these synonymic relations result in the formation of an opposing image of the settled who, lacking these attributes, can be described as being suppressed, cautious, and calculative. This association is automatic and is produced as result of the way in which language – and therefore the mind – works.

The dichotomy between global nomads and the settled is not the invention of global nomads. Their namesakes, pastoral nomads, were long opposed to farmers in the same way (Khazanov, 1994, p. 160). Nor is the discourse of adventuring new. It has a long history in travel writing and fiction, particularly in Romantic imagery. The Romantics defined adventuring in terms of close calls and suffering, often putting their heroes on the stormy seas and on desert islands where cannibals reigned, as these experiences were thought to measure them as men (see Thompson, 2007). In global nomads' stories this glorious past and the present of travel entwine seamlessly. 'I lead a very romantic life, I can't deny that', says Phoenix (49), and details, in the spirit of the Romantics, the price of his manifold adventures.

> I've spent more nights lying in freezing mud or snow, steaming jungles, ditches, trenches, with things crawling over me, had more tropical diseases, been through more hardships and almost lost my life more times than anybody would want to even think about. I have bullet holes, knife holes, burn scars. You might say I've earned my twenty years of alternative living the hard way. (PHOENIX, 49)

Phoenix's story is not one of a kind. Other participants, both men and women, also draw attention to hardships, which range from Phoenix's rather extreme experiences to minor drawbacks or discomfort. Anick (29), who occasionally receives donations from people who want to buy a dream by supporting her travels, reminds us of these less drastic occurrences.

> They [the donators] see my life as a temporary realisation of a dream but it's not my reality; it's not a dream. There are downsides: there's fasting, there's walking forty kilometres because you don't have a ride, there is being tired and sick and having to go to a new place, and constantly taking care of yourself. There's downsides too in this lifestyle. People forget it. (ANICK, 29)

Some global nomads believe it is precisely the pain of travel that makes them nomads. They seek risks in order to test their uncertainty tolerance, which ultimately includes encountering death where and whenever it comes. 'If you're afraid of dying, it's hard to be a traveller. I'm not afraid of dying. If I die, I die. You have to be willing to accept the risk, and I do', says Andy (54), flirting with the theme that is usually avoided in tourism (see Williams and Balaz, 2015; Cohen, 2009, pp. 183–4). The Romantics of the seventeenth and eighteenth centuries, on the other hand, actively searched for close calls, because they hoped to speak more authoritatively on metaphysical themes including religion and philosophy. Travelling for them was a means to experience life in its quintessential form (Thompson, 2007, p. 100), and a similar meaning still persists. In the discourse of adventuring, global nomads are admired role models because of their intense experiences. They are thought to have traversed not only difficult terrains but also made profound discoveries of life. Ingo (36) encapsulates: 'People think my life is glamorous, and they consider me worldly because I've seen so much'.

In participant observation, the aura of adventuring could be seen in many ways. Some of the participants were celebrated heroes in their circles. They visited hospex meetings in their destinations giving speeches and gathering a group of admirers around them. They also received spontaneous invitations from other members to visit their homes, and their references were expected to raise the host's status in the community.

These observations showed that the discourse of adventuring is not a mere story to be told; it actively influences global nomads' practices. Similar discourses exist also among other travellers. While global nomads seek status by ignoring their lifestyles' constraints in order to appear more free, some backpackers smear their backpacks and roughen their shoes to appear more adventurous, or they boast about the diseases that they have suffered (Sørensen, 2003, pp. 856–7. See also Elsrud, 2001, pp. 611–12). The greatest difference between global nomads and other travellers is that for the latter, adventuring is the most common discourse because it is socially acceptable among travellers (see Noy, 2004, p. 90), whereas global nomads also employ another, darker discourse.

Vagrants

Side by side with the discourse of adventuring, within the story of the very same person, there is another discourse, one that characterises location-independence in terms of homelessness and poverty. In this discourse, global nomadism is no longer a celebrated choice of an individual willing to sacrifice his or her own comfort in search of sublime goals. On the contrary, lack of roof and ceiling is viewed as a despicable state, which forces global nomads to sleep like the homeless: in their clothes grasping their belongings. '[I have slept] in bushes, under bridges, city parks, tunnels and caves, sides of roads. Generally, where people won't be able to see me sleeping. Then I'm up at dawn, and back on the road', Scott (33) describes.

Vagrancy changes the agency of the discourse. Global nomads are no longer the heroes of their own lives but instead victims of unfortunate circumstances who are unable to get a grip on their lives. Location-independence might not have been their first choice; rather, they may have been pushed to do something with their lives because of unemployment, death of a close relative, or divorce. Rita recounts the reasons that made her leave:

> I didn't start out expecting to roam the world as a nomad. I thought I was going to spend my life with my husband ... Once I accepted the fact that the divorce was inevitable, I looked around and tried to picture my life as a single woman in LA. My kids, ages 22 and 23, were in Vail, Colorado, and Singapore at the time. I knew I wasn't going to be the kind of mom who moved in down the street and saw them every day. I was too independent for that. And so were they. I also knew that I didn't want to hold my husband hostage for the rest of his life by accepting alimony. We'd had too many years of happiness together to do that. I also hated the idea of being dependent on that cheque. I wasn't going to give that kind of power to anyone, even if it benefited me. (RITA, 72)

The discourse of vagrancy has long roots just like its counterpart (see also Cresswell, 2011b, p. 249). The problem of vagrants became a significant political and social problem in early modern societies (roughly the period between 1500 and 1650). Most of the vagrants were unemployed, seasonal agricultural workers, professionals of rare trades, or peddlers who were floating from job to job, living in alehouses, and sleeping outside. Another group of vagrants comprised of beggars, con men and criminals who rather begged and stole than worked. Under the law, all were treated equally – as criminals (Beier, 2004, pp. 6, 30–31, 35). Officials placed restrictions on their wanderings, arrested them and sent them to workhouses, prisons, and hospitals.

Since the Middle Ages, Western societies have had a hard time trying to draw the line between honest and industrious vagrants living in misfortune and those who simply avoided work. Societies have sought detailed information in order to determine who really needed and deserved assistance, and who were merely exploiting the system (e.g. Beier, 2004). Often the measures the officials took seemed disproportionate, especially considering that as a social group, vagrants exerted very little social power and posed little direct economic, political, and physical threat to the dominant culture (Amster, 2003, p. 196). Exactly the same could be said of global nomads, but despite their small number, they can awaken strong antipathy.

There are material reasons, or more exactly assumptions, for such an antipathy as discussed in the previous chapter. However, these anxieties can also be linked to the unpredictability of travel: travel is believed to have the capacity to radically transform people (Euben, 2006, p. 41). The same reconfigurative power revered in the discourse of adventuring as knowledge producing, courageous, and enriching becomes despicable and corrupting in the discourse of vagrancy. In the worst case, it turns global nomads – former respectable members of society – into criminals and anti-heroes. Some global nomads openly admit that negative changes can take place. 'Travelling has made me more intolerant. You're totally intolerant to stupidity, to intolerant people, to materialism, things that are not important to you. That is something tough to accept', Anthony (35) elaborates.

Just how hard it is for global nomads to produce this discourse, is revealed in Anthony's use of passive 'you' when speaking about his own experiences. This represents a turning point where global nomads are no longer in charge of their lives but victims. Although recognising one's weaknesses is difficult for anyone, in global nomads' case it might be even more so because of the dominant travel tradition that praises sublime transformations such as finding oneself, learning new skills, and broadening one's perspectives. If anything, then, travel is expected to make people more open-minded. This is biopower at work: it guides travellers subtly to 'right' kind of travel.

As these two discourses of adventuring and vagrancy illustrate, travel encompasses various meanings. Most of the current paradoxes related to mobility emanate from the residual meanings of these discourses (see Williams, 1977). They bear meanings that their users are not fully aware of, yet they have a significant effect on their objects; they shape them (see Foucault, 1998b, pp. 369–70). Just like vagrants, global nomads can evoke connotations of both bumming and romantic heroism (see also Cohen 1973, p. 50). More than anything else, these discontinuities show the contradictory meanings that can be created in a particular context, thereby illustrating power at work, in the process of negotiation.

Most global nomads have encountered both interpretations. 'When I'm travelling, some people think I'm on vacation, but usually they think I'm either a millionaire or a vagrant', says Gustavo (51). The first encounter with the two discourses typically occurred at the time when global nomads told their friends and family about their decision to start travelling for a long or an indefinite period of time. While some friends and family members admired their decision, others warned against it. 'Many thought I was crazy. Why would I sleep on the floor and on the streets when I could have a nice job and a comfortable life instead?' Ludovic (32) reminisces.

The discourse of vagrancy indicates that the stigma associated with long-term travel continues (see Bianchi, 2000, p. 109; Riley, 1988, pp. 313–14. Cf. Adler and Adler, 1999, pp. 32, 52–3), also in research as evidenced by the notorious connotations of 'drifting' discussed in Chapter 1. This cultural baggage has many practical consequences. To name one example, the international visa system fails to recognise the phenomenon of long-term travel. Travelling to a country requires a purpose such as tourism, business, or a family reunion. Furthermore, the journey's duration must be limited, evidence of which is often required in the form of an onward or return ticket. Global nomads might have to lie about their intentions, bribe officials, or forge travel documents in order to gain entry. These assumptions of purposes and duration are based on the most common definition of 'travel': it starts from home and it ends at home, which is not the case for global nomads. As George (31) points out: 'I don't have any backup. If I don't make my way, I can't go home'.

The Clash

When and why do these two discourses of adventuring and vagrancy appear? In order to analyse their conditions of production and reception, I asked global nomads how they present themselves to other people and observed them in social situations. The findings show how global nomads govern themselves when searching for command and control in social encounters by adopting norms, or by resisting conventional codes of conduct (see Foucault, 1991b).

Most global nomads tend to keep a low profile when interacting with others by communicating only the most basic details of their lives: where they come from and that they like to travel. They regard telling their story as a hassle because it raises too many questions and suspicions, or conversely, engenders embarrassing and persistent admiration in situations where they would rather go unnoticed. When they do elaborate, however, the discourse of adventuring is usually dominant. After all, why would they purposefully belittle themselves?

Whenever global nomads employ the discourse of vagrancy, it is typically told with less precision and only when they know their discussion partners better. This is not a rule, however. Sometimes global nomads like to provoke, and for this, the discourse of vagrancy offers a perfect means. Stating that one is homeless raises many emotions. 'I think it wasn't a good answer', Michel says laughing (47), describing his experience at the US border with Canada. 'The interrogation took forty-five minutes and all other passengers of the Greyhound bus waited for me'.

For women, the discourse of vagrancy is particularly provoking as it bears the connotation of being morally loose. Although female nomads use both discourses, historically they are masculine and rarely used by or of women (see also Cresswell and Uteng, 2008, p. 2). Female global nomads encounter these gender specific stereotypes especially when travelling in cultures where women are considered homemakers. There they rarely chose to provoke because of the fear of drawing unwanted attention. Instead, they might lie about their marital status, although this does not necessarily save them from questioning. 'I pretended to have a husband but then locals asked, "Who is taking care of the house?"' Anick (29) describes her encounters with locals in Turkey.

When the discourse of vagrancy is employed as a tool for creating a picture of the downsides of location-independence, it is often done so through indirect speech. The respondents quote suspicions and comments they have heard or sensed from other people. When hitch-hiking in the US, Jérémy (27) felt he was looked down on as a beggar or a bum, and sometimes feared as a potential killer or a rapist. Despite his sympathetic manner and appearance, he was stopped 35 times by the local police and ordered to vacate the area, just like vagrants of old.

The discourse of vagrancy might also be projected by global nomads onto other travellers because they do not want to be labelled so themselves. Andy (54) associates vagrancy with heavy-duty travellers who have been on the road for more than two years. This is a group that he represents as well, but he distances himself from the other members by describing himself as an honest person.

If you meet someone who has travelled two years, lock up your stuff. They have to have money, right? Ninety per cent of them will do any kind of compromise to continue their travel. That means if they can run on the bill, they will. You can live pretty cheap if you didn't pay your hotel room and you got people to buy your lunch. These guys, they have no remorse, they are sociopaths. They are more than capable of running into debt and stealing their fellow traveller's guidebook. (ANDY, 54)

When asked who these dishonest travellers are, Andy replies that most of the time they become jewellery sellers. They burn all the bridges in one city and then move on to the next one. 'They are like tramps or bums that way', he says, and after a short pause admits that there is a fine line between a global nomad like himself and a tramp.

As the analysis has showed, there is also a fine line between the two discourses of adventuring and vagrancy. Both spring from the same source merely representing the ambivalent disposition of desire and hate (or pity) that societies display towards location-independent lifestyles or travel in general. For centuries, travel has been considered a double-edged sword. Ethnographer James Clifford (1992) ironically described what seems to count as acceptable travel: it is that which is 'heroic, educational, scientific, adventurous, ennobling' (discourse of adventuring), and only rarely it is 'the movement of servants, slaves, beggars, concubines, mistresses, and wives that represent either the detritus or trappings of the mobility of men of a certain class or race' (discourse of vagrancy) (p. 105).

The latter, negative connotations of vagrancy have been silenced by travellers and researchers alike drawing attention to the beneficial effects of travel. Instead of the substance abuse, bumming, and worthless idling associated with drifting, they rather speak of rites of passage, self-development and the school of life, employing the discourse of adventuring and consciously shutting out the opposing discourse. However, both discourses are equally present in the imagery of travel. They can even be partially united by understanding both as learning experiences or knowledge accumulation.

Both discourses participate in negotiations about who should be let out, for how long, why, and what should be expected from them in return. Opposites, such as those between adventuring and vagrancy, function as vehicles of power distinguishing the desired pole. They represent ideals or warning examples which influence people's lives, travels, and everyday practices guiding them to 'right' kind of travel. By analysing these discursive conditions, the ambiguous meaning of privileges is further revealed: they are dependent on interpretation. What is privileged and ostentatious in one context might be destitution in another. It is an ongoing struggle.

Power and Knowledge

In a world where the majority of people stay in their country of origin, the location-independent need to justify their lifestyles, and when doing so, they participate in negotiations about preferred forms of dwelling, living, and travelling. From societies' standpoint, such mobilities are suspicious, because they have the potential to shake the ordinary, the static, and the norm. They can be acts of domination and acts of resistance, and therefore need to be regulated. These circumstances considered, are global nomads able to master their own lives as the discourse of adventuring suggests, or are they structured, as in the discourse of vagrancy? I explore this in the following analysis where I build on my earlier discussions of Giddens's structuration theory and search for the Foucauldian answer to this dilemma by focussing on issues of power. At the end of the section, I address the criticisms Foucauldian theories have received in order to take their limitations into account, and direct the discussion to avenues that might otherwise be ignored.

Giddens's and Foucault's works largely revolved around the same subject, the relationship between the individual and society, but from different angles. My intention is not to build a synthesis of the two but rather offer a more nuanced perspective for discussion. While Giddens made an extensive effort to understand society through structure – his ambition was to establish an ontology of human society (Gregory, 1989, p. 239) – Foucault approached the issue from an epistemological perspective focussing on the relationship between knowledge, power, and subjectivity. These topics are central to this work in which societal questions are addressed from micro rather than macro perspective. Therefore, analysis of subtle forms of power that exert influence through everyday discourses and practices is needed, rather than study of laws, government regulations, policy texts, and committee papers (cf. Hannam and Knox, 2010).

As my aim indicates, the goal of the analysis is not in discourses and practices but rather in the development of tools with which questions of power can be approached. Simply studying what global nomads' discourses are about and how they are constructed is not enough; what is more important is what those discourses tell us about ongoing power struggles. In the previous analysis, this question was approached by investigating the conditions that allow the two discourses to be created. They can be encapsulated in a few simple questions: who speaks to whom, how, and why (Foucault, 1969, pp. 68–74).

These questions draw attention to the fact that knowledge – whether everyday knowledge or scientific – is neither neutral nor innocent, not even in studies that strive for objectivity as their premises are merely concealed, not missing. Therefore, rather than assuming, for instance based on the discourse of adventuring, that global nomads represent a mobile elite because they travel a great deal and seem to exert their agency, Foucauldian approaches guide us to ask what advantages we are talking about and from whose point of view. By considering the two discourses together, a somewhat different image is formed where it is no longer possible to unambiguously define the global nomads' social standing. It depends on the context and the power struggle between the two discourses.

Knowledge, Foucault maintained, always implies struggle. Whenever discourses produce knowledge, that knowledge is open to dispute (1981, pp. 52–3). Because of this contested and contextual character, discourses always tell us more about power conflicts than about the objects they represent. Consequently, the two discourses do not reveal a societal truth about location-independence; what they offer is an instrument with which societies' norms, dominant values, and ideals can be analysed.

While Giddens spoke about such conditioning factors as structure, Foucault defined his own terminology and systematically refused to accept the usual sociological categories (2002d, p. 17. See also Dreyfus and Rabinow, 1983, p. 113). He addressed a comparable although not a directly parallel concern: he spoke of the 'regime of truth' (or stratum of knowledge) specifying the factors which enable and restrict what people can think and do in a given domain, society, and period.

> Each society has its regime of truth, its 'general politics' of truth – that is, the types of discourse it accepts and makes function as true; the mechanisms and instances that enable one to distinguish true and false statements; the means by which each is sanctioned; the techniques and procedures accorded value in the acquisition of truth; the status of those who are charged with saying what counts as true. (Foucault, 2002e, p. 131)

Like structure, the regime of truth works in a dual way. When individuals draw from discursive rules and resources, they at the same time reproduce them. In global nomads' case, for example, they draw from the old binary opposition between nomads and the sedentary, or from the residual images of adventuring and vagrancy.

The existence of such regimes of truth raises an interesting question: if people say only what they are able to say, then who or what is it that dictates the rules? What are the limits within which global nomads are able to represent their lifestyles? Note that when answering this question, Foucauldian analysis seeks no authority or institution that would use power over people. Power is implicit and anonymous. It works through subtle methods such as dominant discourses, subjectivities, emotions, lifestyles, and peer pressure that are discussed in more detail in subsequent chapters. It also pervades all social relationships and fluctuates between the parties (Foucault, 1978, pp. 93, 102, 1991a, p. 26, 1998c, p. 451), which means that power not only constrains global nomads' discourses but also enables them. When global nomads, for instance, create the binary opposition between themselves and the settled, they promote their own lifestyle and agency but at the same time they tie themselves tighter and tighter to dominant discourses.

In this complex network, the crucial question is not ontological – what is power – but practical: how is it exercised (Foucault, 1998c, p. 452, 2002c, p. 336. See also Deleuze, 2006, p. 71). This leads us to analyse everyday discourses and contexts where power is at work rather than to analyse power within the context of domination from above or transformation from below by competent agents, as Giddens suggested. Notice that although these subtle forms of power that are to be studied are invisible and extend their reach even to our subjectivities, they are not ideologies with which people's minds would be played with. Foucault purposely used the term 'relations of power' so that people would not immediately think of a static political structure such as a government, a state apparatus, or an elite

(Foucault, 2002c, p. 337; Foucault, 1997c, p. 291). Power pervades the whole of the social body from bottom to top and the other way around.

The close relationship between power and knowledge, however, has led many researchers, including influential ones, to use 'discourse' as a synonym for 'ideology' (e.g. Giddens, 1989, p. 290; Beck and Beck-Gernsheim, 2002). These conceptions have also gained ground in some lifestyles mobilities studies (e.g. Benson and Osbaldiston, 2014; Cresswell, 2006; D'Andrea, 2006; Torkington, 2012), and as such, they deserve a few words. The discussion on ideologies has risen, in part as a criticism to second modernist theories' inflated view of individualism. However, mostly because of the absence of a broad theoretical framework from which to draw, these discussions have remained at a rather superficial level, sometimes lapsing into Marxist conceptions of 'material reality', 'hegemonies', and 'state apparatuses', which imply a narrow view of power as repressive. Such conceptions are rarely unbiased, as the underlying world view behind ideology and discourse theories is quite different.

While discourses are observed to create realities (Foucault, 2002e, p. 119), 'ideology' derives from the Marxist conception of base and superstructure, where base has an aura of 'real' – the ultimate reference point – and superstructure only reflects the material reality. This changes analysis drastically. Had my interpretation been that global nomads' discourses were mere reflections of reality, I would have probably viewed adventuring as a misguided representation while granting the discourse of vagrancy the status of truth. From the point of view of the chosen discourse theory, however, there is no absolute reality that would supersede discourses, because reality as such is a social construction. Or, if taking a more agnostic stand, at least we can only grasp 'reality' with discourses.

Discourses are ontologically neither true nor false as each society has its own types of discourses that they accept. This, in fact, is the whole idea of the regime of truth. There is constant struggle in which dominant discourses are reproduced, recreated and modified, because they are challenged and altered. There is never a consensus or a cunning master plan in which people's minds are played with. Even dominant discourses are not *the* dominant discourses, because different regimes of truth reign in different societies and social circles.

While Marxist ideology theories have made a considerable contribution to the study of power, and although some of them are no longer tied to the old idea of base and superstructure, they remain limited in fine-tuned analysis. If power is merely viewed as repressive and as something that people try to escape, why would anybody consent to it, as Foucault pointed out. Power is effective because it is attractive and alluring.

> What makes power hold good, what makes it accepted, is simply the fact that it doesn't only weigh on us as a force that says no; it also traverses and produces things, it induces pleasure, forms knowledge, produces discourse. It needs to be considered as a productive network that runs through the whole social body, much more than as a negative instance whose function is repression. (Foucault, 2002e, p. 120)

In this context, power is no longer reducible to simple binary oppositions or class conflict; instead, it works in everyday settings where structure and agency are at constant interplay being both enabling and constraining. In global nomads' case, some forms of power limit their travels by saying no, other forms limit their travels by seduction, and yet others are merely enabling as the subsequent chapters will show.

Discourses are therefore not just about semantics. They are models of thought and action that comprise a whole world view including a conception of society, its organisation, and individuals' role in it. For Foucault, this regime of truth was 'essential to the structure and functioning of society' (2002e, p. 132). For society to change, the regime of truth also needed to change: 'The problem is not changing people's consciousness – or what's in their heads – but the political, economic, institutional regime of the production of truth' (Foucault, 2002e, p. 133).

While my idea is not to try to change current regimes of truth with this book – global nomads and the chosen discursive arena are too marginal for that – I will point out challenges that location-independence poses to these regimes, particularly through such concepts as 'home', 'citizenship', and 'nationality', as Chapter 5 will show. My aim is more modest: by indicating contradictions within the contemporary society, I identify current constraints and possible future avenues. In order for something to change, awareness is needed, and this is perhaps the best research can do.

As can be expected with such a sensitive topic as power, there are no unproblematic approaches. Although Foucault has been hailed as pioneering a 'properly philosophical form of interrogation' (Deleuze, 2006, p. 49), his theories are among the most controversial in the twentieth-century Western philosophy (e.g. Habermas, 1987, p. 276; Žižek, 2000, pp. 174, 251, 257). Most critics have concentrated their efforts in contesting his idea of the everpresence of power. Philosopher Jean Baudrillard (2007) related Foucauldian 'power' with Gilles Deleuze and Jean-François Lyotard's 'desire', and viewed it as lacking in transformative potential: 'It [power] is there in the same way as desire in Deleuze and Lyotard: always already there, purged of all negativity, a network, a rhizome, a contiguity diffracted ad infinitum' (p. 35). Literary critic Terry Eagleton (1991) argued, in a similar vein, that if there is nothing beyond power, 'then there is nothing that is being blocked, categorized and regimented, and therefore absolutely no need to worry' (pp. 7–8). In both cases, ubiquity is viewed to render power powerless. Similar arguments have also been presented of Giddens's structure which, according to critics, relegates individuals to replication (Archer, 2010, p. 231. See also Gregory, 1989, pp. 200–201). I will come back to these arguments in Chapter 7, when I have examined the whole research material and have more evidence at hand.

While Eagleton did not deny the importance of power, he wanted to reserve the concept for major power issues. However, determining how to decide which are major issues and which are not is already a power struggle. Research is not exempt from these struggles, even (or particularly) when trying to maintain objectivity as I will later show on several occasions. From the Foucauldian viewpoint, objectivity

56 *Global Nomads and Extreme Mobilities*

is not attainable as every statement is already grounded in a battlefield. In order to be open about the major paradigmatic assumptions and goals of the study, researchers need to acknowledge the power networks to which they belong by clearly stating the subject positions they have taken.

In this chapter, a pluralistic approach was chosen in order to analyse power struggles related to global nomads' lifestyles. In this context, power is not reducible to simple binary oppositions such as domination and transformation or class conflict; instead, it works in immediate everyday settings where structure and agency are at interplay, enabling and constraining location-independence and producing complex subjectivities. The fierceness of these power negotiations shows that mobilities move people, not only literally but in the sense of making them feel passionate or threatened. These reactions reveal that we are dealing with important topics that deserve closer analysis. Mobilities are not in the margins of societies but at the very centre of it (see also Söderström, Randería, Ruedin, D'Amato, and Panese, 2013), affecting our everyday lives. But what, in turn, are the factors that affect and direct mobilities? This is the topic of the next chapter where I examine global nomads' social relationships.

Chapter 4
Adrift

When I got to know 36-year-old Ingo in Buenos Aires, Argentina, at the beginning of our trip, I had no idea that he was a global nomad – after all, at that time, I had not yet even devised a name for our own lifestyle. Ingo attended the same English language group, where porteños, people of Buenos Aires, practised English with foreigners, and foreigners benefited by socialising with locals. Ingo was an active member of one of the many groups in the city. He had a circle of admirers and he loved to party. Everybody still remembers when Ingo sang 'What a Wonderful World', imitating Louis Armstrong to perfection.

Ingo grew up in former East Germany and started to travel 'as soon as they let me', as he puts it. When the Berlin Wall fell and Ingo's studies in the university were finished, he left to study management in the United States. He was fascinated by the country and wanted to live there. Later he chose to work from Buenos Aires. He is hired in electoral observation missions around the world, his assignments usually lasting from weeks to months. Long duration assignments are particularly profitable for him as salary is paid on a daily basis and hotel costs are covered.

Although Ingo has attained everything he dreamed of, he is not completely satisfied with his current situation. Travelling has cured his restlessness, and now he would like to live a more settled life belonging to a community and perhaps raising a family. Like most solo travellers, he has had his share of encounters on the way. 'Basically I've had a woman in every port, many women at the same time. Nothing stable and long-term', he says.

Ingo has been living nomadically for 15 years, and he analyses the lifestyle more critically than any other participant. 'Travelling makes you a bit cynical, less naïve, less idealistic. You don't buy so much bullshit. It also makes you more tired. I'm definitely more tired after fifteen years', he sighs. Ingo points out that there is a significant difference between traditional and modern-day nomads. While pastoralists travelled with their families, contemporary societies are individualised. Ingo tries to establish roots whenever he is in a new place because 'nobody can be alone for long. We are not made for that', he says. However, as he usually stays in his destinations for a short time and does not necessarily ever return to the same place, he has not received the same kind of support as people who live in a community which has been built, maintained, and fortified over decades.

Instead of working alone, Ingo would like to do something with other people. Working as an independent consultant, he is not integrated in the everyday life of locals. He has a dollar income and does not face the same issues and problems locals do. 'It's a bubble', Ingo describes.

Many wage earners would probably seize the opportunity to switch places with Ingo, or would they? Would they exchange their stable social circles for rootlessness, loneliness, and exclusion? Essentially, these questions can be encapsulated in the two discourses previously analysed. While the discourse of adventuring portrays global nomads in an appealing light, the discourse of vagrancy instead provides a warning example of the perils of long-term travel. In this chapter, I analyse what kind of subject positions these two discourses propose to global nomads, and what kind of power relationships are entailed. These power relationships are among the most important in global nomads' lives, as they might make them reconsider their lifestyles.

The theoretical theme of this chapter, subjectification, remains an under-explored area in lifestyle mobilities. Most of the studies deal with 'identity' from the individual's point of view (e.g. Bousiou, 2008; Cohen, 2010a; Desforges, 2000; Galani-Moutafi, 2000; Korpela, 2009; O'Reilly, 2000). Here, on the other hand, 'subjectivity' is regarded as one of the most important vehicles of power in the contemporary society (see Foucault, 2002c, p. 331). While in the past, power was exercised more through repressive measures such as the imposition of laws and their violent enforcement, today subtle measures of biopower attach individuals to temporary points of attachment, to subject positions (see Hall, 1996, p. 6). Power, therefore, works through us – through our choices, practices, lifestyles, and our very being. My aim in the following analysis is, through the examination of global nomads' most meaningful relationships, illustrate how they are constituted as subjects who exercise, submit to, and resist power relations.

Sex and Companionship

Sex and the need for social contacts are some of the most powerful drivers in life, and they also influence global nomads' travels and choice of destinations, or give a purpose to their otherwise aimless wanderings. Global nomads' stories about their intimate relationships varied significantly in the interviews and observation situations, depending on which of the two discourses, adventuring or vagrancy, was selected. These subject positions provide me with an opportunity to analyse one of the most significant discrepancies in their lives: the need to stay independent and the need to be loved and share their lives with others. The same dilemma is also familiar for many people leading a more settled lifestyle. As Beck and Beck-Gernsheim have sarcastically noted of contemporary relationships: 'Each partner wants his or her freedom and at the same time to be chained in the hands of the beloved … No one has the answer as to how this will work' (2002, p. 212. See also Elliott and Lemert, 2006, p. 3). In the following analysis, I examine this dilemma and the ways in which global nomads attempt to solve it. I identify the subject positions that are available to them in the two discourses, how their subjectivities position other people, and what kind of alternatives they have tried in order to overcome the constraints of their lifestyles.

The Myth of the Lone Ranger

Most global nomads are solo travellers, and in the discourse of adventuring, they cherish their solitude (see Riley, 1988, p. 324; Elsrud, 2001, p. 604). Michel (47) encapsulates: 'I don't want to argue about decisions. I like mute boyfriends who are shy and just follow me – who agree and let me make all the decisions'. Although Michel is half joking, global nomads' travel style is individualistic. They avoid serious involvement with people who could compromise their freedom using biopower, for example emotions such as guilt, sympathy, or love (see also Adler and Adler, 1999, pp. 44, 51). Global nomads have adopted the strategy of avoidance. This was also their namesakes', the pastoral and warrior nomads' approach, although in a slightly different manner. While pastoral nomads avoided the constraints of societies, they travelled with their significant others, as Ingo pointed out in the beginning of this chapter.

The discourse of adventuring offers global nomads various subject positions, but some are more dominant than others. This is typical for subject positions. They are not mutually exclusive, as people slide in and out of them all the time. Among global nomads, the subject position of 'the lone ranger' is dominant due to the great number of solo travellers. The lone ranger is a solitary wanderer who replaces intimate relationships with one-night stands, paid services, or conscious abstinence. None of these options requires commitment, which seems to suit global nomads' purposes. Stefan (47) explains: 'If I started to date, it would have to be a perfect match. Maybe I will start missing it, but I enjoy my freedom now. I have my encounters. They're brief and they're quickly over'.

Solo travel, and particularly sex without commitment, was not an easy subject to talk about for all, because they can be associated with sex tourism. Although this is a major form of tourism in the world (e.g. Kibicho, 2009, p. 18; Enloe, 1990, p. 36), it is usually concealed as it is considered socially unacceptable and exploitative (e.g. Ryan and Hall, 2001; White, 2008). My position as a married female nomad likely made the situation even more awkward for some. Had the researcher been a single male, the responses would have probably been less evasive and defensive. In some cases defensiveness seemed to compel participants to accentuate their singleness through the discourse of adventuring, emphasising the upsides of solo travel, although this was not necessarily their dominant discourse otherwise. Another popular reaction was to refer to the 'fact' that 'with this kind of lifestyle, maintaining a relationship is impossible'. A third alternative was to shrug the question off with a retort or a joke.

> In Asia I was often asked where my girlfriend is. I always told them that I'm engaged to my bicycle and we will get married as soon as our trip is over. People were always happy with my answer and accepted me. They understood how unfortunate my situation is. (JUKKA, 27)

While defensiveness shows that global nomads find their relationship status difficult, or at least in need of an explanation, humour renders it to their favour. They are able to step aside from their subject positions and make detached observations and even joke about them.

Although both male and female global nomads can be lone rangers, this subject position is, relatively more likely to be popular among men for the simple reason that males dominate among global nomads. Wandering, in general, has been represented as a male challenge, as Cohen also implied by referring to the drifter as a 'he' (see also Enloe, 1990, p. 21; Cresswell and Uteng, 2008). This is biopolitics at its barest: it defines norms, in this case what acceptable behaviours are for men and women. It assesses individuals according to the norm limiting their subject positions. Therefore, when assessed from this gender-specific point of view, the lack of women seems to be attributable to the fact that the prospect of bringing up children on the road is not appealing to women.

The myth of the lone ranger springs from the genre of adventure, the Western, where the lone ranger is a courageous, lonely man searching for a way out of organised society and living in a world where tramps are harsh, manly men (e.g. Chopra-Gant, 2006, pp. 55–6; Bazin, 1971, pp. 144–5). The myth first appeared in folk tales and ballads, and it gained its glorified status in James Fenimore Cooper's Leatherstocking stories and later in the heroes of the Wild West movies (Western, s.v.).

When the myth was born, historian Todd De Pastino (2003) has argued, it was a protest against traditional family values. Single wandering men, whether law-defying cowboys or hobos riding the rails, shook the delicate balance between work and home, public and private, men and women that the American middle-class considered crucial to the social order. Home was the civilising and restraining realm, and the men who rejected it were regarded to be on the way to becoming tramps or hardened criminals (p. 25).

The myth turned the cult of domesticity upside down by making the lone ranger an admirable ideal. The myth is still alive among travellers if travel literature and solo global nomads are to be believed (e.g. Davidson, 1980; Grant, 2003; Vollmann, 2009). George (31) explains his solitary wanderings: 'It's really hard to find company for the kind of trips I do [going by bike and staying with locals]. I did a lot of really risky travelling and I never had a girlfriend that really wanted to do a lot of those things'.

The myth offers global nomads a limited amount of subject positions (see also Euben, 2006, p. 30; Elsrud, 2001, p. 614; Cresswell, 1999); for men as lone rangers who need to avoid emotional entanglements, and for women as frail homemakers who would be better off at home, or, if women insist on travelling, they have to be willing to accept that they will be regarded as morally loose. To maintain this gendered world view, some lone rangers seem to be attracted to settled men or women. By choosing partners who are not willing to travel, they manage to avoid serious relationships.

> My first few years of travelling, I was definitely more social with men. My first year, I was crazy, I was totally promiscuous having a great time, I've had I guess three relationships since I started travelling. The third one was with a Bedouin in Jordan. He wanted to marry me and I actually considered it until I realised that the cultures were just too disparate. (ELISA, 54)

If lone rangers one day found a partner, they would have to reconsider their subjectivities. For this, the incentives need to strong. Although global nomads have changed their approach to their subjectivity almost entirely when adopting the location-independent lifestyle, making this transformation anew appears much more difficult, particularly if it leads to readopting some features of their former lifestyles.

While being the lone ranger allows global nomads some degree of freedom, this subject position is not unproblematic, either for global nomads themselves or for others. It can make travelling with another global nomad challenging if not altogether impossible, because they are not necessarily ready to commit to anything, as I witnessed during participant observation. When I was already hundreds of miles on my way to an agreed meeting that was scheduled to take place in two days' time, I learned, from the participant's public travel letter, that he had left the place and continued his travels without bothering to tell me. It is easy to imagine that issues of commitment and trust pose even greater challenges in intimate relationships. If something is not working out, one or the other will just pick up and leave. This is not a rule, however. Global nomads include many kinds of people, and the situations change. Sometimes the desire to have company makes even the lone ranger compromise, at least temporarily.

> If you want to travel with me, it's fine, but I find it difficult. It's difficult to compromise what is the next path and what will be the leaving time. I tried to do that with some guys I was interested in. It's possible to compromise for a few days or weeks, but it needs some planning in advance, and some nomads are really reluctant to plan so it's difficult to find the balance between compromise and sacrifice. (ANICK, 29)

It seems that when assuming lone rangering, global nomads are not willing to confront power issues on a regular basis. Although they are flexible in dealing with changing conditions on the road, they are not as flexible in regard to other people. They want to do things their way. When my husband and I were being hosted by one of the participants, we soon learned that the house had a great number of rules, for instance how to open and close the kitchen cupboards so that they would not make noise, what dishes could be used, what kind of cooking was allowed (none except boiling water for making tea or coffee or instant noodles), whether windows and balcony doors should be opened or closed, where to hang the clothes and wet towels, and how long showering could take. To maintain the order and minimise the possibility of errors, the host did almost everything by himself, including his many guests' laundry and dishes.

The Curse of the Outcast

While the discourse of adventuring emphasises global nomads' control of themselves and also of others, the discourse of vagrancy drastically changes the picture. Being single is no longer a choice that guarantees freedom but instead is an unwanted destiny that leads to loneliness and alienation. This is also true historically as loneliness and idleness have been considered the most important signs of vagrancy (Langan, 1995, p. 87). Encounters on the road are transient; they include neither commitment nor long-term reciprocity, and therefore interaction often remains shallow. Such relationships are also exhausting because they require individuals to constantly meet new people (see also Adler and Adler, 1999, pp. 5, 47, 51; Vogt, 1976, p. 37). While some of these encounters may lead to long-lasting relationships that are maintained on the internet, most fade away as a result of absence.

What solo global nomads find particularly hard in the discourse of vagrancy is not having a partner they could share their experiences with (see also Cohen, 2011, p. 1,548). 'I have never been in a situation where there was a special person who could travel with me. The odds of finding someone of similar interests, someone open-minded enough, and someone who you are attracted to are astronomically low', Jeff (25) laments. Note the shift in agency in the middle, which generalises Jeff's situation. It implies that loneliness relates to his lifestyle rather than to himself as a person. If Giddens is to be believed, loneliness could be an even more general consequence of the radicalisation of modernity. When the protective frameworks of communities and traditions break down, 'the individual feels bereft and alone in a world' (1991, pp. 33–4). This is the downside of the culture of self-responsibility, although Giddens exaggerated it in a typical and contradictory manner: while he overemphasised individuals' own agency and will, he also considered individuals as extremely frail and in need of secure structures.

Global nomads deal with their loneliness in different manners. Those who consider location-independence as a temporary passage in life take it more lightly than those who consider their journey indefinite. Most of the temporary nomads are young. They expect, or at least hope, that their family and old friends will be waiting for them upon their return, and they will have time to invest in intimate relationships when they are again settled. In other words, they expect the situation at home to freeze so that they can pick up where they left off. However, the subject position of the outcast may haunt them after the return as the following quotation shows (see also Pocock and McIntosh, 2011).

> The trip itself was enjoyable but coming back is always difficult. You have no job, no flat, no insurance. This time my girlfriend – who had been travelling with me – broke up with me, and I didn't know how I was going to live. The economic and media context had changed, and it was more difficult to live from the conferences and writing that I had earned a living from over the last fifteen years. (CLAUDE, 50)

Claude seems to be a special case in the sense that many of the temporary global nomads have not found themselves a partner willing to travel with them, and they usually reject the idea of having a long-distance relationship on the road, presumably because that would make travelling harder, thus pulling them back to more conventional lifestyle. They delay the need for relationships into the future, which is in an interesting contrast with their will to live in the present moment. It shows that for global nomads, any long-term and emotionally loaded relationship is a significant risk unless their partner is sharing the same lifestyle (see also Giddens, 1991, p. 12: Elliott and Lemert, 2006, p. 9). Consequently, global nomads' relationship to places, as well as their social relationships, become transitory. Consider the following statement where Ingo describes his life using the metaphor of 'patches':

> It's a very transient existence. You're always feeling you're building something like a patchwork. I feel my life is a bit like that. I have all this life and it's in these patches. Whenever I go to a new place, I have a new patch, but patchwork jackets are not as good as solid leather jackets made of one piece so even though it looks interesting and it's got interesting stories, it doesn't feel like one solid life. (INGO, 36)

In his statement, Ingo seems to reproduce dominant discourses: he represents nomadism as vagrancy, which is not as 'good' as living a settled life. This is not unusual, particularly among solo global nomads. They do not consider their situation as desirable in the long run, yet they might hold on to the subject position of the lone ranger, even when it turns them into outcasts. Freedom is their ultimate goal, which they are not ready to give up even when they have to face its flipside, the culture of individual responsibility. They waver between the two subject positions, unaware of or ignoring the inconsistencies. While the lone ranger courageously assumes self-ownership, the outcast represents the downsides of such risk-taking.

Risk, second modernists argued, is fundamental in how we organise the social world, and it seems that global nomads epitomise many of their views. Second modernists, however, were not unanimous in their descriptions of risk. While Beck argued that even day-to-day life is now inherently more risky than in prior eras – after all, our lives are now risky experiments (Beck, 2009, p. 7) – Giddens has taken a more cautious stand. For him, risk means 'living with a calculative attitude' and assessing various possibilities, which relates to his views of individuals as rational decision-makers (Giddens, 1991, pp. 3, 28, 123–4). Although Beck's accounts can also be criticised for rationalistic constructions of uncertainty (see Elliott, 2002), the concept of risk also remains important for understanding the contemporary society when viewed from other aspects of human life, including the irrational and the illogical. As Giddens maintained, there are always unacknowledged conditions and unintended consequences of action that influence our lives. The following analysis shows that such unanticipated events can lead to major transformations in global nomads' subjectivities.

Adjustments

Scholarship has posed the question whether solitary life outside stable communities and without solid relationships can be pleasurable in any way (Franklin, 2007, p. 138; Larsen and Urry, 2008, p. 98. See also Adler and Adler, 1999, p. 53. Cf. Urry, 2007, p. 47), and it seems that some global nomads would also rather choose the metaphysics of presence. Their stories revealed interesting shifts, where some subject positions had been pushed into the background or rejected, and new ones had been adopted. Most of these transformations had been brought about by a new relationship status or a membership in a community. Another kind of transformation is visible in global nomads' relationships to their family and old friends. These adjustments are my next topic.

Families and Communities

Thanks to the two-year time span between the interviews, observations, and follow-ups, I had an opportunity to analyse changes in global nomads' lives. Although this is a short time compared, for example, to statistical studies which can extend over decades, it gives the ethnographic perspective of sustained contact (e.g. Brewer, 2000, p. 166). Even during this time, a great deal had happened. Some participants had started a family, while others had searched for a community.

Phoenix (49), who at the time of the first interview was still single and conformed very much to the myth of the lone ranger who leaves broken hearts behind him, had found a new love with whom he now has a baby. He had also assumed a more settled and conventional lifestyle having a steady job and a house in his country of origin. Phoenix reflects how his views had changed:

> One thing I learned travelling, maybe the most important thing, is that I want to have a home. I want stability, my own piece of land in nature, where I can build a little house for my family and have a garden, and be off the grid and surf and hike and do yoga and the things we love to do. Travelling, if you don't ever have a home to return to, is not travelling, it's being a constant nomad; and that's very different from being a traveller. I don't want to raise my children being nomads, nor do I want to be a nomad, but the place I live must be perfect for me and my family, and that means our own land, in nature, by mountains and an ocean, with surfing and hiking, and far from any cities or development. (PHOENIX, 49)

The birth of his child appeared to have altered Phoenix's subject positions completely, perhaps because of conventional expectations of what parenthood means, or because of his own experiences on the road. If the reasons were related to conventional expectations, it would be biopower persuading global nomads to offer their children a stable living environment. The notion of 'stability' in Phoenix's statement seems to suggest this. In many Western welfare societies, states have a say in how to bring up a child. In the case of global nomads, these biopolitical measures can make them move back to their country of origin so that their children get a proper health care and education in their mother tongue. Whether having a family always includes a rejection of location-independence offers an interesting aspect for future research, but for this a longer time span in interviews and observations and a different research focus is needed.

Another interpretation, which seems to hold, also in Phoenix's case, is that those who have lived most of their lives on the road without having their own home find the settled subject positions and the idea of their own place and family at some point attractive. The opposite is also true, where some of those who have lived most of their lives in a house, want to liberate themselves from solid structures and tight social relationships. Both solutions can be interpreted as a particular kind of search for novelty: global nomads are eager to try out subject positions of which they have no previous experience.

Global nomads' couple relationships included other kinds of changes. Some couples had split, and new relationships had emerged. Those relationships that lasted were usually long-lived and formed before leaving. As these partners are usually together 24/7, the relationships are rather tight, but this is regarded as rewarding. One of the couples, Glen (53) and Steve, had already spent all of their time together in their previous settled life in England where they had a business together.

> In actual fact, since we met, the longest time apart is one week, so we're pretty close to joined at the hip. We have actually been together 24/7 since 1985 when we bought the business. We're best friends and maybe because we met when we were very young, we grew up together. We sort of melted together. We wouldn't have it any other way. We are very lucky. (GLEN, 53)

Those couple relationships that were formed on the road were more easily dissolved, or ended up in marriage and a more settled lifestyle. Some of the global nomads had encountered their spouse on their nomadic journey, and either returned to their country of origin or settled down in another country. As these examples show, global nomads are not immune to biopolitical networks, particularly to the kind of power related to personal relationships. The line between the settled and the location-independent is thin, as global nomads readily admit.

Those who had not found or searched for a partner had, instead, looked for a solution to their need for connection in local communities. Cindie (51), who had settled down in India, reflects her reasons: 'I became real detached from my family and friends and I felt a real need to connect with a community. I ended up in Dharamsala teaching English for Tibetan refugees and going to Dalai Lama teachings and I found a community I could connect with'.

What global nomads mean by a 'community' remains unspecified in most cases. It does not necessarily mean returning home to their friends and family, as Cindie's example shows, nor living with a group of people in the same house sharing everyday life and household tasks. For Cindie, community meant that she was no longer so much centred on the 'duty to herself', but on duty to others.

Social wise I like staying better because I build friendships … On the road everything was short-term and it seems like I kept saying the same thing all the time. I was just talking about myself. It seemed so me-centric: I'm doing this, I'm going there, I need this, I want that … Look what I'm doing, it's a great thing. Now it's much more like, 'Hey can I help you, what do you need?' It's more anonymous and more focussing on other people instead of myself. (CINDIE, 51)

In stereotypes, individualisation means a me-first society, but there is no obligation to make an either/or choice between collective networks and individualised subjectivities (Beck and Beck-Gernsheim, 2002, pp. xxii, 38, 212; Mythen, 2005, p. 143; Elliott and Lemert, 2006, p. 7; Rojek, 2005, p. 12). In fact, the Greek meaning of the 'care of the self' was bound with the care for others. It was a precondition that had to be met before one was qualified to attend to the affairs of others or to lead them (Foucault, 1990, p. 73, 1997f, p. 288).

'Community' for global nomads might also mean working together with other people, as Ingo's story in the beginning of this chapter indicated, or doing otherwise meaningful things with others. Most of all, however, the word seems to express a wish to have company. In his book *Community* (2001a), Bauman argued that such wishes arise from the modern experience of fragmentation. As such, 'community' is not to be taken literally; it is more likely to express individual anxieties that arise from the risks and downsides of individualisation (see also Papastergiadis, 2000, p. 198).

The alternative Cindie chose will probably attract some other solo global nomads. It offers a transgression, which is situated between the location-independent and the settled lifestyles. In this scenario, global nomads are offered the opportunity to both stay put and search for novelty within the local culture. Unlike lifestyle migrants, global nomads are not attracted to the nomadic communities of Westerners that can be found in touristy destinations such as Ibiza, Bali, and Goa. Although many of them have been to these places, they seem to find it hard to adjust to the rules and obligations that collective living requires. This indicates that any tight communal solution with strong biopolitical networks will likely fail to satisfy global nomads in the long run – although some occasionally dream about it, forgetting the limitations that it brings along. However, if the community is local, global nomads are more eager to make compromises because they regard it as a cultural challenge as will be detailed in Chapter 6, whereas in contacts with other Westerners such challenges are perceived to be lacking.

If the number of global nomads grows in the future and they want to connect with each other, new types of location-independent communities are likely to emerge. Most of these communities will probably be virtual because of the high mobility and individuality of global nomads, but some might be temporal in specific geographic locations. I have stumbled upon a few examples among Russian and Serbian backpackers who form travel clubs (Travel Club, 2013; Academy of Free Travel, 2002). One of the club activities is to collect donations in order to rent an apartment in a chosen destination for a couple of months, and offer accommodation for free to both members and non-members. Similar arrangements might offer global nomads refuge when life on the road feels too consuming and lonely. On a small scale, such communality already exists. Whenever global nomads stop somewhere and rent their own apartment, they usually host hospex guests, not just for company but also in the name of reciprocity, as they tend to more often be on the receiving end in hospex organisations.

These kind of temporary communities are, whether big or small, 'cloakroom communities', which people join by virtue of shared interests, and which they are free to leave at any time (Bauman, 2007. See also Maffesoli, 1996; Kozinets, 2002). They have limited liability, and they supersede the meaning of shared history and traditions that are linked to more binding arrangements. Critics will probably be quick to point out that these are not 'real' communities at all, because they do not offer long-term caring and sharing. However, cloakrooms produce a 'momentary experience of community', which might be the best there is available to us, if second modernists are to be believed (e.g. Bauman, 2001a, p. 3). Communities, in these definitions, are 'imagined', just like nations in Benedict Anderson's (1991) famous formulation.

Aliens

Another interesting transformation can be seen in global nomads' relationships with their old friends and family. It shows that not all changes are sought out and desired.

> You set out travelling thinking it changes you and then it does, but never in the way you thought it would. It takes something from you. You can never return to where you were again. You never fit, you basically become an alien. You will never be able to interact with people in the way you used to do. You lose that kind of comfortable bliss. (MAX, 39)

In discourse analytic terms, travelling estranges global nomads from the dominant discourses in their country of origin and the related subject positions. After seeing the world as their playground, they might find it difficult to join, for instance, nationalistic hubris. 'Travelling has made me probably unable to really live anywhere. I can no longer drop into a culture and live there thinking that the government is good or the society is kind. It's just a construct, an illusion', Max (39) elaborates.

Location-independence includes considerable changes in subject positions (see also Cresswell and Uteng, 2008, p. 2). Leaving one's country of origin behind is the first visible change, and it also marks the decisive point after which returning back to a more conventional lifestyle and re-establishing old ties may be difficult. In some cases, global nomads feel that their new subject positions have resulted in the dissolution of former friendships as an unwanted side effect (cf. White and White, 2007, pp. 95–8, 100); in some other cases, they have deliberately freed themselves from old ties. Global nomads want to avoid a fixed subjectivity, which would bind them to the past (see also Bousiou 2008, 129).

> I lost some friendships because of my lifestyle and I also chose to disregard some of the relationships because of my lifestyle. Now I pretty much only have people in my life who support it. I forced people to look at the choices they were making. We make people uncomfortable sometimes. (BARBARA, 52)

The 'we' in Barbara's statement implies that the hardships of location-independence may bring the members of this loose anti-community of individualists together. Although they do not necessarily want to socialise and spend time together, they feel some kind of solidarity with each other because of the similarities in their lifestyles (see also O'Regan, 2013, p. 40).

This group of 'us' most notably distinguishes global nomads from their old settled friends, who may have perceived location-independence as a provocation. Leaving one's familiar surroundings can be interpreted as a deliberate disinterest towards others. Jacques Derrida accurately remarked that the departed become foreigners in their countries (p. 141), or, as Georges Van Den Abbeele (1992) maintained, they die in the eyes of their communities (p. 24). Stefan (47) illustrates the idea by describing the cold reception he received in his former home town in Austria: 'Old school friends didn't know how to deal with me. They didn't even want to hear my stories. They were just shutting them out like I hadn't been away at all'.

Ignoring or making something a taboo subject is the most common way to practice biopower on deviancy. Sociologist Mike Featherstone (1987) offers an interesting viewpoint, arguing that differences must be socially recognised and legitimated, because '[t]otal otherness like total individuality is in danger of being unrecognizable' (p. 60). In other words, when global nomads reject dominant discourses and subject positions, they are no longer within their friends' and family's comfort zone. In order to smooth over this discrepancy, some global nomads consciously downplay the experiences travelling has brought them by assuming some of their old subject positions. When I asked them if travelling had changed them, they denied it had (cf. Desforges, 2000, p. 938).

> The core is still here. I am a good man because my parents made me a good man. They took us to church, they taught us right and wrong, they taught us that a good person is trustworthy, a bad person lies, all these value systems are still there. What's changed is my global point of view. (ANDY, 54)

It seems here that dominant discourses intervene in global nomads' answers. Explicitly stating the difference their journey has made, would only make their new subject positions visible, separate them from other people and make communication difficult. Andy (54) confirms by saying: 'The better my life becomes, the more I lose friends. I don't gain more friends, I actually lose friends because they don't want me to be so different than they are. This is a horrible problem'.

Backpacker researchers have made similar findings. Travellers end up hiding some aspects of their new self upon return, if these no longer fit with prior expectations held about them (Desforges, 2000, p. 942). Therefore, while mobility is an opportunity to free oneself from dominant discourses and subject positions, the other side of the coin might be exclusion, if such a change is too visible (see also Butcher, 2010, p. 29).

Most relations, including family ties, need an investment, which requires compatibility in dominant subject positions. They also need to be supported by particular structures, physical proximity being the most important. Although absence itself does not alter global nomads' subject positions, it can make maintaining old relationships difficult. Mere or mostly virtual presence is insufficient for many people. 'I've lost my sedentary friends, because I don't live with them any more', Michel (47) says.

In the era of the network society, however, absence is not an anomaly among the settled either. Their relationships involve a similar combination of proximity and distance, and they continuously shift between being present with some and absent with others (Urry, 2002a, p. 256). Furthermore, in case of physical absence, there might be an imagined or virtual presence through multiple connections (Büscher and Urry, 2009, p. 101. See also Bauman, 1998, p. 13; Frello, 2008, pp. 32–3).

The concept of 'network capital' has been used in similar situations to refer to the capacity to establish and maintain social relations with individuals who are far away (e.g. Bærenholdt, 2013, pp. 22, 30; Larsen and Urry, 2008, pp. 93–5). In these relations, trust rather than physical distance is crucial (Giddens, 1990, p. 35). If there is no trust, there is no intimacy either, no matter how small the physical distance. As global nomads' relationships require a high level of trust because of their mobility and transformations, some of their relationships outlast these tribulations while others fade away. 'Contacts get lost, friendships break but our families are always there. We [Jens and his wife] learned that everybody around the world is searching for the same thing, love', Jens (30) says.

Jens's statement implies that global nomads' family relationships might be the most accommodating and enduring in regard to transformations, but this is not always the case. While some of the participants feel they have their family's support, others admit that their choices have caused friction, or at least worry (see Riley, 1988, p. 319). Michel (47) laughs sarcastically when asked about his family's views, 'They don't think about my lifestyle, they think about my retirement. The closer they are, the more they worry. Others are jealous'.

Worry can be reciprocal. Ageing parents are, together with intimate relationships, one of the reasons that may make global nomads compromise their will to travel, at least temporarily. Claude (50) explains why he returned to Switzerland: 'My parents are quite old. As I lost my brother, I'm the only one remaining. I feel I have to spend more time with my parents now. If I went to the other side of the world, maybe one of them or both would die'. If Western welfare societies can no longer offer elderly care facilities in the future, there will probably be pressure for the emphasis to shift from duties to oneself to duties to others.

As these findings show, major transformations are never easy. Subjectivities make individuals who they are. While people always shift between different subject positions, most often without their even noticing it, some of these positions are more dear to them than others. Solo global nomads have invested so much in the subject positions of the lone ranger and the outcast that they might find it hard to give them up by making compromises, particularly if these lead to the rejection of their lifestyle. However, all the transformations analysed in this chapter show that lifestyles – and the reflexive project of the self in general – are evolving processes. Particular lifestyles and concerns are suited to particular phases in life. While the idea of location-independence might have arisen after a breakup or loss of a job, it could be compromised later because of family reasons, for example the sickness of a close person, as happened to one of the participants of this study. Giddens calls these situations 'fateful moments' (1991, pp. 142–3). They can make individuals seek refuge in dominant discourses, or detach themselves from such predetermined factors and move into new modes of being. According to the pluralistic approach chosen here, both apply.

Power and Subjectivities

Sex and love represent the seductive forms of power, which make people accept the inevitable constraints that intimate relationships involve (see Foucault, 1997f, p. 298). For global nomads, these are among the most critical factors that can make them reconsider their lifestyles and seek a change. In order to analyse these transformations in more detail, I continue the discussion at a metalevel reflecting the advantages of the concept of 'subjectivity' compared to 'identity'. The discussion includes a comparison between Foucault's and Giddens's approaches, which, in this respect, are contradictory in a multitude of ways. These contradictions reveal an interesting power struggle between residual and emerging theoretical discourses regarding the self, where rational and unconscious elements collide. By analysing this discrepancy, my intention is to show that subjectivity is not only one of the most important vehicles of power in the contemporary society; it also encapsulates important power struggles in research. At the end of the chapter, I discuss how theories of subjectivity have been criticised in order to open new horizons for further discussions.

To start from the Foucauldian perspective, people's selves are neither viewed as coherent nor guided by unambiguous motivations. This is, in fact, one of the advantages of Foucauldian theories: it takes into account that people's acts can be contradictory. Solo global nomads, for instance, can be both lone rangers and outcasts at the same time, and while suffering from loneliness and longing for a partnership, they might still hold on to these two subject positions, rejecting intimate relationships. These kinds of contradictions arise because we do not entirely control the discourses we use. Discourses speak us, and the other way around, which brings an unconscious element into our actions. Foucault argued: '… there is no power that is exercised without a series of aims and objectives. But this does not mean that it results from the choice or decision of an individual subject; let us not look for the headquarters that presides over its rationality …' (1978, p. 95).

Foucauldian theories are in complete opposition to Giddens's who, in turn, emphasised individuals' knowledgeability and self-mastery (1984, p. 3). Although Giddens also mentioned that individuals are not in complete control of their acts because actions can have 'unacknowledged conditions' and 'unintended consequences' (1984, p. 8), he has not theorised how this unconscious and irrational side of human reflexivity works. He merely argued: 'The realm of human agency is bounded', adding that 'the production of constitution of society is a skilled accomplishment of its members, but one that does not take place under conditions that are wholly intended or wholly comprehended by them' (1993, p. 108. See also 1979, p. 78). In order to avoid difficult questions regarding the consolidation of agency and structure, Giddens merely ended up exaggerating one at the cost of the other. He viewed power either as transformation or as domination. From this stance, global nomads' would be interpreted either through the subject position of the lone ranger or the outcast, which freezes their subjectivities into one form of coherent and cognisant self.

Giddens stressed coherence because he viewed it as necessary for individuals' ontological security and psychological well-being (e.g. 1991, pp. 54, 58). While he was sensitive to the complexity of individual identifications, he still argued that individuals have 'true' selves and motives, and 'original' acts of thinking, feeling, and willing (1991, p. 191). Giddens largely based his accounts on developmental psychology, particularly on the ideas of Erik Erikson, Sigmund Freud, and Jacques Lacan (see also Gregory, 1989, p. 211; Meštrović, 1998, p. 3), but ignored their conceptions of the unconscious and promoted agency instead. Such rationality is attractive because it is self-explanatory and requires no other approaches (see Goldthorpe, 1996, p. 485). However, it is rarely fruitful, because it ignores significant realms of human existence. Why is it, for instance, that we do not always work toward achieving our aims but rather sabotage them by our behaviour? Nor does it consider risk properly: what if we have a lapse of judgement (as we all do)?

Giddens is not alone in defending individuals' need for stability in spite of obvious intrinsic contradictions. Similar incongruences, where residual theories collide with emergent theories of identities as processual and developmental are present in all second modernists' works. While Giddens is influenced by psychology, in some other cases the contradictions have to do with researchers' ethical subject positions. They sympathise with individuals who, in the midst of the changing world, desire permanence while their actual experiences speak of fragmentation and continuous insecurity.

Bauman (2008), for instance, has regarded the individuals' pressure to adopt various subjectivities as a rather undesirable modern survival game (pp. 138, 187). Those who are able to cultivate various sides of themselves as a result of better life chances are the winners, while those who are condemned to one invariable set of values and behavioural patterns are increasingly viewed as socioculturally inferior or deprived (ibid., p. 24). Such interpretations convey hidden class discussions of the privileged and the deprived, creating binary set-ups. Readers are required to take sides against the madness of the current age rather than being allowed to take the view that these oppositions are politically laden constructs that are used to appeal to emotions. Even the most prominent advocates of individual choice and agency waver between residual and emerging discourses as if uncertain whether plurality really is the desired direction for change, although they see it as inevitable. Beck and Beck-Gernsheim have expressed their concern saying:

> People end up more and more in a labyrinth of self-doubt and uncertainty. They are constantly asking themselves 'Am I really happy?', 'Am I really fulfilled?', 'Who exactly is the I saying and asking this?' In their quest for self-fulfillment, people travel to the four corners of the earth; they throw away the best marriages and rapidly enter new ties … They pull themselves up by the roots, to see whether the roots are really healthy. (Beck and Beck-Gernsheim, 2002, p. 38)

This quotation could well describe the global nomads in this book, if viewed with the discourse of vagrancy: they are the unsure individuals of second modernity who are unable to find direction but are forced to make choices. The Becks nostalgically look back to the 1950s and 1960s, when people, they argue, gave a clear and unambiguous answer to the question of their goal in life. It was a happy family, home, a new car, a good education for their children and a higher standard of living (ibid.); in other words, they had clear and stable material anchors for life. Conversely, people's answers today, particularly those of the better educated and more affluent young people, revolve around issues of self-expression, experimenting, and risk-taking which relate to plural subjectivities and search for more immaterial and mobile anchors for life.

Laments such as the Beck's are nostalgic wishes for a unified and uncomplicated past that is contrasted with the unpredictability of the contemporary world. Second modernists seem to be particularly drawn to such conceptions, supposedly because that supports their thesis of the radicalisation of modernity (e.g. Giddens, 1991, pp. 183–5; Bauman, 1991, 2008, pp. 135–6, 189. See also Curran, 2013, pp. 44–5; Bleicher and Featherstone, 1982; Elliott, 2002; Goldthorpe, 2002, p. 21). While I do not want to contest their well-meaning message that capitalism has perhaps gone too far in creating such insecurities and something needs to be done, my point is that research is not just innocently observing and analysing the contemporary world but actively participating in power negotiations, although in subtle and often hidden ways, in this case through discussions on the self.

If research is bound by political agendas and residual discourses, it is no wonder that laymen's discourses are as well. Although global nomads like to live precariously and try out new things, some of them would also rather stick to one subject position instead of many. For solo global nomads, the subject position of the lone ranger has become a kind of fact of life. They cling to it believing that their lifestyles make intimate relationships difficult. So dear can this subject position be that a strong incentive is needed for a transformation, even in situations where lone rangering no longer offers them sufficient rewards – in other words when unintended consequences (loneliness) have started to dominate over the intended purposes (independence).

Some of the global nomads justify the need for one subject position with the explanation that other people may find it hard to deal with their changing selves. Although such changes happen all the time in interaction, they are often ignored or explained away, for example, as illogicalities, changes of mood and views, or humour and irony where people visibly take a different stance. If taken more seriously, these can be analysed as different discourses and subject positions. They effectively question the sovereign agency of individuals and the validity of any theory that emphasises agency over structure, or cognition over unconscious. Foucault usefully paid attention to the double meaning of 'subject' when explaining contradictions: subject is not only an agent but subject to power (2002c, p. 331).

This dualism of subject is central for understanding the main difference between Giddens and Foucault. While Giddens attempted to transcend it, Foucault argued that it is a precondition for any field of inquiry. Human sciences were made possible, he maintained, 'when man constituted himself in Western culture as both that which must be conceived of and that which is to be known' (2005, p. 376). In other words, individuals are not only problem solvers but also the core of the problem. As such, this dualism was not meant to be solved; it is a major enabling factor without which human sciences would not exist (Smart, 1982, pp. 132–6. See also Dews, 1979, pp. 149–50). The next question is how to address a subject who is an agent and an object at the same time. As this chapter has shown, the advantage of 'subjectivity' is that it does not privilege one form of coherent self but allows contradictions and change (see Hall, 1996, p. 10), therefore enabling power analysis.

Among critics, Beck argued that under such changing and evolving circumstances, 'it makes little sense to talk about subject positions because the subject is so constantly in motion' (Beck, Bonß, and Lau, 2003, p. 23). However, let us remind ourselves that 'subject position' is not an essence. It is merely an analytical tool with which such motion can be examined. On the other hand, the more serious criticisms, that can further the discussion on subjectivity presented thus far, can be encapsulated in two strands. The first argues that subject positions make individuals mere standardised products (Habermas, 1987, p. 293), while the second calls for a systematic model with which such standardisation could be predicted and exploited in research (Hall, 1996, pp. 10–14. See also Bianchi, 2009, p. 490)!

Starting from the latter argument, critics have pointed out that subject positions have become a priori categories which individuals seem to occupy in an unproblematic fashion, while the theory lacks the means to examine how and why various subject positions are occupied.

> … what remains to be accounted for is a theory of what the mechanisms are by which individuals as subjects identify with the positions to which they are summoned as well as how they fashion, stylize, produce and perform these positions, and why they never do so completely, and some never do, or are in a constant, agonistic process of struggling with, resisting, negotiating, and accommodating the normative or regulative rules with which they confront and regulate themselves. (Hall, 1996, pp. 13–14)

Although it would be convenient to see a theory with which the success of discourses and subject positions could be forecast, all knowledge is contextual and therefore analyses are tied to specific research material. They cannot be simply and straightforwardly replicated in another environment, or abstracted into a set of universal rules or mechanisms. Foucault's accounts, for instance, were never even intended as a theory, as Hubert Dreyfus and Paul Rabinow (1983) have pointed out. Rather, they offered a grid for analysing how power works (p. 184). Furthermore, individual behaviour cannot be easily predicted or fit into any categories.

Jürgen Habermas (1987), representing the other line of criticism, argued that subject positions have a 'cloning' effect that belittles individuals: '… socialized individuals can only be perceived as exemplars, as standardized products of some discourse formation – as individual copies that are mechanically punched out' (p. 293). While Habermas is right in the sense that all individuals act within particular conditions of production and reception of discourses which direct their acts, he failed to take into account the multitude of subject positions, their combinations, and the ways in which they are adopted and recreated. The concept of 'subjectivity' does not imply that subject positions were adopted uniformly by a particular group of people, or even by members of that specific group, as the previous analysis of global nomads clearly demonstrates (see Mills, 2001, p. 103; Teun van Dijk, 2006, p. 162).

What should also be remembered is that subjects have a capacity to resist, which means that they are not merely effects of power relations. They have an agency which – according to their awareness, courage, and will – can be used or left unused. As Foucault famously pointed out: 'Where there is power, there is resistance'. Power includes its own criticism, and therefore subjects can, at least in principle, always modify its grip (1978, p. 95; 1988, p. 123). Whether this is the case, and how resistance works in practice, needs evidence. I will continue this discussion in the next chapter by broadening the perspective on global nomads' societal relationships where both sovereign power and biopower guide them to specific subject positions entailing opposition and submission. We will see the conditions in which their resistance, if present, takes place.

Chapter 5

In or Out

Max (39) works in IT and has the ability to work from anywhere. Every six months to a year he picks a new city somewhere in the world he is interested in, gets an apartment and lives there. 'I get a new bakery, a new place to do my laundry, and a new set of people to hang out', he describes. A new place is not a big deal for him. There is almost zero interruption in his work, and his largest challenge is organising high-speed internet in the apartment.

Post-9/11 made Max change his lifestyle. He realised he no longer wanted to live in the United States. 'What bothered me was the kind of police state that the US turned into. Suddenly they were wanting to search my bags in the subway, and every time you would get into an elevator, there would be a message to be afraid. I didn't feel comfortable any more'.

Max had been successful in the things that Americans consider successful, but he found it a hollow victory. He started to look for something more interesting and came up with travelling and the challenge of languages. He was not a novice when he left. When he was 16, he hitch-hiked around the United States and met a friend in Hawaii who got him hooked on the idea of going abroad. One year later Max was in Europe hitch-hiking from town to town. He lived for a year in Bavaria, Germany, earning his living as a dishwasher, bartender, and waiter.

When Max returned to the US, he started studying philosophy but ended up getting hired by a dot.com company. He lived nine years in Manhattan, wrote some patents for speech recognition technology, played a lot of a computer game called Everquest, and had a couple of love affairs.

Max still likes big cities that have a lot of activity going on to keep him from getting bored. 'I've pretty much got two options', he says with a mischievous twinkle in his eyes, 'either living in a place with a huge amount of activity, or go and try find myself in the East and discover my inner source of discomfort and dharma. In the short term, I think I'll go for the urban solution'.

When travelling, Max has three motivations when choosing a place to stay: food, girls, and a liberal government. 'I don't have a great love for people who are telling me how to live, where to live, or what to live', he explains.

Max considers himself one of the pioneers of digital nomadism. Not being a prisoner of geography, he represents the prototype of an entrepreneur that the information society admires. For nation-states, however, the likes of him are a threat. Having a portable occupation that allows them to earn money without licenses, permits, or a permanent place of business, they are beyond taxation and lawsuits. Even the idling global nomads fall into the same category, because governments consider them tourists who are just passing through. The location-independent thereby effectively make the limits of state power visible, although this threat is mostly negligible considering their small number. States are more interested in labour migrants, refugees, and asylum-seekers, all of whom pose a bigger risk to the status quo (see also Warnes and Williams, 2006, p. 1,266).

States and power are tightly knit. As Foucault maintained, 'To live in society is … to live in such a way that some can act on the actions of others. A society without power relations can only be an abstraction' (2002c, p. 343). Power, in societies, is practised in two forms: through sovereign power that is guided by laws and regulations, and through biopower which is present in social encounters as the previous chapter detailed. By analysing these forms of power, particularly the latter, I am able to examine to what extent societies and dominant discourses intervene in global nomads' lifestyles and subjectivities.

To start with, a definition of 'society' is needed. Are societies networks of social relationships? Social orders? Systems? Clusters of institutions? (see Urry, 2001, p. 7; Elias, 2001, p. 3). When formulating the mobilities manifesto, Urry (2001) suggested that if the concept makes sense at all, it has to be embedded within the analysis of nation-states. British historian Eric Hobsbawm drew the same conclusion by quoting political theorist Miroslav Hroch, who viewed nationality as a substitute for factors of integration. 'When society fails, the nation appears as the ultimate guarantee' (Hroch in an unpublished paper 'Nationale Bewegungen früher und heute', as cited in Hobsbawm, 2000, p. 173. See also Sassen, 2008, p. 281).

Today the nation-state – a state whose boundaries are congruent with the limits of nations, in other words a state of and for a particular nation – is the norm of political organisation (Brubaker, 1996, p. 63. Cf. Held, 2004; Held and McGrew, 2003). It consists of a set of institutional forms of governance, and it maintains an administrative monopoly over a territory with demarcated boundaries (Giddens, 1985, p. 121).

The most interesting question in regard to global nomads is how states and societies shape their location-independence with sovereign and biopower – do they live in or outside of societies, or more accurately, can there be any life outside societies? The following analysis focusses on nationality and citizenship. The two concepts are tightly linked and establish the meaning of full membership in society (Holston and Appadurai, 1999, p. 187) offering me an opportunity to examine whether global nomads can dodge societies' power networks as Caren Kaplan's definition in Chapter 1 stated. Within the concept of nationality, I explore the realm of feelings that global nomads relate to their country of origin, and within the concept of citizenship the legal side, particularly the privileges and responsibilities that citizenship entails. This categorisation is purely analytic because nationality and citizenship often overlap, and both can raise strong emotional reactions as we soon see.

Passport and Toothbrush

Global nomads try to detach themselves from some of the dominant discourses in their countries of origin and in the Western world in general, as discussed in Chapter 2. This seems to imply that they might also reject nationalistic affiliations, which was confirmed in the interviews. Unlike expatriates, who create home-like environments in their new destinations (see Butcher, 2010, pp. 27–8), global nomads do not experience homesickness. For the great majority, their home countries' cities, sceneries, nature, and culture failed to evoke nostalgia. Only a few mentioned mountains, lakes, and national parks, or a specific regional culture to which they feel attached. When nationalism was born in the nineteenth century, it was most often these kind of cultural bonds and natural sights that were used to imagine one's home country and the nation (Anderson, 1991). Even rebellious hobo culture was nationalistic. Author Jack London (2006), who was a fierce critic of middle-class values, proudly stated, 'I was the American hobo' (p. 59).

For global nomads, home country is an empty concept like places in general. It is not a bounded territory, nor is it an imaginary community of anonymous compatriots. It consists of their friends and family – wherever their loved ones happen to be. A sense of having 'roots' exists if global nomads have significant others in their country of origin, otherwise the connection is bound to weaken.

Global nomads are critical towards nationalistic discourses in general in the same way as they are critical to other ideals of dominant discourses. Rita (72) encapsulates: 'I'm not in the least interested in being an American in the world, I'm much more interested in being wherever I am'. Global nomads want to connect with locals and learn about their cultures, and in this task nationalism can be a mere obstacle, particularly if it incites hate, as is demonstrated in the next chapter. Global nomads would rather see nationalistic discourses disappear: 'I would love a world without cultural, mental and physical borders where there would be an understanding in every way', Ciro (29) says.

From the point of view of location-independence, nation-states and borders are a constraint. They limit, channel, and regulate movement (Cresswell, 2014, p. 718; Hannam, Sheller, and Urry, 2006, p. 11). On the other hand, nation-states also enable mobilities because they are the sole guarantors of mobility to other states. Therefore borders are not only places of resistance but places where people use different tactics and strategies to cope with, transcend, ignore, overcome, use, and build borders (Bærenholdt, 2013, p. 31. See also Beck, 2007, p. 696).

Global nomads are prime examples of such border artistry, which may include bribing, talking oneself out of some obligations, or sometimes just abiding by the rules. When no considerable alternatives for states exist, global nomads are practical even though they might dream of more freedom. They learn how to avoid unnecessary contacts with state officials, and how to deal with the obligatory formalities and requirements. In Beck's terms, this is a form of 'experimental cosmopolitanism from below' (2007, pp. 697–8), which can sometimes lead to complicated situations. Consider the following statement, where Anthony describes his experiences in Central Africa:

> We [Anthony and his partner] had three big bags. At the border the guy told us: 'I'm in a good mood today. You can choose which one is for me'. The border guards can be stoned or drunk, and they are heavily armed, sometimes having machine guns. You have to be very patient and start negotiating so that he doesn't get one of the bags. I usually have a packet of cigarettes although I don't smoke so that I can offer one. (ANTHONY, 35)

Sometimes global nomads' nationality or skin colour helps them, at other times they are an obstacle. From global nomads' point of view, the lack of alternatives is one of the greatest problems of nationality. Nationality cannot be chosen, nor can it be renounced unless it is tediously and expensively exchanged for another. Here the second modernists' theories of choice no longer apply: nationality is a structural condition which can, at best, be ignored or considered a mere commodity like passport and toothbrush.

> When someone becomes a traveller they slowly come to realise that nationality no longer matters, as blood type or other trivial things we are born with, yet have no control over. My home country has never been defined, except by passport. Norway, Canada, America? For me, I would be unable to give a home country if someone were to ask for it. Those terms simply don't register as comfortable for me. (JEFF, 25)

Nations are mandatory communities entered by birth and exited by death only, which is in an interesting contradiction to human rights. Governments have unilaterally imposed nationality and citizenship, and assumed arbitrary jurisdiction over their citizens – after all, no one was born as a citizen of any state. Citizenship and the set of responsibilities entailed were simply designated to them (e.g. Wolff, 1996, p. 45). This is a strong measure of sovereign power in which individuals have little to say. It also contains a threat: if the state can give individuals rights, it can also take them away at any time. States are therefore both a source of security and danger to individuals.

However, the contemporary, powerful role of the state is a result of a fairly recent development of the nineteenth century. If we go further back in time to ancient Rome, for instance, the Latin 'patria' was a much more layered concept that allowed multiple attachments (see Arnold, 2004, p. 147; Held, 2005, p. 10). Global nomads would prefer this option. 'I see the world as a house. My kitchen is France, my recreation centre is maybe South America, and my den or sort of is Poland. They are just neighbourhoods in my little village', Max (39) elaborates. Note that Max intentionally omits his country of origin, the USA, from the list. This seems to suggest that he and the other location-independent have elected 'a deliberate, chosen strangeness' of their home country. They have instead become 'enmeshed' with the people, places, and cultures they visit, to borrow the words of Scottish nomadic author Alastair Reid (1990, pp. 31, 36).

If nationalism is put aside, the constitutive factors of society are harder to pin down. This is because the aim of nationalism is precisely to bind disparate spheres, such as culture and politics together in order to form a whole. Therefore the concepts of 'society' and 'nation-state' seem entwined, perhaps in an inexorable manner. Although there is also the possibility of integration through values, which was the driving force of classical sociology, it is now viewed sceptically among sociologists. Beck and Beck-Gernsheim, for example, have argued that as people make varying connections, the very foundations on which value communities could be based are eaten away (2002, pp. 17–18).

If the question of what makes up a society is approached from the Foucauldian point of view, it can be tentatively defined as something that is kept together by dominant discourses and biopower (2002b, p. 404). They produce collective practices that people follow trying to ensure desirable behaviours (1991a, pp. 183, 199, 304). These practices define how people view themselves, other people and the society, and how they organise their lives together.

What these dominant discourses are, the kind of practices they involve, and how they are maintained and reproduced is my next topic. These questions lead me to analyse subtle measures of biopower, which cannot be found in government regulations or committee papers. They manifest themselves in people's everyday practices, speeches, and codes of conduct only. The main question in regard to global nomads is, are they more likely than the settled to manage to detach themselves from their country of origin by rejecting nationalistic subject positions and criticising the current system based on nation-states? The analysis aims to show the ultimate level to which global nomads are either detached from their origins or still tied to them.

Cultural Baggage

The dominant discourses under scrutiny are part of the tacit knowledge. They are functional in the sense that they free people from having to constantly consider behavioural choices and alternatives (Giddens, 1994, pp. 22–3). The downside is that their existence is rarely even noticed. This is an effect of power, as discussed in the previous chapter: they have become naturalised.

Although global nomads, for instance, do not consider themselves patriots, they are not immune to nationalistic discourses. Consider the following quotation, where Jukka (26) ponders what he is missing from his country of origin: 'Especially in Asia and Africa when I was buying groceries, I would have liked to be able to get all the stuff from the same place, also milk. Everything just works so much better in Finland. But I didn't really miss anything'.

Why travel if everything is so much better at home is an inevitable question that this statement evokes. However, Jukka also seems rather content with his present stateless life ('I didn't really miss anything'). Similar contradictions between residual nationalistic discourses and emerging discourses of statelessness were present in all interviews illustrating the strong position of dominant discourses. Even after being exposed to different regimes of truth for years, global nomads still travel with their home society.

Dominant discourses are a result of a long process of internalisation through parents, teachers, colleagues, friends, and the media – and most importantly – by ourselves, as we enforce these discourses in order to be accepted by others. Nationalism is just one example of these vehicles of biopower. They cover all areas of life from working to consuming, and the more closely they are related to values, the more significant are their effects, particularly if they lead to fear and prejudice. Travelling is one of the most effective ways to become aware of the existence of dominant discourses, and it is also the reason why travelling is restricted in some countries. It changes the individuals' conception of norms.

> We have seen different ways of living, different religions, different people. Earlier we thought that some things are good for us and some things are bad. Now everything is normal for us. We will never judge anybody for their way of life. We try to live the same way and find the best parts of this lifestyle. It makes us more universal and adaptable. (AJAY, 24, and MARIA, 32)

In discourse analytic terms, travelling means being at the limits of one regime of truth and at the beginnings of another, which produces an alienating effect (Foucault, 2005, p. xxii, 1998a, pp. 178–9. See also Simons, 1995, p. 90). Travellers notice that the same discourses, which facilitate their everyday life in their country of origin, make them feel confused elsewhere. Paradoxically, this feeling of alienation is perhaps the best way for travellers to learn – not about foreign cultures – but of their 'own' society (see also Euben, 2006, p. 24; Geoffroy, 2007, p. 281). The same contradiction reigns in travel literature. It tells more about 'home' than 'abroad' because home is where the writer's and the audience's frame of reference is (e.g. Lisle, 2006, p. 42).

From the point of view of research, dominant discourses are the key for understanding the tourist experience, but studies tell us surprisingly little about them (see also Wilson, Fisher, and Moore, 2009, p. 17). The questions that Erik Cohen asked about drifters in the 1970s – has the drifter's attitude toward his own society changed? In what ways? – remain unanswered (1972, p. 179). Instead, studies have focussed on the other culture and its impact on travellers, or on individual psychology, while ignoring the broader social, political, economic, and cultural contexts involved, the travellers' home context included.

For global nomads, getting rid of dominant discourses is an ongoing challenge. These discourses cannot be forgotten at will; they need to be questioned, criticised, and replaced with other discourses (Foucault, 1997d, p. 117, 1997e, p. 97. See also Habermas, 1987, p. 84).

> I'm trying to strip away everything that is not necessary. Probably 90 per cent of what we do is scripted. What I want to achieve myself is I want to be able to consider myself completely human instead of some other label, to be without

prejudices, like national. I try to look at things as if I were coming from another world, and to be able to judge things that way. (GEORGE, 31)

The scripted, in the language of this research, consists of dominant discourses which might emphasise, for example, the value of hard work and accumulation of wealth, and each citizen's responsibility towards their home country. Unlearning these 'truths' requires a view of subjectivity as an evolving process. Some participants, however, hold on to their cultural baggage, such as the value systems taught at home, considering them to be the core of their personality. 'I don't think it's [travel] changed me at all, but peeled away the shells of my cocoon. Surely the butterfly is the same creature as the caterpillar ...', Scott (33) reflects. This latter approach explains why biopower has such a strong influence on our lives. Dominant discourses feel natural to us as if they originated in ourselves and in our own desires.

Note that when comparing these two different conceptions of 'subjectivity' as evolving or as constant, there is no moralistic statement involved. Everyone's cultural baggage contains both positive and negative discourses, and it is merely the individuals' task to assess them and distinguish which to retain and which to discard. This – unlike nationality – is a lifestyle choice in the sense that second modernists formulated it: it is one's own making. Cindie (51) describes the discarding process she is going through: 'I have a lot of things to digest, a lot of things I learned on the road ... I don't fit back into society. I just have to assess what I'm happy with'.

Trying to get rid of dominant discourses is not easy. It is a struggle against particular forms of subjectivity (Foucault, 2002c, p. 331), and raises the question how successful global nomads' attempts eventually will be. Some global nomads believe they have not been able to shed their baggage. Despite their attempts, the home context is still what they know best. Others fiercely deny their ties.

> Wherever I go, I'm Portuguese whether I want or not. Whenever I go abroad, I don't ignore it. I was living 24 years of my life in Portugal. (CIRO, 29)

> I not only have nothing to do with the American people, I have taken a set against them. I truly and ardently don't like them, and would never associate myself with this nationality. (JEFF, 25)

In both cases, global nomads remain within the regime of truth of dominant discourses. Either they recognise these discourses in themselves or they oppose them. As Foucault researcher Sergei Prozorov (2007) has maintained, power cannot be escaped; indifference is perhaps the only means to resist it. If power is hated and confronted, or loved and followed, these passionate attachments merely turn resistance into new, and possibly even more intense forms of subjection (pp. 20, 145).

Although indifference sounds like a mild form of resistance, if it is resistance at all, it promises global nomads relative freedom from dominant discourses. Biopower cannot work alone but needs the cooperation of individuals. This is its weakness. However, resistance never seems to lead to a complete detachment either, although global nomads might like to think so. The more they oppose, the more they enforce dominant discourses, as their travel practices already demonstrated in Chapter 2. When attempting to detach themselves from the monetary economy, for instance, they might develop an even stronger attachment to it if their lives become consumed by the practice of living on the cheap. The same applies to their criticism against states and borders. Every time they cross borders, they encourage their making and maintenance and the related power structures. Borders also attract and organise global nomads' mobilities in many ways, and add to their travel experience no matter how much they resent them. The more borders global nomads cross, the more grows the number of countries visited, which is something the settled always ask as a proof of their travel experience. Even though global nomads do not believe in these structures, many of them keep country lists and gather knowledge of border crossings to show their travel expertise.

Dominant discourses, therefore, cannot be avoided, not even by opting for location-independence. Borders and national regulatory regimes do not let foreigners 'forget who they are and where they come from' (Butcher, 2010, p. 33. See also Conradson and McKay, 2007, p. 169). Nor would global nomads themselves, in most cases, want to renounce their nationality. Thanks to their mostly Western passports, they can travel almost anywhere in the world. Therefore, nationality for them is not an obstacle; it is one of the keys for location-independence. A similar attachment, that ties global nomads to their country of origin, may lie in citizenship.

Citizens and Freeloaders

Just like 'society', 'citizenship' has been understood from varying and often confusing perspectives (Sassen, 2008, p. 287). In the most general sense, citizenship has come to mean the right to receive the protection of the state, for instance police protection and welfare, and the opportunity to exercise political rights such as voting (e.g. Arnold, 2004, p. 20; Rosanvallon, 2008, p. 20; Beck, Cohn-Bendit, Delors, and Solana, 2012). In practice, however, citizenship has been configured under the rubrics of national identity and economic independence. To be a citizen, one has to acknowledge territorial belonging, to be economically independent, and make a contribution to the market (Arnold, 2004, p. 166. See also Malkki, 1992, p. 27). Although political equality in the liberal capitalist state has, in principle, been guaranteed regardless of economic status and spending, this has not been achieved, political researcher Kathleen Arnold argues (2004, p. 5). Contemporary society engages citizens primarily as owners and consumers. Bauman (2007) confirms: in the society of consumers, 'the invalids earmarked for exclusion … are flawed consumers' (pp. 28, 56).

The predominantly economic character of citizenship was already present in Aristotle's work. Property was viewed as a moral and political phenomenon, which was 'both an extension and a prerequisite of personality', as historian J.G.A. Pocock argued (1985, p. 103. See also Rousseau, 2002, p. 164; Simmel, 2004, p. 317; Weber, 1978; Barbalet, 2010). Property and taxes paid are all measurable, and therefore suitable criteria for citizenship. Another question is, how do these criteria fit with the location-independent. Global nomads do not, for the most part, adhere to nationalistic discourses as seen in the previous analysis, nor do they want to belong to any places. They do not necessarily contribute to their home market either, nor consume avidly. It is worthwhile to ask whether they are fit for citizenship at all or are they just freeloaders.

For a national economy that seeks continuous growth, everyone leaving the system is a freeloader if they get more from the society, for example in the form of education and health care, than they have given back. However, how to calculate who has received more than their fair share is a question that has puzzled many influential writers and statesmen since antiquity. While my purpose is not to engage in these discussions, I reflect some of their main arguments that relate to global nomads. These are, once again, important power negotiations where global nomads need to justify their lifestyles in regard to the settled.

From the economic point of view, the notion of productiveness and unproductiveness has been one of the main ways to distinguish citizens from non-citizens (Byrne, 2005, pp. 24–5). Being homeless and jobless, or working in the informal economy without paying taxes or by structuring their activities to avoid taxes, global nomads do not seem to be productive in the required sense. Michel (47), for instance, tries to keep his income so low that he does not need to pay taxes, whereas Andy (54) systematically avoids taxes. 'United States has a special rule that says you can earn 88,000 dollars and not pay taxes if you are outside the country 335 days a year, so I can stay in the United States 30 days. I spend about 10 days at a time', Andy explains.

Global nomads' other financial practices, downshifting and exchange economy discussed in Chapter 2, are also controversial in the view of citizenship. At a personal level these practices only have an effect on global nomads and those close to them, but on a nation-wide and global scale downshifting would mean rethinking the way economies work. This is because the growth of an economy requires debt that fuels the creation of new money. Here, the banking sector has a central role. It has the ability to create credit and money out of nothing. All that is needed is the decision of the bank to extend credit (Schlichter, 2014, pp. xiv). Most of the money in national economies is created either when banks give loans to their customers, by quantitative easing, or by printing more money. To fuel debt, people have to be encouraged to consume more than they earn so that they will borrow money. Mostly debt-free and low-consuming global nomads do not participate in these activities that boost national economies, nor do those settled, for example, who are not in the process of buying their homes.

Because of their alternative practices, global nomads raise strong controversy in the manner of vagrants of old despite their small number and influence. My husband and I have received an outpouring of negative feedback from other Finns who are afraid that we might one day return back to Finland and exploit social security without having contributed to it for years (see also Warnes and Williams, 2006, p. 1,267). For them, we are irresponsible deserters and parasites of the discourse of vagrancy. We had received free education without giving enough back.

The participants reported slightly milder reactions. Anick (29) related stories of elderly men who had been worried about the example she sets. Their reactions had been aggressive, and Anick speculates where they come from: 'They are worried that their grandchildren would do the same'. Many global nomads have been asked what would happen if everyone worked and consumed less, or just travelled around without contributing and being productive. The question reflects the old fear related to vagrancy. The example of idling is believed to have an infectious, negative effect poisoning the minds of other people. At a societal level, this fear implies a threat of disintegration, which could undermine the legitimacy of states.

Mobilities are a threat. While the notion of citizenship in principle includes the right to move, to travel within and across borders (Cresswell, 2013, p. 106), states also want to control movement. Elaborate bureaucracies and technologies have been created for monitoring citizens through collecting varied data. This includes fingerprints, DNA, blood samples, medical records, location information, and bank account information (Torpey, 2000, p. 16). In the streets and public places, cameras follow people; passport RFIDs (a microchip that broadcast information for remotely identifying a person), mobile phone SIM cards, and bank transactions provide authorities with location information; banks are required to release financial information about their accounts and transactions; internet users are spied on through email and online transactions; shopping malls and stations have surveillance systems that have been compared to the Panopticon – a prison with a particular architectural structure allowing prisoners to be viewed without their knowledge (Foucault, 1991a, pp. 201–2, 2002d, pp. 58; Urry, 2002b, p. 134).

All of these controls represent anonymous networks that lack a single source of responsibility (Arnold, 2004, p. 41). They enable abuses of power. This spread of legal regulation and surveillance has the structure of a dilemma, as Habermas maintained: 'It is the legal means for securing freedom that themselves endanger the freedom of their presumptive beneficiaries' (1987, p. 291. See also Sassen, 2008, p. 284; Bauman, 2008, p. 14). As Max's example in the beginning of this chapter showed, some global nomads have left their countries as a protest to such violations of freedom and privacy.

The gathering of this data has been legitimised by biopolitical care: the state has an opportunity to help its citizens if necessary. The passport, for instance, should vouchsafe the issuing state's aid to its bearer while she is in the jurisdiction of other states (Torpey, 2000, p. 160). However, there is also another reason, state control over individual movement for maintaining and strengthening state power.

This is one of the reasons why the push and pull model has been so popular in migration studies; the state and its interests have guided studies.

For individuals, citizenship is not a mere formality but a question of physical existence (Arnold, 2004, p. 131. Cf. Holston and Appadurai, 1999, p. 190). Without the state issued documents that are needed to establish identity, they lack recognised status. The states are also able to practise sovereign power over citizens by restricting the kind of identity they are allowed to choose, and individuals are not free to reject these identities. Political philosopher Giorgio Agamben (1993) explained: 'A being that were radically devoid of any representable identity, would be totally irrelevant to the state' (p. 85).

While granting global nomads freedom to move, the concept of citizenship therefore poses significant constraints, both to their location-independence and their subjectivities. The same is true for the stateless, the homeless, and the poor, who all challenge the existing notion of citizenship. Sociologist Saskia Sassen (2008) has, rather accurately, called citizenship 'an incompletely specified contract' between the state and the citizen (p. 277). It is a form of sovereign power that leaves both citizens' rights and duties open, allowing accommodating new conditions at will (ibid., p. 321). But even though citizens are states' property, this is of course a bargain: citizens gain rights in return for obligations. At a global scale, however, there are no opportunities to opt out of the bargain. Even global nomads need to negotiate their benefits and duties with their respective country of origin.

Welfare

Upon leaving their country of origin, global nomads retain their formal citizenship, but they also renounce most of their benefits. In Europe, this means public health care and social security, the contents of which vary according to country (see also Gangl, 2002). For global nomads, keeping official residence in their country of origin may maintain some of their rights to public services, but every country has its own policies as to what kind of absences are accepted. The threshold might be half a year or one year, and in case of long absences, some rights might be removed. For instance, in the UK, citizens lose their voting rights after 15 years of absence.

Some participants have purposely detached themselves from welfare, while a few have tried to maintain benefits by making regular visits, having a house for rent and keeping a postal address there, or by officially stating that it is their country of residence. The latter option usually entails duties. 'In Switzerland, you either have to declare you leave your country for an indeterminate time, or you keep your official address and then you have to be insured', Claude (50) illustrates.

The question about the participants' right to welfare was in some cases answered evasively, and not all of them were sure about their status, because the rules are not clear. Therefore, it is impossible to give an exact number of participants who still enjoy benefits. In a couple of cases, at least some of the benefits were retained.

However, to be able to use public services, global nomads would need to stay in the country, as states are not willing to give such benefits for people who are spending their money and time abroad.

The majority of global nomads have deliberately detached themselves from the system, and they have little trust in societal structures. A similar phenomenon has been studied in relation to lifestyle migrants, who offer an interesting comparative material for global nomads. Some British lifestyle migrants, for instance, have moved to Spain because they had doubts about the real value of UK pensions, or the ability to rely on sickness or unemployment benefits in times of need. By moving, they expected to gain a better quality of life for less money (O'Reilly, 2007, p. 281. See also Hoey, 2009, pp. 31–2). At the same time, however, they lost the right to use the National Health Service in the UK, and they also severely reduced their entitlements to pensions and other social service benefits ending up being socially excluded. Many of them work in the informal economy paying no income tax or national insurance contributions in Spain, and they rely on emergency state health provision or inadequate private insurance (O'Reilly, 2007, p. 283. Cf. Warnes, King, Williams, and Patterson, 1999, p. 737).

Although most of the global nomads are in a similar situation, they do not consider themselves as socially excluded. Their lifestyles rather seem expressions of neoliberalism in terms of the reduced role of the state, although their resentment of capitalist greed is contrary to this interpretation. As discussed in Chapter 2, it is increasingly difficult to put people in any slots according to social class, because they tend to represent different and contradicting trends, exercising self-categorisation rather than being categorised.

Another interpretation for global nomads' self-exclusion is that Western societies' welfare for them is 'illfare' in the sense that it involves features they are not ready to accept such as materialism and high-pressured working cultures. They see no point in socially adapting to a 'dysfunctional society' (see Laing, 1967, p. 120). Global nomads rather believe that self-exclusion has enabled the mastery of their own lives. 'A traveller has a life purpose, and has chosen travelling as a lifestyle choice. We're not victims, we travel by choice', Barbara (52) states.

So far, scholarship has not thoroughly considered the possibility of exclusion being chosen, which would have implications for agency. For sure, 'social exclusion' also implies agency, as sociologist David Byrne (2005) has remarked, but it is 'something that is done by some people to other people' (p. 2). The emphasis is on society and its best interests instead of individuals.

Self-exclusion requires risk-taking and includes many downsides as discussed in the previous chapter in relation to social ties. At a societal level, risks are very different for European and American participants. Americans consider these risks smaller than Europeans because of lack of health care and social security in their country (see Sassen, 2008, p. 285; Walters, 2004, p. 243). In the United States, lack of services is a mechanism which maintains flexibility in the labour market. It makes it relatively easy for Americans to move if they lose their job, whereas in Europe, movement is limited by administrative barriers and language.

The United States holds a competitive edge provided people remain within its borders, because it reduces the cost of labour, but as soon as educated people start moving abroad, it becomes a debt because they take their talent elsewhere.

Many of the American global nomads found my question about health care merely hilarious and said they pray the president will fix the system. For them, moving out of the country was rather a solution than a problem.

> Ha, ha, ha. That was another reason why I left. When I lost my job, I lost my health insurance. I was uninsured for six years and in my country, I don't have a pension. I don't have social security, I don't receive any money. I got unemployment benefits for six months and that was it. (ELISA, 54)

This may be an increasing trend also in Europe, as will be discussed later in Chapter 7. Even in the so-called welfare states, citizens might no longer get any help from society; they need to help themselves to live better lives. If global nomads can offer us any glimpse to the future, how do they get by without society's safety nets? Although the biopolitical government of the last two centuries has limited citizens' freedom of choice, it has indisputably also made significant advances in medical and social care, education, and the establishment of certain guarantees of positive equality. To seek liberation from biopower, or to be deprived of it against one's will, means losing these benefits (Prozorov, 2007, p. 143. See also Giddens, 1991, p. 115).

The benefits of citizenship represent the alluring side of biopower. Functional welfare societies, for instance, liberated people to do other things in life than the sheer necessities, for example to travel rather than to stay at home taking care of their ageing parents as discussed in the previous chapter. Most of the benefits, however, keep people at home and limit the length of their journeys so that their personal benefits, particularly health care, are retained.

As drastic as the question of losing these benefits seems for the settled, most global nomads do not believe that societies can offer them any security. For them, welfare is just another way of disempowering people. 'It creates a victim cycle where people become reliant on insurance and retirement and all other stuff that are being sold as a security. You can lose that in an instant. I know there is no such thing as security in this world', Barbara (52) says.

The structures which seem important to the settled sit on thin ice. In a moment a job can be lost and the dearly-paid insurance and life savings can vanish when insurance companies and banks go bankrupt. Global nomads do not believe in these soothing structures but rather stand on their own. The same was true already for their namesakes, pastoral nomads, who aimed at self-sufficiency. In fact, one of the central features of the nomadic lifestyles has been the maximisation of unit autonomy: each household is responsible for its own resources. Once a household establishes its autonomy, its success or failure is also individual (Barfield, 1993, p. 104). For global nomads – and for all people according to second modernists – the same promise of individual success and threat of failure persists. The latter represents itself in the discourse of vagrancy where the protagonist ends up in the gutter.

Half of the global nomads do not buy insurance either for the same reason: they do not want to be controlled (see also Riley, 1988, p. 319). 'Things like social security and health care do not even exist in my mind. Purely out of convenience, I do not even use a bank. I have not used insurance since I was a teen for the same reasons. I think these dependencies tie us down', Jeff (25) argues. Many global nomads view insurance companies as mere rip-offs. They do not want to pay out, and they charge too much money for what they do. 'They make a lot of money. I don't want them making mine', Tor (61) remarks.

While some participants rely on emergency health care in case of need, others have bought insurance when they have aged, worried that they might fall ill. Sometimes insurance is bought to appease global nomads' loved ones, or to fulfil visa requirements or regulations of a transportation company. In these cases, insurance represents both sovereign power which works by force, and biopower which is practised by a subtle threat: 'What if?' However, even when having insurance, not all problems are solved, as studies on later-life migrant populations have shown. Even though health care might be available, care might be a problem – either at the hospital or after discharge when recovering at home (e.g Warnes, Friedrich, Kellaher, and Torres, 2004; Warnes and Williams, 2006).

For global nomads, travel insurance is more expensive than for holidaymakers, because most insurances are tied to the social programmes of the traveller's country of origin. Upon leaving or having been away for a certain amount of time, global nomads lose access to public services and therefore also to travel insurance in most countries. The private insurances that are available are costly. With the same amount of money, global nomads can visit a doctor dozens or even hundreds of times on the road.

> I had a treatment in the Philippines where it cost me 150 USD. The same would have been around 2,200 USD in the United States. As long as it's not a major thing, like a cancer when you need a million dollars, I can afford to do my own health assurance. (ANDY, 54)

Even if there is public health care available in global nomads' country of origin, it might be cheaper and faster to find another solution. 'In Portugal, health care is very expensive even if it's public. I rather go to see a dentist in India', Ciro (29) says. This is also one of the reasons why medical tourism is such a fast growing branch of the tourism industry, even among the citizens of welfare societies.

If global nomads bought health insurance, it would be of limited use, because insurance is not valid in countries where travelling is not recommended. For Americans, about a half of the world's countries are not covered. Of global nomads, only a minority worry about their safety, and even those found it unnecessary to make a fuss about dangers (see also Jarvis and Peel 2010, p. 25). Most avoid war zones and areas that are infested with disease, and a few mentioned thefts, muggings, robberies, and traffic accidents (see also Riley, 1988, p. 320). Considering the current fear of terrorism, it is noteworthy that no one mentioned terrorist attacks. Although belittling risks might be self-aggrandising, most of the risks global nomads take are psychological rather than physical. Leaving the biopolitical networks in the form of health care and social security in order to live homeless on the road is one of the most risky steps one can take, at least from the point of view of the settled (see also Nudrali and O'Reilly, 2009, p. 149; Warnes and Williams, 2006, p. 1,261. Cf. Elsrud, 2001).

Life without Signs of Respectability

Homelessness is the factor that most visibly distinguishes global nomads from their compatriots and the settled in general. It is therefore a good starting point for the discussion on citizens' duties, with which they are expected to pay back the services they have received, and the ways in which global nomads cope without having this important sign of respectability.

In societies, having a home is tightly knit with the concept and criteria of citizenship. It signifies citizens' ability to contribute to the market, pursue long-term goals, and maintain a social network. Home also means being rooted, which is necessary for having a nationality and a citizenship, as both are based on the idea that everyone naturally belongs in one place. In this context, home is the precondition for any degree of citizenship (see Arnold, 2004, pp. 3–4, 17, 27).

Home, having such great importance in dominant discourses, makes homelessness seem like a predicament to be concealed (e.g. Dordick, 1997, p. 182). However, homelessness increasingly touches ever more people today (Bell and Ward, 2000, p. 91), and can therefore hardly be bypassed as an anomaly. This is also true historically. The ideal of home and particularly home ownership as a basis for citizenship, security, and identity – just like nationality – are only recent inventions of the nineteenth and twentieth centuries (DePastino, 2003, p. xxi). This ideal was fuelled by capitalism, which stressed property ownership.

Knowing how dearly home is regarded in dominant discourses, global nomads provoke the settled by celebrating their homelessness as a cherished choice in the same way they celebrate statelessness and rootlessness. With these provocations, they consciously distance themselves, physically and mentally, from the commitments and attachments that citizenship and home entail (see Euben, 2006, pp. 24–5). 'I don't live anywhere, that's a sentence where people have to change their mindsets', Anick (29) describes.

Although it is controversial to juxtapose oneself with the homeless because it means ignoring the power asymmetry at play, as discussed in Chapter 2, it is also illuminating and not as far-fetched as one might think. Both global nomads and the homeless are outcasts according to the prevailing formulation of 'citizenship'. The main difference is that global nomads can usually determine the duration of their slumming experience unlike the unwillingly poor who anguish over begging money and food and protecting themselves (e.g. Dordick, 1997, pp. 6, 192). Although global nomads are a very small and, so far, mostly invisible challenge to society, their provocations make visible the current restrictions of citizenship (see also Warnes, Friedrich, Kellaher, and Torres, 2004, p. 321). They remind us of the fact that anyone can move both upwards and downwards in the social hierarchy, and this might not always be their cherished choice. While elective downward social mobility seems more understandable because it is a trade-off in terms of lifestyle aspects, the non-elective is the great fear of the middle class.

For societies, all homeless citizens alike, regardless of the reasons why they find themselves in that situation, pose a challenge. Footloose, they are not easily controlled by authorities. They cannot be reached when necessary, which is an unwritten duty of citizens. Having a permanent address, for instance, is a prerequisite, for social security (see also Dordick 1997, p. 58). The homeless are also perceived as having less to lose in material terms, and also in respect to other rights attached to citizenship. Householders or renters, on the other hand, have their house or their dignity in the eyes of other people, at stake. However, this argument ignores that the reputational stakes of the homeless are even higher because their status lies completely on themselves (ibid., p. 30). The same is true for global nomads who cannot establish their rank with possessions or professional status.

Although global nomads do not consider the lack of address, stable living conditions and possessions as a distress or an involuntary peril, it nevertheless causes occasional inconvenience for them. Consider the following statement, in which Scott describes his attempts to find work:

> I spent three months hitching around my favourite country in the world, mostly the North Island, knocking from door to door at Montessori schools, asking for a job. I was barefoot, sleeping in the woods every night, smelt of the road's asphalt, with a knife on my hip, no qualifications and no palpable experience. I never got a job. (SCOTT, 32)

The self-irony shows that for Scott, slumming is a play. He knows his efforts must have looked weird in the eyes of the settled but he is not representing himself as a victim; he could have chosen differently. Still, lack of home, address, and work make many everyday things difficult, and all of these tend to be related. When global nomads have no home, searching for a job is challenging, and without a pay slip, they may not be able to rent a place. The same applies to credit cards. Card holders need to prove that they have a steady inflow of cash for paying the bills.

Travelling without a mobile phone can also pose problems, because a telephone number is required in many places, sometimes even in immigration. A mobile phone can also be a prerequisite for purchasing airline tickets online in addition to a debit or a credit card. The buyer receives a PIN code via SMS to the mobile phone, which then has to be typed into the online payment system. Without these necessary signs of respectability global nomads are outlaws, but with experience, they learn to play the game without anchoring themselves in things.

> People ask for your permanent address, it's difficult sometimes. Sometimes you have to create an appearance of stability in order to make people comfortable. It's

for other people. Then you have a common language with them and you don't
have to explain your whole lifestyle to them. I can play the game, I clean up nice.
(BARBARA, 52)

The game of 'cleaning up' boils down to different discourses. When speaking
and doing business with the settled, global nomads mirror dominant discourses in
order not to raise suspicion, fear, or questions. When they learn the game, they no
longer need to employ things as a proof of their identity and integrity. They rely on
their ability to switch discourses and subject positions so that possible frictions are
smoothed over by using other people's assumptions in their favour.

All the challenges described imply power relationships that are not commonly
addressed in tourism studies. The underlying assumption is that the individuals are
on a temporary escape, which does not alter their basic coordinates (see Franklin,
2007, p. 139). Tourism has traditionally been viewed as reinforcing societies' values
and norms rather than confronting them. This partly derives from the heritage of the
industrial age. Leisure and tourism were harnessed in the service of productivity by
considering them as breaks from the everyday, which could increase individuals'
fitness to work and responsible citizenship (see Rojek, 2010, p. 2). Rather than
enabling mobility and difference, this notion of travel is limiting. It merely offers
biopolitical incentives for people to stay at home.

Due to their location-independence, global nomads make visible the current
restrictions of nation-states. However, they cannot remove them. Although they
attempt to reject states' sovereign power in their lives, they are still tied to it, not
least by their citizenship, which alone allows them to travel and hold an official
identity. During their travels, global nomads also need to collaborate with other
states by going through, or trying to circumvent, the process of applying for
visas. They remain, therefore, within societies' power networks. The reasons and
implications of this predominance of the state is my next topic.

(Bio)power and States

Despite the widespread hype of globalisation, we are not living in a global world.
State economies are still managed according to national principles counting the
losses and profits such as migration flows and tax income at a state level, while
the capitalist market is global. The allocation of citizens' rights and duties is also
tied to the nation-state, even though mobilities have increased (see also Held,
1989, p. 176). For the location-independent, this leads to a paradoxical situation:
they need to retain a home territory in order to be mobile.

The world is at best contradictory, due to the clash between residual
nationalistic discourses and the still emerging discourses of globalisation. Residual
discourses never die, and they rarely even wither away (Smart, 1982, p. 123).
The same grass roots level discourses that were visible in the global nomads'
interviews, those between their old nationalistic and new stateless discourses, are

also at work in societies and in research where they have deeper implications. When only citizens are considered to be fit for mobility, a large number of people are shut out (Cresswell, 2014, p. 713. See also Bertram, 2005, p. 75). Although the location-independent are privileged compared to the homeless in the streets, the stateless, refugees and illegal immigrants, the current conceptions of citizenship make extreme mobilities difficult for them, sometimes even impossible.

While scholarship has suggested that the power of the nation-state has already diminished in citizens' lives due to the emergence of new spaces of citizenship such as global cities (Cresswell, 2013, p. 109. See also Sassen, 2008, pp. 169–71, 314–18. Cf. Holston and Appadurai, 1999, p. 189), this is a theoretical notion which ignores the everyday problems of the multi-mobile. Global cities do not reinvent anybody's nationality nor do they resolve their ID or visa problems (cf. Sassen, 2005, p. 81; Ong, 2006, p. 500–501). As this chapter has shown, even people with a valid and widely recognised passport need to use loopholes in the system, or break the rules in order to be mobile. The research interviews and global nomads' trajectories showed that these tactics can be tiring in the long run. Some of the global nomads were considering returning to their country of origin, or settling down in a location where they can stay without having to constantly negotiate and bribe.

In order to enable location-independence, the notion of citizenship would need to confer political equality regardless of economic status, race, nationality, gender, or differences based on lifestyle. If this were the case, citizens would no longer need home and home country for essentialising subjectivity, nor for proving that they are respectable citizens, because this merely creates inequality (see Arnold, 2004, p. 160).

This dilemma and the suggested demands are not new. Jean-Jacques Rousseau already argued that citizenship rights should be translated into human rights, which they intrinsically are (see Rousseau, 2002). Among second modernists, Giddens has raised the same question (1989, pp. 269–70), and Beck actively advocated cosmopolitan society (e.g. 2000, 2002; Beck and Sznaider, 2006). However, whether such ideals can ever be achieved in practice is not a question of problem-solving but of politics, as Foucault pointed out when summarising the key lessons of Deleuze and Guattari's *Anti-Oedipus* (1972). Any idea of restoring individuals' rights merely means reinforcing power since the 'individual' and the 'rights' are just another product of power (Foucault, 1983).

Research is not immune to these political struggles either. On the contrary, it often maintains state power either by adopting the state as a primary category of analysis, or by opposing it. While studies and topics have become more mobile, researchers' gaze remains fixed, as sociologist Barak Karil has pointed out (2013, p. 312. See also Beck and Beck-Gernsheim, 2002, p. xx). This is particularly the case for migration studies, as discussed earlier in relation to the push and pull model, which is based on the premise of the state (see also Söderström, Randería, Ruedin, D'Amato, and Panese, 2013, p. 10). The same assumption also reigns in many other fields including history, economics, and statistics (e.g. Piketty, 2014. Cf. Savage, 2014, p. 595). Even second modernists are bound by it. Giddens, for instance, has formulated his accounts of power largely within the framework of the state discussing at length the development of modern state and its infrastructural power (Giddens, 1985). To understand what kind of limitations this leads to, I now shortly analyse the conditions of production of these nationalistic theories. I use Giddens's power theories as an example in order to explicate, at the same time, what I meant in Chapter 2 when saying that his power theories are not suitable for this work.

A few basic conceptual clarifications are needed so that Giddens's basic premises can be understood. Giddens spoke of two forms of power, dominance and transformation, which represent a shift from his early work influenced by Marxist theories to his later works on second modernism. By domination Giddens means 'structured asymmetries of resources' (1981, p. 50. See also 1979, p. 93), which depend on two types of resources, allocative and authoritative. Allocative resources refer to capabilities that generate command over objects, goods, or material phenomena, while authoritative resources refer to types of transformative capacity that generate command over persons (1984, p. 33).

In modern capitalist societies, Giddens argued, power asymmetries arise primarily from allocative power (1981, p. 4; 1984, p. 258). However, what remains unaccounted for in this analysis, is how the state is articulated to capitalism (Jessop, 1989, pp. 121–4). If the modern nation-state is said to be capitalist, how can we reconcile this with the fact that capitalism has a global reach?

It seems that Giddens produces a similar contradiction between residual nationalistic and emerging global discourses as was identified earlier in this chapter, which merely reveals its widespread popularity. This contradiction produces significant problems in research. While any investigation of power must also scrutinise the logics of the state to some extent, the state is merely a site of exercise of power, while it possesses no power of its own.

If the state is assumed to be the primary research object, the explanation for power is sought out in state institutions, which leads to explaining power by sovereign power (see Foucault, 2002c, p. 343). The questions that these studies can ask are limited: who can be let out, when, and where (see Bærenholdt, 2013, p. 26). They focus on states' coercive measures such as laws and regulations, overt control and surveillance, or unequal resource endowments leaving the subtle forms of biopower unaddressed. In the name of fairness, Foucault was not immune to these residual discourses either but stated:

> … the state is not simply one of the forms of specific situations of the exercise of power – even if it is the most important – but that, in a certain way, all other forms of power relation must refer to it … power relations have come more and more under state control … Using here the restricted meaning of the word 'government', one could say that power relations have been progressively governmentalized, that is to say, elaborated, rationalized, and centralized in the form of, or under the auspices of, state institutions. (Foucault, 2002c, p. 345)

By emphasising the role of the state, Foucault also ended up being a prisoner of a discursive network, inadvertently proving his idea that discourses also speak us. The same naturally applies to this research. I leave it to critics to point out the discrepancies and further the approaches presented here.

While Foucault shifted more and more towards positive conceptions of power in his work, Giddens's accounts enforce the primary position of the state, remaining blind to the problem of methodological nationalism in his own work but criticising it in others: 'The undue reliance which sociologists have placed upon the idea of "society" ... should be replaced by a starting point that concentrates upon analysing how social life is ordered across time and space' (Giddens, 2003, p. 60).

In order to switch the viewpoint from the state to the mobile, a top-down and bottom to top approach is needed. From the point of view of location-independence, the aim is to study individual mobilities and socialities that actively participate in the making and unmaking of societies (see also Bærenholdt, 2013, pp. 20–21, 26, 31), but without ending up in a mere reversal of the dichotomy where society would be replaced with individual mobilities, as Urry (2001) initially suggested in the mobilities manifesto. Instead, the interplay between the two needs to be analysed.

Another problem arises if the state is merely replaced by places (e.g. Urry and Sheller, 2004. Cf. Cresswell, 2008b, p. 137) as the result is the same: the individual point of view is disregarded. As discussed in Chapter 2, from the point of view of location-independence, places are mere platforms for individual mobilities. They gain meaning in relation to other places, people, and the travellers themselves.

When the focus is on the interplay between sovereign and biopower through individual movements, as in the case of global nomads, a more nuanced analysis can be constructed. In this context, power is no longer about empowerment or disempowerment, access or exclusion only; instead, the complex, situated and contested nature of power is taken into account. As this chapter has showed, biopower is crucial for this analysis. It represents a strong integrating force that binds citizens to society, even when they are overtly against it. Although most global nomads, for instance, have rejected nationalistic subject positions, social security, health care, insurance, permanent address, and the security of a steady job in their country of origin, they are still tied to it. Dominant discourses intervene in their thoughts and actions, their identity is state-issued, and even their opposition is based on dominant discourses.

While there are yet few studies on how citizens' mobilities are being reconfigured (Cresswell, 2013, p. 121), Foucauldian theories seem to offer interesting horizons for this shift. It focusses on those forms of subjectivity that are linked to the state instead of viewing the state as an exploiter and primary user of power. Global nomads have offered fruitful material for analysing this shift. Lack of a permanent domicile, constant border crossings and extended stays in various countries effectively test the limits of mobilities revealing contradictions.

In societies, these contradictions have an effect on everybody's lives. Although mobilities have been promoted and encouraged for example in the European Union area, these efforts do not necessarily produce the desired effect because of the residual discourses that constrain mobilities. As long as mobilities are expected to contribute towards home either financially or by strengthening the dominant discourses, the location-independent and other multi-mobile people remain anomalies who are not recognised in international policies. The current national regimes, therefore, at the same time both make extreme mobilities possible and negate them. This represents an interesting statement in discussions on mobilities. It shows how contradictory mobility policies are, and how perplexing the current social situation is interpreted to be when the global and/or European wide perspective should be included (see also Warnes and Williams, 2006, p. 1,270). In the next chapter, I increase the challenge by broadening the analysis to this global perspective.

Chapter 6
A Sisyphean Task?

Rita (72) has been wandering since her divorce at the end of the 80s. She sold everything she had and just took off. While she had been interested in anthropology and would have liked to have seen more of the world earlier, her husband was phobic about planes. When Rita no longer had to make compromises, she had mixed feelings. She was excited about the opportunity, but she was also afraid of the smallest things like eating a meal by herself in a restaurant. It was not something that she was used to doing.

Rita had been a stay-at-home mother writing and being active in the community, for example, taking part in protests against the Vietnam War. When she and her husband moved from New York to Los Angeles, her lifestyle changed radically. 'We ate in the best restaurants, went to the Academy Awards and the Grammies, and had a high profile list of friends'. Despite all the glamour, Rita didn't like the place. She didn't like to wear fancy clothes and she found many of the celebrities that she and her husband knew very superficial. 'Los Angeles made me realise I wasn't experiencing life', Rita summarises.

Now in her seventies, Rita has taken on a mission to encourage American teenagers to take a gap year abroad. This has slowed down her own travels, as she has been going from school to school talking about her journeys. Her travel tips to the young are: 'Smile a lot, talk to strangers, accept all invitations, and eat everything you are offered'. Rita admits that she is a tourist of the human condition rather than a tourist of things. 'I have to be dragged kicking and screaming to see this building and that cathedral', she says laughing, 'That's not what I'm there for. I'm there for people'.

When I ask what has been the most memorable moment of her travels, Rita tells me a story of her visit to a local village on the island of New Guinea. She and three other women had arrived in a tribal village where men were wearing nothing but penis gourds. 'They were all sizes, all shapes', Rita describes laughing, 'and we were sitting, the four of us, covered from the tops of our heads to the bottom of our feet because this is a malaria country'.

The guests and the hosts had one common language: singing. The women sang American songs including the nursery rhyme 'Old McDonald', and challenged the men to perform in their turn. 'Glongkakaglonkakaglongkaka, auaaa auaaa, auaa, piipapapiipapapiipapapiipapa', Rita imitates the different parts of the tribal song the men performed, and describes the dynamics of the event: 'Tears were streaming down my face. They couldn't have been further away from where we came from, in the spectrum of life on earth. We were both ends of it, yet we sang to them and they sang to us. We were one, there was no question about it'. With a twinkle in her eye, Rita adds: 'The PS to the story is that when we continued to the next village the following day, they were eagerly waiting for the travelling minstrel show'.

Global nomads seek to cross barriers between peoples and cultures. While individuals sharing a similar social position are viewed to interact socially with their peers rather than with members of other groups (Bottero, 2005, p. 4), global nomads deliberately try to overcome social distance. Distance may be due to different ethnic background, religion, income, or way of living. All these classify, categorise, and rank people.

Overcoming barriers is not an easy challenge. Although people look for something different, they have limited abilities to deal with the difference, as tourism researcher Petri Hottola has argued (2004, p. 449; 2008, p. 35. See also Cohen, 1972, p. 166). Global nomads' will to engage with other cultures and regimes of truth, and at the same time distance themselves from their 'own' facilitates the task (Hannerz, 1992, pp. 246–8. Cf. Skrbis, Kendall, and Woodward, 2004), but it does not remove it as the title of this chapter implies. In Greek mythology Sisyphus, the former king of Corinth, was condemned to forever roll a huge stone up a hill in Hades only to have it roll down again on nearing the top. Whether global nomads' task is as futile remains to be seen, but one thing is clear: mobilities are not innocuous. They can be a major source of advantage for individuals and groups (Urry, 2007, pp. 51–2. See also Bianchi, 2009, p. 498), producing a highly complex system of social differentiation where individual travellers can only have a limited influence.

My intention is to examine how global nomads participate in creating and dissipating global power asymmetries. While many of their experiences described in this chapter could happen to any tourist or traveller, they are rarely spoken about as pointed out in Chapter 2: they are not part of the socially acceptable imagery of travel, which should be entertaining and relaxing, or educational and ennobling rather than shameful and degrading. Global nomads, on the other hand, offer us more examples of negative experiences both in their relationships with locals and with other tourists, thus enabling us to ponder whether these difficulties can be overcome. The theoretical focus of this chapter is on power dynamics in global nomads' personal encounters. They are examined through two discourses, the ethical and the ethnocentric, that make visible the huge stone that global nomads are rolling up the hill: they struggle with the dilemma between their will to learn and understand local cultures and people, and their own cultural baggage which hinders the task.

Going Native

Although global nomads avoid tight social relationships in order to maintain their location-independence as discussed in Chapter 4, their attitude towards locals is different. Locals can offer them the necessary introduction to different cultures and ways of life, which global nomads consider a critical success factor of their journey. They have developed various practices to facilitate establishing rapport with people in their destinations, which are analysed in this section, as attempts with which they try to even out some of the global power asymmetries.

'Locals', in this context, is a broad concept. It includes all the people global nomads meet in their destinations. They are naturally not a homogeneous group but represent various ethnicities, races, nationalities, religions, world views, personal features and lifestyles, and their lives are not static but changing just like global nomads'. In the following analysis, I seek to narrow down this group of people in order to understand what global nomads mean when they say they try to 'live like locals'.

When investigating global nomads' relations, I use the concept of the 'Other', the not-I and the not-us. It is based on the idea that differences are socially constructed through power struggles (e.g. Hall, 1992, p. 279, 1996, p. 4; Grossberg, 1996, p. 94). The concept has often been used when analysing relationships between former colonisers and the colonised (e.g. Pratt, 1992; Ashcroft, Griffiths, and Tiffin, 2002; Spivak, 1990; Wearing, Stevenson, and Young, 2010, pp. 53–71). The Other, as a negation of the self, is feared and approached at a distance, and in order to meet the Other as a fellow-being, separation and prejudices have to be overcome (Derrida, 1997, p. 278). It is precisely this mix of attraction and fear that creates the myths and fantasies that are considered fundamental to tourism and ethnography alike (Geertz, 1984, p. 275; Wearing, Stevenson, and Young, 2010, p. 62; Galani-Moutafi, 2000, p. 220; Franklin, 2003, p. 214).

The tourism industry is used to seeing the Other as the exotic local. The West is the norm from which other nations and races deviate. The approach taken here, however, is different. I turn the opposition upside down in order to examine what happens when global nomads are treated as the Other – how do they represent this subject position and what kind of challenges does it pose to their attempts to approach locals. While maintaining the unequal power relationship, the reversal shows the double meaning of 'subjectivity'. Global nomads are not only exerting their agency and doing things to others. When they choose to engage themselves in local life, they become subject to others. This complex dynamic is approached in the analysis through the topics of race, wealth, and nationality.

Racial Discrimination

Discrimination based on white or fair skin colour is rarely spoken about, but for many global nomads it is part of everyday life. The participants were not necessarily conscious of their skin colour before travelling, especially if they grew up in only white areas, but their travels have made them realise the affect it has. Tor (61) discovered racism for the first time when he was sailing in the British West Indies in the 1970s where, at the time, the atmosphere was not favourable for those who looked different. 'Mostly it's a kind of rudeness, short answers, if they would give you an answer at all', Tor describes.

Racial discrimination is tightly bound with colonialism. In former conquered countries, white people embody the cultural baggage of European imperialism. As such, they are often treated as representatives of their race and nation first and human beings second. Even though some global nomads themselves come from former colonised countries, they carry the same burden. Sometimes this colonial-based racism manifests as arrogance and aggressiveness as Tor's statement illustrated, at other times as submissiveness. It is a 'parody of human relationships', tourism researcher Malcolm Crick described (1996, pp. 29, 35–6).

Certain situations seem to trigger racist reactions more easily than others. Those global nomads, who are looking for company, summon up recollections of colonial times, which can result in outbursts of anger from the locals. If a foreign man and a local girl, or vice versa, are seen together, this can be associated with prostitution. Sex replaces slavery as Others are viewed to belong to the white race, literary scholar Mary Louise Pratt explained (1992, p. 97). Tourism researchers have, perhaps not in vain, considered that sex tourism is a particularly insightful aspect of intercultural relations (e.g. Wearing, Stevenson, and Young, 2010, p. 54).

The classical sociologists, including Karl Marx, Emile Durkheim, and Talcott Parsons, believed that racial divisions would lose their significance in the modern period. They regarded these divisions as mere by-products of other processes, particularly the competition over economic resources (see Bottero, 2005, p. 61). However, as global nomads' experience shows, these divisions remain an enduring basis of conflict. Still, global nomads seem to feel that the subject is not appropriate for discussion. Only a few participants spoke openly about their discrimination experiences. This further illustrates the constraints of production of discourses analysed earlier in relation to the discourse of vagrancy (Chapter 3): discrimination has been a taboo subject in travel.

Global nomads' reaction to racism when it was brought up in the interviews was either to dismiss it because they felt uneasy saying anything negative about local cultures, or to try and frame the discrimination in a positive light. A couple of the participants thought they heard wrong when asked if they had ever been discriminated against. Quite surprisingly, even some of the non-Western participants also ignored and dismissed racism. Among others, Alberto (39) spoke about 'curiosity' and 'cultural ignorance' instead, paying attention to the fact that discrimination is a subjective notion. 'I think they [locals] don't know my culture, but I didn't feel it as discrimination'. I call this discourse *ethical* to make the following of the analysis easier.

Another option was to speak of 'positive discrimination'. Global nomads reported, for instance, that they had been pushed to the front of the line in shops, they had been better catered to than locals, or that more had been allowed to them than to locals because they were white or looked otherwise different. 'Being French helped me a lot. Also the fact that I'm white and tall makes it easier for me. If I were black, sad to say, my journey would have been a lot harder', Ludovic (32) assesses.

Positive discrimination – as the term explicitly states – does not mean lack of discrimination; locals just discriminate against themselves in favour of foreigners. Inequalities remain, or they may even become more prominent. Positive discrimination maintains, for instance, one of the most common unequal power relationships in tourism: the relationship between hosts and guests (e.g. Aramberri, 2001; McNaughton, 2006; Molz and Gibson, 2007, p. 12; Sherlock, 2001; Smith, 1989). According to the dominant code of conduct, guests are in a destination by the grace of their hosts, and if they complain, they transgress the norms of good behaviour. This discourse has been criticised for presuming a static territorial belonging and notion of 'place' (e.g. Aramberri, 2001). It fails to take into account people's mobilities and changing identifications, merely using places to exclude Others who do not belong (Harvey, 1993, pp. 3–4).

Few global nomads spoke openly about their experiences. Jukka (27) told me of a shop in Iran where they refused to sell him anything because he was a foreigner. In Ethiopia, local children had a peculiar way of welcoming him into their country: they threw stones at him when he bicycled by. 'Obviously they were frustrated or something, had nothing else to do. When I stopped to talk with them, they were OK. Perhaps throwing stones was a local replacement for a Playstation', Jukka (27) suggests playfully, subduing discrimination with humour.

The ethical discourse usually activates in situations where global nomads suffer from downsides of their lifestyle such as culture confusion and stress, or when they witness disadvantages of tourism such as congestion, pollution, and overpricing (see also McCabe, 2005, p. 100). In principle, global nomads' stress could be taken out on local people and culture, but as ethical travellers they do not want to create power asymmetries between them and locals, because that would make their task of getting to know local cultures more difficult. Rather, they criticise other tourists, usually their compatriots. As discussed in Chapter 2, global nomads project negative interpretations of others onto their former compatriots, consciously forgetting that not everyone in their country is the same; they are also individuals. This simplification is their way to use biopower over others in order to emphasise their own individuality. Ajay and Maria target their disciplining to Russian tourists:

> Most of them are rich and rude. They think local people are stupid and they treat them like slaves. If locals don't understand Russian, they just shout louder. We try not to be in contact with this kind of tourists. We are different. We come to a place and stay one month, two months resting and trying to live like local people. We are not in a rush. We think the best name for this is traveliving.
> (AJAY, 24, and MARIA, 32)

What is forgotten in such disciplining acts is that you are also a tourist, as Dean MacCannell pointed out (1999, pp. 1, 9). This disregard is exemplified in Ajay and Maria's use of the phrase 'we are different', which shows the process of Othering in action. For MacCannell, on the other hand, the tourist is a prototype of modern man, and by examining it, we can better understand ourselves.

MacCannell's metaphor offers an insightful perspective as it focusses the attention on global nomads rather than on the objects of their criticism. If we look at their criticism more closely, it is not so much targeted at badly behaving tourists; it is directed at *the ethnocentric discourse* that makes tourists – including global nomads themselves – sometimes behave in a rude and arrogant manner towards locals. In other words, global nomads recognise that the unfavourable discourse of privileges awarded based on race, relative or assumed wealth and nationality, is prominent in themselves. As it would be too uncomfortable to admit that they are not so different from other tourists after all, they rather project this ethnocentric discourse to other tourists (e.g. Bowins, 2004, p. 10). Such projections are well-known coping mechanisms which are activated in stressful situations. They show that although global nomads seem flexible, their lifestyle pushes them to the limit. While challenging themselves has been their aim, it might sometimes wear them down.

In the interviews, most global nomads carefully concealed the ethnocentric discourse, but it sometimes came out when unexpected questions were asked. Max (39) burst out laughing when hearing the question about discrimination: 'I'm white, Anglo-Saxon, two meters tall. If I was discriminated against, I guess I just didn't notice it'. In this ethnocentric subject position, global nomads do not bother to appear sympathetic and understanding to the less advantaged, yet fully enjoy their superior position.

Both ethnocentric and ethical discourses severely constrain global nomads' attempts to get to know local people and cultures. While the former creates master-servant types of relations where most locals are seen in instrumental terms as mere service providers, the latter views locals as objects of charity who need to be taken care of. Instead of lowering the threshold, the two discourses end up making inequalities more visible, and therefore work against global nomads' aims.

Wealth

Skin colour is not the only basis for discrimination. Power requires a manifold and refined system of differentiations that permits some people to act upon the actions of others, as Foucault maintained (2002c, p. 344). Status is one of the most common instruments of discrimination (see Chan and Goldthorpe, 2010, p. 11), and as material possessions make comparisons between people easy, status often boils down to wealth, or more accurately, to perceived or assumed disparities of wealth.

In developing countries, white global nomads are believed to be rich regardless of their income, possessions, spending, and travel style (see also Lea, 2006, p. 56; Saldanha, 2007). '[Locals] are nice to you because they think you come from a rich country. Sometimes it's fake. Money is very important in how people look at you', Jérémy (26) observes. The mindset equating foreigners, travelling and riches is bound up with the history of travel and tourism. In the old days, wayfarers were preyed upon on the roads and boats, and various attractions were built in order to plunder tourists in a legal way as far back as antiquity (e.g. Caner, 2002, pp. 29, 62; Dietz, 2005, p. 13. See also Aneziri, 2009, pp. 230–31).

Most global nomads have stumbled upon bribe requests or double pricing where foreigners have one price and locals another. Foreigners might also be forced to buy higher class transportation while cheaper classes are reserved for locals. They are often cheated in commercial transactions, and beggars may harass them more relentlessly than locals. Some participants regard these as discrimination, for others they are simply part of business: 'Don't let the stupid keep their money'. Ciro (29) reflects his experiences: 'Overcharging happens in many countries, even in Europe, but either you learn all the tricks beforehand, or you learn as you go. Sometimes they get you, but after a while it becomes harder and harder'.

Although global nomads learn the tricks, being constantly milked for money, gifts, and alms can be a frustrating experience particularly because it places global nomads in the ethnocentric subject position of a wealthy white person and thus makes the encounter an instrumental one based on monetary exchange (see Lea, 2006, p. 56). Many tourist researchers are sceptical whether any other kind of social interaction can ever exist in tourism (Aramberri, 2001, p. 746; Molz and Gibson, 2007, p. 7), and some of the participants expressed similar thoughts. 'Sometimes they see you as a walking dollar or euro rather than as a person that they can have interaction with', Ciro (29) admits.

Two opposite reactions can result from such irritation. Global nomads may think that locals have nothing but hidden agendas on their mind (ethnocentric discourse), or they may remain blind to various cheating attempts and rip-offs in an anti-imperialist appreciation of the Other (ethical discourse). Both discourses appear in the following statement where Claude (50) describes his experiences in African countries.

> Of course because I'm white, I'm by definition rich so sometimes you have to fight for the price. Sometimes you just get fed up, you feel discriminated against, but it's not all the time. Maybe you get cheated one time, but then you're invited to people's homes a hundred times. It's a balance to find. I would do exactly the same if I were African. [Imitating 'Africans' with his voice] 'Want to buy tomatoes from me, I make you a super price!' (CLAUDE, 50)

The active 'I' and the passive 'you' in the statement represent different subject positions. The 'I' speaks as the ethical traveller who understands overpricing, whereas the passive voice expresses annoyance and tiredness with such behaviour ('Sometimes you just get fed up, you feel discriminated against …'). While the ethical traveller refuses to criticise locals, the ethnocentric traveller makes his criticism a universal claim: everybody gets annoyed by overpricing, it is only human.

The two subject positions lead to different reactions. While the irritated imperialist might confront locals, the ethical traveller happily pays more because from his viewpoint it is only fair – after all, he comes from a rich country and he can afford it (or at least he feels guilty for having more than locals). Both behaviours maintain the unequal power relationship. Either global nomads pose themselves as victims of cheating attempts, or they treat locals as objects of charity who must be helped.

Most global nomads shift between these two discourses and their variants. They try to respect other cultures and they also want to be seen as respecting them, but they do not shy away from criticism either. For them, respect might mean that they take off their shoes before entering a temple or somebody's house, and that they are polite, humble, and act otherwise decently. Their criticism, on the other hand, is related to those situations where locals want respect to be shown with money rather than by behaviour. Consider the following statement, where Andy (54) vents his anger at the hawkers in the Dominican Republic: 'It's time to recognise I'm a person. Every day there's the pitch. Here they are aggressive and it's quite annoying. They don't recognise your face. People don't pay attention to people'.

As discussed in Chapter 2, global nomads avoid instrumental relationships that are based on monetary exchange and favour direct contacts instead. These immediate contacts show similarities between people rather than differences, and therefore even out some of the asymmetries. Naturally, no encounter is completely equal, because there are always differences at play. For a fruitful relationship, however, it is important that power fluctuates between the participants. If one is completely at the other's disposal, there are no relations of power; it is mere domination (Foucault, 1991a, p. 27).

During their travels, global nomads have had time to experiment with various means in order to overcome the shortcomings of the ethical and ethnocentric discourses. These include patient politeness, humour, and sarcasm. Anick (29) recounts an incident in a Peruvian shantytown. An old woman grabbed her hand and said: 'You gringita, you are rich, you have millions and millions', to which Anick replied, 'No, I have a student loan of twenty thousand'. How these attempts are taken depends largely on tone of voice, gestures, and the other person. What also needs to be remembered is that wealth is always relative. While global nomads are wealthier than some locals, they are also poorer than other locals. For global nomads, the only solution to deal with the assumptions of those who ask money from them might be a constant and polite 'No thank you'.

Such power asymmetries are most striking in transitory encounters, which seems to imply that time and patience are the most effective means in overcoming unfavourable effects of power. For this, global nomads' lifestyles pose perhaps the greatest of constraints. They will always leave, and often before sufficient time has passed to affect the power dynamic. Consequently, saying that global nomads 'immerse into local cultures' is rather exaggerated; it would be more appropriate to speak about 'connecting'. It means simply establishing a rapport with locals without making any statement of the depth of the relationship. Whenever global nomads do have the patience to stay in one area for a longer period of time, they might get further. At some point street sellers and beggars might start to recognise their face and change strategy, becoming curious about the Other.

Nationality

Travelling in places where global nomads draw attention because of their race, appearance, or assumed wealth can be tiring. In some cases, nationality can have the same unwanted effect. There are two rare issues where global nomads' nationality has a noticeable effect on their lifestyles: citizenship, as discussed in the previous chapter, and discrimination. Discrimination based on nationality was most prevalent for Americans, particularly during the Bush era when the United States' international policy led foreign politicians to stir hatred against Americans. Elisa (54) describes her visit to a local hospital in Egypt at the time: 'I had stepped on a coral and I had a really bad infection. It was a tiny little hospital with two employees and a camel tied out front. The doctor, when he was giving me all the shots, was saying all kinds of bad stuff about the States. I didn't feel comfortable'.

A few other Americans reported that purely upon seeing their passport, people will treat them differently. They had sometimes lied about their nationality saying that they come from Canada instead in order to avoid explaining and justifying their nationality. Therefore provocation, particularly if it makes global nomads feel uneasy or threatened, can be one of the triggers that pushes them to the ethnocentric subject position. Sometimes the attacks against Americans are not only verbal but physical, and the mere anticipation of them can make global nomads take precautionary measures, pushing them further behind the barriers of ethnocentric discourses.

> In a lot of former Soviet countries they have a real grudge against Americans. They have a very suspicious mindset about us and they believe a lot of conspiracy theories. They believe we were trying to infiltrate them, caused their downfall, and were stealing from them. There is a lot of random violence in those countries. Here [in the US] we have random shooting sometimes, but it's not something you walk around expecting to happen. When you live over there, you expect it. You don't speak loudly or look out of the ordinary because you are afraid that you are going to get attacked, jumped by the guys at night. It does happen. (GEORGE, 31)

Whether the threat is actual or based on a feeling is irrelevant, because both lead to the same situation. Whenever global nomads feel the need to defend and justify themselves, a barrier between them and locals appears and blocks communication.

Other nationalities, including other world powers – Britain, Germany, and France – did not mention any incidents related to their nationality. Either they had no bad experiences, or they ignored them. The effect of nationality is also relative and depends on the relationship between global nomads' country of origin and the destination, as Andy describes in the following statement.

> As a white American coming to Africa, I'm instantly regarded a very high status person. If I'm around a British person, they consider us the peasants. The Netherlands person treats us as equals. Scandinavians treat us like we are not

> as educated. Spanish … they don't really know what they're doing. There is no culture that is better. There are cultures that are more honest but at the end of the day, it's just a different channel. (ANDY, 54)

The statement's many stereotypes remind us of the fact that stereotypes prevail when talking about nationalities or any other type of Othering. The fear of the Other makes people settle for their prejudices. In their attempts to rid themselves of the dominant discourses of their respective society, global nomads try to question what they are told about other races, countries and nations at home, school, work, and in the media. 'Instead of being afraid of the other, I walk towards it', Anthony (35) explains. Some participants have also taken on the challenge of encouraging others to do the same, as Rita's (72) story in the introduction to this chapter showed. This seems to indicate that although global nomads do not see any hope for societies in general, they believe in individuals as motors of change. Rita explains her motives:

> Most of the country is fearful of foreigners. It's common in many parts of the United States, and I just think that if we're going to be part of the world, we have to know it better. I'm convinced that anyone who goes out into this world, discovers that we are really all the same and it will be much harder to drop bombs on people who are us. (RITA, 72)

To avoid exaggerating global nomads' success at establishing meaningful relationships with locals or in encouraging others to do the same, it should be safe to say that they are at least willing to engage with the Other, and that they also actively seek these encounters (see Hannerz, 1996, p. 103). While many anthropologists will undoubtedly belittle such experiments and consider them as superficial and naïve, Bauman represents another interpretation. Even the most modest encounters with Otherness are important, he argued, because they can be a start for discovering new modes of coexisting, both for foreigners and locals (Franklin, 2003, pp. 214–15).

Dealing with Difficulties

Discrimination seems difficult to avoid as the world consists of pre-existing relations of inequality, which provide the context of our interactions (Bottero, 2005, p. 3). Whenever global nomads move, they carry with them markers of country, gender, race, ethnicity, class, and social status (see also Sheller, 2004, p. 21). The main question, therefore, is not how to avoid power asymmetries but how to deal with them. In the following analysis, I examine the culture confusion that occurs when encountering cultural differences and how global nomads cope with the resulting power asymmetries. Additionally, I examine the frustration that the ever-present tourism industry seems to cause for global nomads.

Culture Confusion

All the participants are familiar with culture confusion (see Hottola, 2004), which occurs whenever they have to encounter new regimes of truth. Global nomads might find themselves, for instance, stressed and perplexed when learning new things or facing unexpected difficulties or unacknowledged consequences of their own or other people's actions.

> There's a sense of unexpected. You know you're gonna do something different. You push yourself, you meet new people. You learn a lot. You don't have a routine, it can be good but it can also be bad. You have to make your body adjust to a different reality every day, different food, different climate, keep yourself fit. It can be demanding. You have to communicate in a foreign language. It can be mentally exhausting. (CIRO, 29)

Although queue-jumping may sound like a banal and insignificant issue, it is one of many similar small everyday occurrences that create culture confusion (see also Levine, 2006, p. 115). When in foreign locations where queue-jumping is the norm, global nomads' rules regarding how they treat other people and how other people should treat them back no longer apply. This change to the rules of the game is confusing and requires them to make a mental adjustment. An even bigger adjustment is needed when global nomads travel in cultures where social relationships are based on distrust, and they have to be constantly alert.

Culture confusion can be tackled via various means. Lifestyle migrants find relief from the stresses of their new home country by surrounding themselves with like-minded people. Backpackers spend time in tourist enclaves, which combine both the familiar and the new, therefore increasing their feeling of being in control (Hottola, 2005, pp. 2–3). More conventional tourists, on the other hand, may isolate themselves completely in all-inclusive resorts.

While these types of refuges provide shelter, they also prevent their residents from experiencing local cultures as intensively as they might like to. The reasons for seeking refuge can be many but most importantly, enclaves save the residents from uncomfortable situations where they would need to deal with their inferior power position as foreigners (see Casado-Diaz, 2009, p. 96; O'Reilly, 2002, pp. 186–7). Or, those who seek out these refuges might simply be more oriented towards the possibilities that the enclaves and the other residents provide them with than towards local life.

Global nomads usually like to challenge themselves by seeking action and expanding their comfort zone as the discourse of adventuring showed in Chapter 3. Some of them feel that even taking photos on their journeys alienates them from the immediacy of experience. 'It seems kind of silly to me that you go somewhere and you're in the midst of an experience, and the first thing you do is take yourself out of the experience to remember to take pictures so that you can tell someone else about the experience', Max (39) explains. The person behind the camera becomes the surveillant in the same way that the person who withdraws to an enclave does. As anthropologist Ulf Hannerz (1990) has argued: 'Tourists are not participants; tourism is largely a spectator sport' (p. 242). Those who are gazed at are subjected, which turns the power relationship in the observer's favour.

Rather than retiring to a place to gaze at others, global nomads experiment with the subject position of the Other. They lower their status and let themselves be gazed at. They might sleep on the floor in their host's living room, or in the backyard of a petrol station in the open air. Even when they pitch up their tent, things are more likely done to them rather than the other way around. Jukka (26) illustrates: 'One Ethiopian guy came to my tent to wake me up at six o'clock in the morning and told me, [after seeing Jukka's bicycle] 'Don't you know man, it's much more comfortable to travel by plane'.

Being objects that are gazed at is part of global nomads' strategy of letting go. They surrender to unfavourable power relationships where they might be vulnerable (see also Molz, 2007, p. 70). Barbara (52) explains:

> One of the things you learn when you're a true traveller is that you have to extend yourself and your boundaries if you want to have the full experience. You could always choose to be an observer, and only look outside without exposing yourself who you truly are instead of being open and vulnerable to the people you come in contact with. (BARBARA, 52)

The experience of being the Other can be tiring in the long run but global nomads always have the option to leave whenever the experience is too much for them, as discussed in relation to their homelessness in the previous chapter (see also Butcher, 2010, p. 31). They have 'no firm commitment, no fixed date of staying', as Bauman has described nomads (Franklin, 2003, p. 207). Instead of going home to rest and digest their experiences like other tourists, global nomads might choose a less challenging destination and resume their encounters with the Other later. Such places of rest are also needed for physical recovery, as long-term travel is also a test for the body.

But although global nomads' option for relief may be to make a quick escape, this is not always the case. Sometimes the mere possibility of being able to withdraw at any point of time is enough to relieve culture confusion. 'I can live in shitty conditions as long as I know that I can leave whenever I want to', Claude (50) says. In other words, global nomads get relief from the temporary and changing character of their lifestyles and use it as a motivator. As discussed in Chapter 4, solo travellers use a similar technique when postponing the establishment of intimate relationships until they are again settled, which disrupts the experience of living in the present moment. This seems to suggest that in such situations global nomads find culture confusion particularly hard to endure, and various mental techniques are needed in order to overcome it.

If, rather than make a quick escape, global nomads choose to stay, they have a few approaches available for dissipating culture confusion. Whenever they have no place of their own to which they can retreat, they can produce a similar effect by searching for like-minded company among locals, for example with the help of a hospex organisation. This illuminates a more general globalisation development in which class and education rather than nationality and culture unite people across borders (e.g. Bergesen, 1990, p. 73; Urry, 2003, pp. 4, 61). It also shows that although global nomads seek to cross boundaries between peoples and cultures, they also find relief in socialising with individuals who share a similar social position.

Talking and staying with like-minded locals gives global nomads perspective and reminds them of the fact that cultures are not homogeneous; they are heterogeneous. Culture confusion is, to be precise, not so much produced by the country and culture itself but more so by encountering groups of people one would not necessarily socialise with in Western countries. Being with Indian hospex hosts is a very different experience than socialising with Indian street sellers, rickshaw drivers, and beggars.

Obviously, this leads to a particular elitism where global nomads are in a position to pick and choose, and it is true that 'locals' for them are a fairly select group of people. For instance, being a member in a hospex organisation requires that hosts have a house or an apartment in which to receive guests. They also need an internet access and language skills. Therefore they are not just any men or women off the street.

Another approach for dissipating culture confusion is seeing the Other in oneself (see Ricoeur, 1992, p. 3), for which global nomads' own experiences as the Other prepare them. They learn to see that the Other is, fundamentally, within themselves and not outside, which neutralises power positions. 'I look at everyone as brothers and sisters. Regardless of religion or country, we are all one', Ludovic (32) opines. It is not in vain that encountering the Other has been viewed as the truest test for human respect. Similarly, by letting themselves be treated as the Other, global nomads might experience the hardiest test for dealing with culture confusion.

Avoiding Tourists and Tourist Traps

Although global nomads shift between subject positions, they are not free to experiment with just any subject position. They are tied to several conditions of production and reception of discourses. Of these, the tourism industry is among the most important. It is one of the fastest-growing sectors of the economy today (Wearing, Stevenson, and Young, 2010, pp. 2–3), and it has already swallowed groups that were once marginal, including backpackers who are now crucial for certain destinations and types of travel products (e.g. Cohen 1972, 1973; Riley, 1988, p. 322; Speed, 2008, p. 63). Although global nomads try to steer clear from the tourism industry in order to maintain their unique status, they are already within its power networks which both enable and constrain their lifestyles.

For global nomads, the main problem in tourism lies in locals' assumption that all foreigners are either holiday-making tourists or expatriates at a work assignment. Noam (32) describes: '[I see myself as] someone who lives abroad. I like to think about losing this "this is your country, this is not your country" mentality. Many people see me as an expatriate but I don't'. These assumptions are prevailing. As much as global nomads would like to distinguish themselves from the mass of foreigners, locals fail to recognise the difference (see also Moufakkir and Reisinger, 2012).

Similar labelling, categorisation, and positioning are deeply rooted in human interaction. This is also true in science, for what would I call, and how would I define, the location-independent if not with a concept? This is an inherent weakness in language, where meanings can only be created through difference, as discussed in Chapter 2 in relation to places. Language has to be dealt with as a tool, which has both strengths and weaknesses. Many global nomads, however, are tired of people's assumptions. They would like to stop labelling and stereotyping altogether, but when they do so, they usually just perplex other people.

> It makes some people uncomfortable that you don't have a fixed identity. Sometimes I'm a translator, sometimes a traveller, a crewman of a boat, or a financial manager, but they try to put me in a box. It was the same in the university. You have to choose your major. I was interested in everything: mathematics, philosophy, economics. (GUSTAVO, 51)

Refusing labelling can be interpreted as a biopolitical act with which global nomads intend to take the lead and rewrite the rules of the game. Whenever their attempts fail and they are considered as 'mere' tourists, they are expected to behave accordingly: appreciate architectural monuments, take taxis, eat in restaurants, and buy souvenirs. This is the point where interacting with locals can get tiring for global nomads. They might need to explain their lifestyles over and over again by answering such questions as: 'If you are in Cairo, why don't you go to see the pyramids?' 'What is the point of travelling if you don't want to see any sights? Why not stay at home instead?' (see also Cohen, 1973, p. 102). In these situations, they might assume the ethnocentric discourse just to drive locals away and be left in peace.

As a general rule, the more touristy the destination, the harder it is for global nomads to approach. When locals view them as yet another tourist, their chances to familiarise themselves with local life become poor. Therefore, not being considered as a tourist can be an important success factor for global nomads. Many of the participants were seemingly horrified when I asked them if they think of themselves as tourists. 'No, never!' some of them exclaimed. However, avoiding this subject position might be easier said than done, even among other Westerners, as the following reference Michel (47) received from a hospex member shows. The reference was to warn other hosts of an atypical member. 'If you host Michel be aware that as he says in his profile, he is NOT a typical tourist. He may not have plans to explore your town. He has a fair amount of work to do online'.

Rather than sightseeing, global nomads may want to participate in their hosts' daily chores whether this means grocery shopping, cooking, watching films, going to a bar or a party, or walking the dog. Their approach is not unique. Similar activities, those that are grounded in everyday life, are gaining currency also among more conventional tourists. This trend challenges the view that tourism would be an activity removed from the everyday life, as the old conceptions of travel and tourism suggested; rather, tourism becomes an extension of the everyday (Richards, 2011, p. 1,233).

There might be a difference, however, in how global nomads and more conventional tourists seek these experiences. While the latter may be interested in the everyday life of their destinations as a part of the more generalised motivations of relaxing and enjoying themselves, global nomads actively seek these experiences. As the previous analysis showed, they have developed various practices to better come into contact with locals, which might help them to escape the most crowded tourist zones. When being hosted by locals, for instance, global nomads stay in local neighbourhoods. However, as there is no comparative study to provide insights into the actual differences between the global nomads and the experienced, cultural or adventure seeking individual tourists, further evidence is needed.

Whenever global nomads stumble upon locals' assumptions despite the best of their attempts, humour seems, once again, one of the best approaches available. When Guillermo (42) became frustrated with locals in Africa who failed to see the point of his bicycling – they thought the government was paying him for cycling – Guillermo said: 'On the contrary, I'm paying for the government. Taxes'.

Humour, as Giddens has argued, defends us against the influence of those outside forces that we cannot otherwise cope with (1979, p. 72). In the case of global nomads, it detaches them from the assumed subject position of the tourist in a well-meaning way, at the same time creating the feeling of togetherness with their audience. Humour requires a dispassionate detachment, but sometimes the same result can also be obtained with empathy and passion by refusing categorisations and willingly regarding oneself as a mere tourist:

> What's a tourist? What's a traveller? We are all tourists and travellers, I don't give a shit about definitions. It's snobbish that the traveller wants to be different. We are all tourists. The world was invented by the British in the eighteenth century. We are not inventing anything, we are just buying tickets. (CLAUDE, 50)

Through humour and empathy, global nomads separate themselves from the normative and disciplining aspects of biopower. They identify themselves with other tourists in order not to create power hierarchies that complicate social relationships by inciting status games. Sometimes, however, the emotional baggage entailed in other people's assumptions is simply too much, which might provoke another kind of reaction, especially when it comes to global nomads' status among other travellers (see also Benson 2009, p. 121). When hearing in the interview that my research included over a dozen other global nomads, some of the participants were convinced that the others had to be imposters. They were not aware of their colleagues, nor did they want to hear about them because that would have shattered the illusion that they were somehow unique.

My first thought is: I'm the only nomad I know. Nomad means you go wherever you want to without any itinerary or plan. I don't know very many people that have the money, the ability, and the curiosity to do it. I know some people that have the money and that could wander wherever they want, but they're not wandering around, they plan everything. (ANDY, 54)

Defining others as imposters is an extreme form of Othering. Global nomads might disqualify or belittle their competitors with disciplinary power. This is a status-enhancing practice, which might be based on the number of years travelled or the maximum duration of stay in one place. In participant observation, such Othering was sometimes done through jokes in which the participants' either regarded me either as a 'little sister' or a mentor-like figure, depending on the participant's own travel experience. This naturally could have had an effect on the interviews, as those considering me a senior might have tried to mirror the expectations they assumed me to have of the location-independent lifestyle. In some cases this seemed to lead to sugar-coating at the cost of ignoring the downsides of the lifestyle. Those who were most critical of the lifestyle were usually older and more experienced than I was. In this way, the disciplinary power was at work also in the research process reminding us of how important status is in human interaction. I end this chapter by discussing status and inequality that location-independence brings about at a global level, and how these topics have been discussed in the preceding literature.

Status and Global Inequality

While second modernists believed that status and class have a declining influence on social action and the formation of lifestyles (e.g. Beck, 1992, pp. 88–9), the previous analysis indicates the contrary. Status offers relevant aspects for studying the dynamics of social relationships. People build their lifestyles in relation to other people, which means that an element of competition is included (see also Dunn, 2008, pp. 123–4).

Status competitions are common in tourism, and they are a well noted phenomenon in tourism studies and studies on travel literature (e.g. Cohen, 2010b, pp. 64–9; Dann, 1999, pp. 159–60; Fussell, 1980, pp. 39–40; Huggan, 2001, pp. 193–208; Hulme and Youngs, 2002, p. 7; MacCannell, 1999, pp. 9–10, 104; McCabe, 2005, pp. 92, 96–8; Mowforth and Munt, 2009, p. 70; Munt, 1994; Lisle, 2006, pp. 77–83; Riley, 1988, p. 322; Rojek and Urry, 2003, p. 1; Sørensen, 2003, p. 858; Welk, 2004). Backpackers look down on mass tourists as safety and comfort seeking, associating themselves with the positive connotations of backpacker culture such as freedom, fun, and self-development (e.g. Elsrud, 2001, pp. 597–8; Edensor, 2001, p. 74), and global nomads might emphasise their open-mindedness and respect for local cultures as this chapter showed. Essentially, however, all are part of the same tourism industry.

While travel has always been a way of establishing rank (Adler, 1989), global nomads seek it differently than some other tourists. In their case, as in the case of other budget travellers, money and lavish consumption do not buy the winning position; it is a question of honour (see also Brooks, 2000, p. 50). Weber, one of the classical sociologists who has most thoroughly discussed status, regarded honour as an essential element in it (1978, p. 937). While class was more economically determined, as discussed in Chapter 2, status involved evaluations of prestige and required a wider analysis, which took into account class membership, consumption patterns, and social and cultural affiliations (ibid., pp. 305–7. See also Chan and Goldthorpe, 2007).

In global nomads' case, their status seems to depend primarily on lifestyle factors, which differentiate them along a horizontal axis of non-economic criteria (see Dunn, 2008, p. 123). The most important are their homelessness and the length of their journey – the longer, the better. Other status factors include frequency of movement, which global nomads may define by restricting the time spent in one destination; speed and transport mode that may vary from quick to slow as discussed in Chapter 2; low level of comfort, which gives them an aura of endurance, and geographical distribution of movement that maintains their search for novelty (see Cohen and Gössling, 2015). While more conventional tourists also seek status with iconic places visited, global nomads rather strive for the contrary aim: they build their status by avoiding such places as discussed in this chapter.

Given the relative character of status, in order to understand how these status factors work in practice, the dynamics of social encounters are the key. Status is a competition between the parties who are involved either directly or indirectly. As the presence of other tourists is an integral part of any travel experience, even for the location-independent, tourists offer a natural point of comparison. Furthermore, as locals usually assume that all foreigners are tourists, this means that global nomads need to mark their rank based on these assumptions, if they want to differentiate themselves from the mass.

Locals provide global nomads with another reference point. These competitions – or particularly global nomads' attempts to avoid such competitions – have implications at a global level. As the analysis showed, the location-independent are not innocent bystanders but actively participate in creating global divisions. While they sometimes manage to even out some asymmetries, at other times they stir power struggles. They are not able to dispel the complex system of differentiations that guides people's acts. Maintaining and producing inequality is, therefore, an unintended consequence of their contrary attempts. This reminds us of the unconscious realm of human action, which will be further discussed in the next, concluding chapter.

Global divisions have usually been made with binaries between the people in the rich north and the poor south, the colonisers and the colonised. This partly applies to the location-independent as most of them come from Western countries, but there is also a minority of global nomads from the south. What also needs to be remembered is that the West is not a guarantee of equal rights and opportunities, as discussed earlier in Chapter 2. There are growing third world conditions in many parts of the wealthy nations because of unemployment, denial of credit, loss of affordable housing, and social exclusion (see Reid, 2003, pp. 1–2). Some of these conditions, particularly unemployment, also touches global nomads denying their privileged status, and therefore new, more pluralistic approaches are needed that do not tie analysis to centre-periphery models (see Appadurai, 1990, p. 296).

Some critics have called for a reinstatement of 'social class' in order to ensure that analyses are attuned to inequality, also worldwide (e.g. Curran, 2013, pp. 57–9. See also Atkinson, 2007b). However, class theories tend to be defined in the Marxist terms of economic and political mechanisms by which surplus products or surplus labour is appropriated, which are no longer sufficient class criteria (see Wright, 1989, p. 87), although they might be combined, for example, by looking at how class and gender are interwoven. Still, many factors are ignored, particularly the individualisation of class criteria. What is downgrading for some might be upgrading for others.

Another problem is the related Marxist conceptions of power as domination, which lead to a rather superficial interpretation of inequality. However, this conception appears to have a widespread appeal, also in studies related to mobilities. Geographer Doreen Massey (1993) has argued, for example, that mobility of some groups can actively weaken other people's mobilities, and therefore 'we need to ask whether our relative mobility and power over mobility further increases the spatial imprisonment of other groups' (pp. 63–4. See also Cresswell, 2001, p. 24).

The statement suggests that mobilities are a zero-sum game. If someone wins, someone else has to lose. A discussion on ethics and values is often accompanied raising the question who should be involved in mobilities (see also Reid, 2003, p. 26) – the economic elite who is capable of shutting out the concerns of the poor when forging relationships with fellow elites in other parts of the world? Those who have the 'right' kind of nationality and are therefore able to be more mobile than others, global nomads being one example? Everyone?

These questions are bound with power struggles where the global world order is discussed, and they usually presuppose a particular set of values from participants. In critically oriented research, criticism is targeted at the privileged Westerners in order to defend the underprivileged locals in tourist destinations. Sociologist Karen O'Reilly (2007) offers an example when criticising lifestyle migration, which she suggests is a new form of mobile elitism. Lifestyle migrants take advantage of a cheaper cost of living and a good infrastructure in order to improve their own lives. Migrants 'move on when things get too expensive in an area, increasingly seeking out the cheaper places to exploit' (p. 281).

In such research, travelling and living on the cheap are judged from the disciplining ethical discourse raising such questions as: Is it right that people who have made their money in wealthy Western countries exploit the low prices of poor countries, or exploit income and price differences within the Western world? Are they profitable customers for local entrepreneurs or are they just taking advantage of them? How much money should they spend? These discussions make the same assumptions as do locals in global nomads' destinations – that migrants are wealthy and locals poor, or at least somehow in a less fortunate position. This means taking a political stance, which researchers could perhaps not afford to do, unless they pursue overtly political objectives.

The discourses that become dominant in these discussions eventually influence many people's lives, as some of them are incorporated into administrative policy and praxis. My purpose in this chapter has not been to answer these questions nor defend migrants or the location-independent; rather, I have wanted to offer a metalevel approach to the power struggles involved in order to show that researchers are actively participating in these negotiations, often creating more inequalities with ethical discourses which intend to be compassionate yet objective. As objectivity cannot exist, when viewed from a Foucauldian perspective (cf. Žižek, 2000), research needs to be subjected to the same questions as all other discourses: who is being addressed, when, how, and why, thereby making researchers' own stances clearly visible. Only then is it possible to open a fair discussion on important subject matters such as global inequality.

Chapter 7
Alternatives

This book came about from the realisation that extreme mobilities remain an under-explored area in lifestyle mobilities. Tourism and migration studies have examined more purposeful and place-dependent travel, whereas the mobilities paradigm has concentrated on more general issues of movement and transportation. The aim of this book, on the other hand, was to shed light on the phenomenon that is starting to attract attention in the media and among people looking for alternative lifestyles: location-independence.

Advances in technology have made location less significant, which has far-reaching implications. Work can be done remotely, home associated with several places, and social relationships tied across distances and virtually. While this offers individuals fresh opportunities, it also entails problems. Location-independence may reduce the number of face-to-face contacts and intimate relationships; coordination of networks and knowledge transfer in workplaces become challenging, and work/life balance is increasingly blurred. Societies, on the other hand, need to figure out who benefits and who pays the costs of these lifestyles. Although it may be an exaggeration to say that location-independence has major revolutionary implications, dismissing it as irrelevant may also miss the point. The benefits and the costs of multi-mobility have resonance for an increasing number of people, and therefore they merit more research than has been dedicated to them in the past (see also Cohen and Gössling, 2015).

My aim in this book has been to analyse the phenomenon of location-independence through a group of global nomads representative of a variety of ways in which location-independence can be realised. My approach utilised methods that allowed incongruences without explaining them away. When analysing global nomads' everyday practices, their relationships and attitudes towards the broader social order, these discrepancies were viewed as indicative of power negotiations in which limits of mobilities and models of the good life are discussed. In this concluding chapter, I discuss the theoretical framework used, the findings, and their deeper societal and academic implications.

Controlled Freedom

As assumed in the beginning of this book, location-independence has been revealing of the contradictions in contemporary society. Because of its extreme character, it tests the prevailing norms and values. Fundamentally, all these contradictions boil down to the basic sociological dilemma of the relationship between the individual and society – how people should live and organise among themselves, and whether society has the right to intervene in individuals' lives. I now summarise these findings by reflecting upon the forms of freedom that location-independence can offer to global nomads, the counterparts that exist in the lifestyles of the settled, and how theories of second modernity, structuration, power and subjectivity have both helped and hindered the analysis.

The Logic of Illogic

From the outset, the location-independent seem to represent utmost agency. This is particularly the case if their lifestyles are analysed from the point of view of second modernist and structuration theories. Global nomads seem to be searching for greater individual freedom through self-exclusion, giving up settled and more conventional lifestyles, and silently opposing many important structural pillars in contemporary life. Global nomads have cut geographic ties, the most visible and evident form of social exclusion (Byrne, 2005, p. 117). They have also renounced regular employment and housing conditions, nationalist belongings, and most of their citizenship rights. They do not integrate into common cultural processes in their respective country but seek to belong to the world, and they avoid close personal relationships that could tie them to biopolitical networks and localised communities (see ibid., p. 2).

Global nomads are not unique in their attempts at self-exclusion, as many alternative lifestyles also aim for a partial social exclusion. By adopting a minimalist lifestyle and reducing work, the settled lessen their access to material resources. For societies, this is a worrying development as citizens are expected to contribute financially to the home market. In Japan, governors and politicians are particularly concerned about the satori, young people in their 20s who seem to have overcome desire for material things and participation in consumer society (see Kelts, 2014). 'They don't drive cars, don't wear brand name clothing, aren't active in sports, don't care about career advancement, can't be bothered earning more than enough to cover basic needs, don't travel, don't fall in love much, don't dream of a better life, don't make plans for the future', writer Michael Hoffmann described in an article in *The Japan Times* (2013).

Are the satori and the location-independent exerting their agency, or have they given up? Had I conducted the analysis with structuration and second modernist theories only, I could have concluded that they represent an ultimate form of detraditionalisation and individualisation: they aim to renounce predetermined identities and instead find their own path in life. However, such analysis would have been partial and romanticising, ignoring many aspects of these lifestyles.

As discussed in Chapter 2, location-independence gives rise to discrepancies that question agency. These include the contradiction between global nomads' anti-materialism and their simultaneous, high consumption of tourism and IT related products and services. Another contradiction can be found between their idle and time-crunched lifestyles, and yet another in their constant search for novelty and refusal to give places any meaning. As my further explorations in Chapter 3 showed, discrepancies arise because location-independence gains different meanings depending on the context. Global nomads may represent themselves both as agents and subjects to power. This was the decisive point where structuration theory fell short: it failed to offer conceptual tools for analysing the interplay between structure and agency (see also Archer, 2010, p. 236; Callinicos, 1985, pp. 135, 144; Dallmayr, 1982, p. 27), merely exaggerating individuals' ability to decide about their own lives.

Even when global nomads represent agency as their cherished choice (as in the discourse of adventuring), they may have partly assumed self-ownership from sheer necessity (as in the discourse of vagrancy). Or, what was chosen in one context, may have turned out to be forced in another context, as their yearning for intimate relationships indicated in Chapter 4. Global nomads are torn between contradictory forces. They want to get rid of sovereign power, but they may be attracted to societies' biopolitical care and safety nets; despite their criticism of nation-states, they exploit their citizenship which alone allows them to travel and hold an official identity (Chapter 5). If the concept of power has negative connotations, they can be found here, in people's tendency to succumb to somehow repressive but also tempting subject positions because they seek familiarity, security, and continuity.

The proposed analysis requires tolerance for contradictions, plurality, and irrationality. It aims to gain access to the realm of the unconscious, where the relationship between structure and agency remains suspended like the meaning between two contradictory words in Saussurean theory. For this, Foucauldian approaches offered insightful perspectives. They pay attention to the ways in which individuals are not in complete control of their discourses, nor of the ways in which power works in their lives. Although we speak discourses, discourses also speak us. This contradiction is a gateway to a dimension where thoughts and actions do not have an inner logic that could be revealed through latent or explicit motivations; discourses and power work through and in spite of us. Because of this, despite their attempts, global nomads do not necessarily manage to detach themselves from society. Similarly, researchers and policy creators may end up resorting to residual discourses although they are advocating emerging discourses.

The unconscious is not a widely developed theoretical field, Freud and Lacan excluded (see Smart, 1982, p. 139). These two theorists have very little to do with Foucault's theories. While they were interested in the human psyche, Foucault's work was about social construction through discourses, power, and the formation of subjectivity. However, the concept of 'unconscious' offers interesting perspectives also for the latter. Although unconscious was never an overt theme in Foucault's works, he briefly elaborated on the idea in *The Order of Things* (2005). He maintained that his aim was to reveal 'a level that eludes the consciousness of the scientist and yet is part of scientific discourse' (pp. xi–xii). The unconscious was the negative side of science which 'resists it, deflects it, or disturbs it' (ibid. See also Feldner and Vighi, 2007, p. 9).

While researchers have a tendency to explain away the inexplicable in the name of coherence and logic (see Heaphy, 2007, pp. 169–70, 178), Foucault suggested that the unconscious has an agency of its own. To explain this, no mystification is needed. The unconscious simply reveals the network of discourses and subject positions that works through us, making us both agents and subjects. Although this is not an easy thing for everybody to admit – particularly to those believing in their rationality and sovereignty – we all can probably find examples from our own lives where we think and act differently in different contexts, or we have had to endure an inner conflict These contradictions are a most interesting object for research because they render power visible to analysis. In this study, they have helped me to identify the residual discourses that work against mobilities, thereby allowing me to examine related assumptions, belief systems and ideals, and ask what it is about extreme mobilities that so fascinates and disturbs people. What do these struggles say about society, and what is the role of research in these power negotiations?

I pinpointed the source of these passions to the criticism of the assumed elite or exploitative character of location-independence (Chapters 2 and 5), and showed that these arguments are based on the ideas of nationalist belonging and the states' need to guard their benefits. A similar bias was revealed in locals' assumptions about global nomads (Chapter 6). They are thought to be tourists passing through and are expected to contribute financially to the local economy. These discourses effectively hinder other discourses that might, at the same time, promote tourism and mobilities.

In the analysis, I concentrated on the multiple meanings of mobilities and privileges. Despite being privileged, for example, due to their nationalities, global nomads travels are not unhindered, resource-intensive, disruptive, excessive and visible like scholarship has suggested of some mobile elites (see Birtchnell and Caletrío, 2014, pp. 9–10. See also Freeland, 2012). Rather, global nomads' privileges are relative and need to be examined in their complex contexts. Where some constraints do not apply, other constraints emerge. The same also applies to research, which is both enabled and limited by the choices made, as discussed in the next section where I ponder the limits of this analysis.

Unconscious Awareness

While Foucauldian approaches have been helpful in this work, one of the greatest challenges in applying them is to explain how transformations are possible. While Foucault asked what makes individuals agents, who are able to do otherwise and present themselves with alternative possibilities for action, he never went into sufficient detail when answering this question (e.g. Eagleton, 1991, p. 47; Poulantzas, 2000, p. 149. See also Taylor, 1984; Walzer, 1986). If individuals do not merely internalise the norms and values of dominant discourses, or, as the location-independent show, internalise them but later seek to shed this baggage, how is change possible? The problem is similar to that of Giddens's structure. It seems to come from out of nowhere and trap individuals so that change appears unthinkable.

As the analysis showed, global nomads' actions are indisputably bounded, but their partial freedom from constraints suggests that some kind of transformation and detachment from power is possible. Power is, after all, not just the repressive force in people's lives but also productive. However, when examining how such transformations can come about, we stumble upon problems. If power is viewed as residing everywhere, as Foucault maintained, resistance merely appears a burdensome task. It requires the painful task of encountering power within oneself (see Rasmussen, 2004), most often with a bitter awareness that somehow power will always keep us in its grip, even if in a modified form. How did the location-independent, under the circumstances, become aware of the constraining factors of their previous lifestyles? What made them desire and seek change, and how was change possible? This is one of the most crucial questions that, for example, Giddens never answered in his structuration theory (see Archer, 2010, p. 231; Gregory, 1989, pp. 200–201).

I have argued that the role of mobilities is crucial in global nomads' transformations. Transformations require friction, which reveals the limits of one stratum of knowledge and the beginnings of another. This friction produces the necessary alienating effect, which can help the individual to become aware of power relations (Foucault, 2005, p. xxii; 1998a, pp. 178–9. See also Simons, 1995, p. 90). For the location-independent, extreme mobility and encounters with new cultures enable this change. It lets them 'know how and to what extent it might be possible to think differently, instead of legitimating what is already known', as Foucault once said of critical thinking (1990, p. 9).

This struggle for freedom is not available to everyone, which should be thrilling news and a wealthy source of criticism for researchers who employ the ethical discourse advocating equality and defending those who they consider as underprivileged. Resistance, indeed, is only reserved for the privileged few – not for the wealthy but for those who understand how power works. It therefore involves an active subject who is competent politically and philosophically, as Foucault researchers Dreyfus and Rabinow have noted, concerned about such elitist view of resistance (1983, p. 207. See also Foucault, 1997c, p. 291). And now we encounter a major underlying problem in Foucauldian theories: if individuals are to engage in the projects of the self, do they need to be rational, cognitive and reflective as Giddens argued in his theories?

Based on the research findings on global nomads, the answer is no. While such awareness is required, it does not necessarily need to be a conscious activity; it can also be intuitive. Global nomads' actions are not necessarily well thought out, nor do they have an agenda for their practices, and yet they seem to almost deliberately oppose the dominant discourses in Western societies. Awareness may come later on, as in the case of those global nomads who have realised how excluded they have become from the context of 'home', which makes socialising and communicating with other people difficult, either strengthening or diluting their resistance. But awareness may also remain intuitive or practical as observed in the case of those who believe in a constant and unified self (see Chapter 4). They define themselves with dominant discourses, yet they also exercise opposing practices.

Rationality is not, therefore, a precondition for awareness. None of us are in control of all of our discourses and subject positions – not even researchers as discussed in Chapters 4 and 5 in regard to identity and methodological nationalism. We use residual and emerging discourses which lead to contradictions. In fact, attention needs to be paid to the subtle difference between two attributes that describe critical awareness: 'reflexive' and 'reflective'. As Beck, Bonß, and Lau, (2003) pointed out, people in second modernity do not lead a more conscious life (p. 3); more likely, the opposite is true. They have no time to think, nor can they control the unintended consequences of their actions (see Latour, 2003, p. 36). In this way, the term 'reflexive' better describes how individuals react to changes around them, leaving space for exploring the unconscious factors in our lives.

Although this explains how transformations are possible, Foucauldian theories are not merciful for people who engage in such projects. Reflexive awareness does not make individuals' lives easier or liberate them. This ambiguity could be witnessed in global nomads' struggles to detach themselves from power relations. It is a continuous battle where their subjectivities are in perpetual motion. Perhaps this is what Bauman meant when he lamented the modern individuals' need to assume many subject positions instead of enjoying the peace and quiet of one single subject position and set of values (see Chapter 3). Not many people want to live in a constant battlefield, particularly if that battle is against oneself.

Partial as global nomads' attempts remain, their struggles give them an opportunity to exert some degree of agency. They are perhaps not able to choose freely but they are able to develop a reflexive awareness of the conditions of the choice. This, in fact, might be the greatest privilege (or disadvantage) that the location-independent have. Although they are not able to oust power from their lives, they have become conscious of the ways in which it works. This may provide them with the feeling of 'not being governed so much', which is the closest definition of freedom we can find in Foucault's work (Foucault, 2007, p. 45. See also Prozorov, 2007). Or, it may drive them to exasperation that power really is omnipresent and cannot be escaped. According to the pluralistic approach taken here, both reactions apply. The realisation of power's role in our lives is at the same time a relief and a source of anguish and frustration.

To wind up these trains of thought, I have suggested that, regardless of the theoretical viewpoint and conceptual framework chosen, the question of constraining and facilitating factors is the key for analysing the relationship between individuals, mobilities and society. We can speak of 'structure' or 'regime of truth', but the central question is social organisation and individual mobilities' role in it. I have also proposed that the question of structure and agency should be viewed as an ongoing interaction rather than reducing the analysis to either pole. I also suggest that these questions should be kept separate from dilemmas dealing with ethical questions, which easily lead to normative stances. When privileges are measured, for example, in financial resources, those who have more are viewed to be exploiting others and limiting the choice of others. As a result, agency and structure are projected into different groups of people rather than being examined as present in all individuals. Foucauldian theories offer more refined approaches, of which particularly useful are his conceptions of the subtle ways in which biopower works through our subjectivities. For the location-independent and other multi-mobile people, these biopolitical forms of power are among the most critical. They might make them reconsider their mobile lifestyles and search for a transformation through intimate relationships, or through the safety nets of societies, or simply because they are tired of applying for visas and doing visa-runs. Due to such transformations, studies need to increasingly take into account the ways in which mobility practices are continuously created, maintained, transformed and/or rejected, and be open to simultaneous contradictions. A similar plural approach is also needed when analysing societies and changes within them, as the next section shows.

Voluntary Social Exclusion

Global nomads are symptomatic of the changes in the general mentality, therefore offering an interesting mirror of the contemporary society. These changes are already visible at some levels. Along with global nomads' exit option, people are seeking options to dominant discourses in diverse ways. Non-voting, interest in ecological and anti-materialistic lifestyles, distrust of authorities whether health, state or religious, and the search for new gurus, are some examples of these trends. They represent a growing dissatisfaction of state control and surveillance, and attempts to increase individual agency at the cost of structure. Rather than trying to change society, people might end up choosing to socially exclude themselves, to varying degrees.

In the case of global nomads, social exclusion is partial and opportunistic. They are not overtly political, and their 'statement' consists of indifference towards those structures they are able to dodge, as the definition of global nomads in Chapter 1 assumed. Whenever needed, in other words when the rewards are higher than the costs, global nomads abide by the rules. Similar features can be found in alternative lifestyles among the settled. People who choose to live in communes might nurture their own lifestyles, accepting some parts of dominant discourses while opposing others. They might prefer alternative medicine to conventional medicine, organically and locally produced food to industrial products, or home-schooling to public or private schools for their children. Some people join a cooperative in order to reduce their dependency on the public sector combining resources with other members, sharing goods and services such as food, shelter, and health care, while also using some public services.

To call these lifestyles 'countercultural' would be misleading (cf. D'Andrea, 2006). This interpretation draws mostly from early cultural studies in Birmingham School that examined youth subcultures as either conforming or resisting the dominant culture (see also Veal, 2001, p. 366). The latter were more interesting for researchers, and therefore they drew more attention (see Hall and Jefferson, 2006; Hebdige, 1979; Roszak, 1969). However, most of the contemporary lifestyles that bear the label 'alternative' have no agenda. They are loose groups, at best cloakroom communities that draw people together for a short period of time to be later forgotten. People adopting alternative lifestyles rarely imagine that society's values ought to reflect or absorb their own (e.g. Gelder, 2006, p. 22; Hall and Jefferson, 2006. Cf. MacBeth, 2000, p. 29; D'Andrea, 2006); more likely, they represent a weakening of social and societal bonds (e.g. Clarke, Hall, Jefferson, and Roberts, 2006, p. 48).

Global nomads' practices, for instance, indicate that their criticism towards societies is at best selective and self-centred. They are not aiming to change society or the world; they change their own life, in ways that suit them best, and perhaps encourage a few others to do the same. They utilise the benefit of their citizenship, often paradoxically re-enforcing the current dominant discourses and practices rather than opposing them, and they practise indifference towards those power relationships they are able to dodge. The same may also have been true for the original drifter introduced in Chapter 1. Although the drifter was identified as countercultural, Cohen described him as 'anarchistic' and 'disdainful of ideologies' referring to the drifter's individualistic rather than to his confrontational characteristics.

To call global nomads' relation to societies 'social exclusion' is disputable. The excluded are usually viewed as disempowered, whereas social exclusion for the location-independent can be a necessary precondition for their lifestyles and subjectivities. Their lifestyles are not compatible with the kind of integration that societies long for, because integration assumes territorial belonging and financial contribution to the home market.

Upon closer inspection, the location-independent remind us of the ambiguity of 'social exclusion': it can be bad for the excluded, and it can be bad for the society (Barry, 1998, p. 3). For societies, social exclusion is a threat, because it weakens the loyalty and sense of reciprocity between individual citizens and the state thus having the potential to destabilise the meaning of citizenship. Unemployment among the young, for instance, may lead to weakening ties to the labour market, which was once thought of as a crucial socialisation mechanism (Sassen, 2008, p. 285).

Unemployment and other major crises in society are important motors of change where dominant discourses are challenged. Those individuals who are ready to master their own lives, are not waiting for the stiff and sluggish societal structures to respond to changes. If circumstances are not pleasing, they will move on, either literally or figuratively, and start searching for alternatives. Second modernists believe that this is what individualised societies in fact tell people to do: to seek personal solutions to social problems (e.g. Beck, 1992, p. 135; Beck and Beck-Gernsheim, 2002, p. xxii. See also Elliott and Lemert, 2006, pp. 9–10).

This has already happened on a small scale in Schengen area where people can live and move around relatively freely, and there is also an increasing number of young moving from Europe to former colonies including Brazil,

Mexico, and Mozambique for work and for better quality of life (e.g. Beck, 2012; Callegari and Cintra, 2012; Sarcina, 2012). The more the media present examples of alternatives, the more people are likely to reconsider their options (Papastergiadis, 2000, p. 47). Although this does not necessarily lead to action, the growth of lifestyle migration, for instance, has been explained by the strong media presence of the pioneering migrants in Spain (O'Reilly, 2000, pp. 1–2). As the media are now becoming aware of the wide array of lifestyle mobilities (e.g. Baker, 2010; Manson, 2012; Snedden, 2013; Weber, 2013), it is probably only a question of time till the featured examples attract people to consider new forms of dwelling and moving. However, the number of people undertaking life changes as dramatic as the location-independent will remain marginal. Location-independence requires greater individual responsibility than many other options and entails the possibility for failure, which can be frightening. People usually consider new risk to be more threatening than keeping themselves within the old familiar risk regime, even when it no longer offers them sufficient rewards.

The increase in mobilities inevitably involves frictions. Societies lag behind new trends, and they are not ready for such large-scale movements as those that take place today. When young and educated people leave their home countries, societies are viewed as having been drained of talent and left as debtors because the focus is on nation-states, their benefits and losses, rather than on a global level. Here, individual choice no longer represents a promoted opportunity; it is a problem. Societies only encourage choice when it is exercised *within society*, reinforcing its norms and values.

Societies' worry about mass movements and social exclusion among those who stay appears to be justified in view of their own existence (e.g. Europe 2020; European Commission, n.d.). At the same time, it is perhaps a bit overblown, at least in the light of this book's findings. Social exclusion rarely means a complete withdrawal from society, as such moves are not made easily. Although the location-independent, for instance, want to reject societal welfare and surveillance – that many socially excluded in societies cannot nor want to reject – there are still some biopolitical benefits that they are not ready to give up. It is only when there is nothing to gain from society that individuals might choose complete social exclusion, and even in this case, exclusion might be difficult if the society tries to push its well-meaning care on the individual. This is of course problematic, for if individuals have chosen to exclude themselves, any attempt to intervene is against their expressed will (Le Grand, 2003, p. 4). However, this is not necessarily an actual problem as welfare states have decreasing resources for performing such interventions.

Considering how well the location-independent seem to be doing with only a little help from the state, it is relevant to ask whether we should speak of 'social isolation', while reserving 'social exclusion' for more serious cases in which isolation occurs for reasons that are beyond the control of individuals (see Barry, 1998). However, just to determine what constitutes a serious case requires taking a political stance and intervening in individuals' lives. Furthermore, this stronger concept better reminds us that voluntary isolation may sometimes lead to social exclusion. This was the case of some solo global nomads whose solitude had turned into an unwanted form of loneliness. This raises the question whether individualisation combined with hyperconnectivity can cause social exclusion on a more general level (e.g. Jan van Dijk, 2006, p. 167; Burns and O'Regan, 2008. See also O'Regan, 2008, p. 127). Increasing groups of Westerners also rely on web presence for maintaining their everyday social relationships, as can be witnessed in the popularity of social media.

The research findings in this book suggest that hyperconnectivity does not eventually lead to isolation but rather to the formation of new and smaller temporary communities. Nor does location-independence necessarily lead to uprooting, although societies fear that it does. While the location-independent search for individuality by taking distance, they also seek to re-root themselves, although in a modified form, for example by settling down in a new country. Rather than collectivities as such, they reject the presupposed identities such as nationality, gender, class, and citizenship. These represent sovereign power that is linked to specific institutional communities leaving individuals little choice and scant opportunities to practise their agency. Relative freedom, therefore, appears to be the only basis on which societies, whether states or other social associations, can be built on in the future (see Bauman, 2002).

Location-independence and social exclusion suggest that the role of the state is, or should be, changing (see also Warnes, Friedrich, Kellaher, and Torres, 2004, p. 310). Some individuals may opt out of the system, and this does not necessarily mean that they are (under)privileged, misguided, or suffer from false consciousness. Rather, they turn this question upside down: what if people want a different kind of society? To avoid merely legitimating the current values, norms, and ideals of dominant discourses, more plural and refined approaches are needed so that individuals are not only considered as subjects to power but also as agents who actively participate in the making of society, whether by being mobile or settled.

Bibliography

Academy of Free Travel [website] (2002). The Academy of Free Travel. Retrieved from: http://avp.travel.ru/AFT-2002.htm [Accessed 17 July 2015].

Ackers, L. and Dwyer, P. (2004). Fixed laws, fluid lives: The citizenship status of post-retirement migrants in the European Union. *Ageing & Society*, 24, 451–75.

Adams, M. (2003). The reflexive self and culture: A critique. *British Journal of Sociology*, 54(2), 221–38.

Adey, P. (2006). If mobility is everything then it is nothing: Towards a relational politics of (im)mobilities. *Mobilities*, 1(1), 75–94.

Adler, J. (1989). Origins of sightseeing. *Annals of Tourism Research*, 16, 7–29.

Adler, P.A. and Adler, P. (1999). Transience and the postmodern self: The geographic mobility of resort workers. *The Sociological Quarterly*, 40(1), 31–58.

Agamben, G. (1993). *The Coming Community*. Minneapolis: The University of Minnesota Press.

Ahmed, S. (1999). Home and away: Narratives of migration and estrangement. *International Journal of Cultural Studies*, 2, 329–47.

Alexander, J.C. (1996). Critical reflections on 'reflexive modernization'. *Theory, Culture & Society*, 13(4), 133–8.

Amster, R. (2003). Patterns of exclusion: Sanitizing space, criminalizing homelessness. *Social Justice*, 30, 195–221.

Anderson, B. (1991). *Imagined Communities: Reflections on the Origin and Spread of Nationalism* (Rev. ed.). London: Verso (Original work published 1983).

Aneziri, S. (2009). World travellers: The associations of artists of Dionysus. In R. Hunter and I. Rutherford (Eds), *Wandering Poets in Ancient Greek Culture: Travel, Locality and Pan-Hellenism* (pp. 217–36). Cambridge: Cambridge University Press.

Appadurai, A. (1990). Disjuncture and difference in the global cultural economy. *Theory, Culture & Society*, 7, 295–310.

Aramberri, J. (2001). The host should get lost: Paradigms in the tourism theory. *Annals of Tourism Research*, 28(3), 738–61.

Archer, M.S. (2007). *Making our Way through the World: Human Reflexivity and Social Mobility*. Cambridge: Cambridge University Press.

——— (2010). Morphogenesis versus structuration: On combining structure and action. *The British Journal of Sociology*, 61(s1), 225–52 (Original work published in 1982).

Arnold, K.R. (2004). *Homelessness, Citizenship and Identity*. New York: State University of New York.

Ashcroft, B., Griffiths, G., and Tiffin, H. (2002). *The Empire Writes Back: Theory and Practice in Post-Colonial Literatures* (2nd ed.). London: Routledge (Original work published 1989).

Ateljevic, I. and Hannam, K. (2008). Conclusion: Towards a critical agenda for backpacker tourism. In K. Hannam and I. Ateljevic (Eds), *Backpacker Tourism: Concepts and Profiles* (pp. 247–56). Clevedon: Channel View Publications.

Atkinson, W. (2007a). Anthony Giddens as adversary of class analysis. *Sociology*, 41(3), 533–49.

——— (2007b). Beck, individualization and the death of class: A critique. *The British Journal of Sociology*, 58(3), 349–66.

——— (2008). Not all that was solid has melted into air (or liquid): A critique of Bauman on individualization and class in liquid modernity. *The Sociological Review*, 56(1), 1–17.

——— (2010a). *Class, Individualization and Late Modernity: In Search of the Reflexive Worker*. London: Palgrave MacMillan.

——— (2010b). Class, individualization and perceived (dis)advantages: Not either/or but both/and? *Sociological Research online*, 15(4). Retrieved from: http://www.socresonline.org.uk/15/4/7.html [Accessed 17 July 2015].

Bærenholdt, J.O. (2013). Governmobility: The powers of mobility. *Mobilities*, 8(1), 20–34.

Baker, Vicky (2010, January 9). The escapees travelling the world while working online. *The Guardian*. Retrieved from: www.theguardian.com/travel/2010/jan/09/nomads-working-travelling-world [Accessed 15 July 2015].

Barbalet, J. (2010). Citizenship in Max Weber. *Journal of Classical Sociology*, 10(3), 201–16.

Barfield, T. (1993). *The Nomadic Alternative*. Englewood Cliffs, NJ: Prentice Hall.

Barry, B. (1998). Social exclusion, social isolation and the distribution of income [Case paper]. London: Centre for Analysis of Social Exclusion. Retrieved from: http://eprints.lse.ac.uk/6516/1/Social_Exclusion,_Social_Isolation_and_the_Distribution_of_Income.pdf [Accessed 15 July 2015].

Baudrillard, J. (2007). *Forget Foucault* (N. Dufresne, Trans.). Los Angeles, CA: Semiotext(e) (Original work published 1977).

Bauman, Z. (1989). Hermeneutics and modern social theory. In D. Held and J.B. Thompson (Eds), *Social Theory of Modern Societies: Anthony Giddens and his critics* (pp. 34–55). Cambridge: Cambridge University Press.

——— (1991). *Modernity and Ambivalence*. Cambridge: Polity Press.

——— (1993). *Postmodern Ethics*. Oxford: Blackwell.

——— (1998). *Globalization: The Human Consequences*. Cambridge: Polity Press.

——— (2000). *Liquid Modernity*. Cambridge: Polity Press.

——— (2001a). *Community: Seeking Safety in an Insecure World*. Cambridge: Polity Press.

——— (2001b). Identity in the globalising world. *Social Anthropology*, 9, 121–9.

————— (2002). Individually, together [A foreword]. In U. Beck and E. Beck-Gernsheim, *Individualization: Institutionalized Individualism and Its Social and Political Consequences* (pp. xv–xix). London: Sage Publications.

————— (2005). *Work, Consumerism and the New Poor* (2nd ed.). Maidenhead: Open University Press.

————— (2007). *Consuming Life*. Cambridge: Polity Press.

————— (2008). *Does Ethics Have a Chance*. Cambridge, MA: Harvard Press.

Bazin, A. (1971). The western, or the American film par excellence. In H. Gray (Ed.), *What is Cinema?* (Vol. 2) (H. Gray, Trans.) (pp. 140–48). Berkeley: University of California Press.

Beck, M. (2012, February 16–22). L'Australie, seconde patrie des Irlandais. *Courrier international*, 1111, 15.

Beck, U. (1992). *Risk Society: Towards New Modernity* (M. Ritter, Trans.). London: Sage Publications (Original work published 1986).

————— (2000). The cosmopolitan perspective: Sociology of the second age of modernity. *British Journal of Sociology*, 51(1), 79–105.

————— (2002). The cosmopolitan society and its enemies. *Theory, Culture & Society*, 19(1–2), 17–44.

————— (2007). Beyond class and nation: Reframing social inequalities in a globalizing world. *The British Journal of Sociology*, 58(4), 679–705.

————— (2009). *World at Risk* (C. Cronin, Trans.). Cambridge: Polity Press (Original work published 2007).

Beck, U. and Beck-Gernsheim, E. (2002). *Individualization: Institutionalized Individualism and Its Social and Political Consequences*. London: Sage Publications.

Beck, U., Bonß, W, and Lau, C. (2003). The theory of reflexive modernization: Problematic, hypotheses and research programme. *Theory, Culture & Society*, 20(2), 1–33.

Beck, U., Cohn-Bendit, D., Delors, J., and Solana, J. (2012, May 12). Let's create a bottom-up Europe. *The Guardian*. Retrieved from: http://www.guardian.co.uk/commentisfree/2012/may/03/bottom-up-europe [Accessed 15 July 2015].

Beck, U. and Grande, E. (2010). Varieties of second modernity: The cosmopolitan turn in social and political theory and research. *The British Journal of Sociology*, 61(3), 409–43.

Beck, U. and Sznaider, N. (2006). Unpacking cosmopolitanism for the social sciences: A research agenda. *The British Journal of Sociology*, 57(1), 1–23.

Beier, A.L. (2004). *The Problem of the Poor in Tudor and Early Stuart England* [PDF version]. London: Methuen (Original work published 1966).

Bell, M. and Ward, G. (2000). Comparing temporary mobility with permanent migration. *Tourism Geographies: An International Journal of Tourism Space, Place and Environment*, 2(1), 87–107.

Benson, M. (2009). A desire for difference: British lifestyle migration to Southwest France. In M. Benson and K. O'Reilly (Eds), *Lifestyle Migration: Expectations, Aspirations and Experiences* (pp. 121–35). Farnham: Ashgate.

—— (2010). The context and trajectory of lifestyle migration. *European Societies*, 12(1), 45–64.

—— (2011a). Landscape, imagination, and experience: Processes of emplacement among the British in rural France. *Sociological Review*, 58(2), 61–77.

—— (2011b). The movement beyond (lifestyle) migration: Mobile practices and the constitution of a better way of life. *Mobilities*, 6(2), 221–35.

Benson, M. and O'Reilly, K. (2009). Migration and the search for a better way of life: A critical exploration of lifestyle migration. *The Sociological Review*, 57(4), 608–25.

Benson, M. and Osbaldiston, N. (2014). *Understanding Lifestyle Migration: Theoretical Approaches to Migration and the Quest for a Better Way of Life*. London: Palgrave Macmillan.

Berger, P. and Luckmann, T. (1966). *The Social Construction of Reality: A Treatise in the Sociology of Knowledge*. London: Penguin.

Bergesen, A. (1990). Turning world-system theory on its head. In M. Feathertone (Ed.), *Global Culture: Nationalism, Globalization and Modernity* (pp. 67–81). London: Sage Publications.

Berlin, I. (2002). *Liberty*. Oxford: Oxford University Press.

Bertram, C. (2005). Global justice, moral development, and democracy. In G. Brock and H. Brighouse (Eds), *The Political Philosophy of Cosmopolitanism* (pp. 75–91). Cambridge: Cambridge University Press.

Bianchi, R.V. (2000). Migrant tourist-workers: Exploring the 'contact zones' of post-industrial tourism. *Current Issues in Tourism*, 3(2), 107–37.

—— (2009). The 'critical turn' in tourism studies: A radical critique. *Tourism Geographies: An International Journal of Tourism Space, Place and Environment*, 11(4), 484–504.

Birchnell, T. and Caletrío, J. (2014). Introduction: The movement of the few. In T. Birchnell and J. Caletrío (Eds), *Elite Mobilities* (pp. 1–20). Oxfordshire: Routledge.

Bleicher, J. and Featherstone, M. (1982). Historical materialism today: An interview with Anthony Giddens. *Theory, Culture & Society*, 1(2), 63–77.

Boon, B. (2006). When leisure and work are allies: The case of skiers and tourist resort hotels. *Career Development International*, 11(7), 594–608.

Bottero, W. (2005). *Stratification: Social division and inequality*. London: Routledge.

Bourdieu, P. (1984). *Distinction: A Social Critique of the Judgement of Taste* (R. Nice, Trans.). London: Routledge and Kegan Paul (Original work published 1979).

Bousiou, P. (2008). *The Nomads of Mykonos: Performing Otherness in a Polysemic Tourist Space*. New York: Berghahn Books.

Bowins, B. (2004). Psychological defence mechanisms: A new perspective. *The American Journal of Psychoanalysis*, 64(1), 1–26.

Braidotti, R. (1994). *Nomadic Subjects: Embodiment and Sexual Difference in Contemporary Feminist Theory*. New York: Columbia University Press.

Brannen, J. and Nilsen, A. (2005). Individualisation, choice and structure: A discussion of current trends in sociological analysis. *The Sociological Review*, 53(3), 412–28.

Brewer, J.D. (2000). *Ethnography*. Buckingham: Open University Press.

Brooks, D. (2000). *Bobos in Paradise: The New Upper Class and How They Got There*. New York: Simon & Schuster Paperbacks.

Brubaker, R. (1996). *Nationalism Reframed: Nationhood and the National Question in the New Europe*. Cambridge: Cambridge University Press.

Burns, P.M. and O'Regan, M. (2008). Everyday techno-social devices in everyday travel life: digital audio devices in solo travelling lifestyles. In P.M. Burns and M. Novelli (Eds), *Tourism and Mobilities: Local–Global Connections* (pp. 146–86). Oxfordshire: CABI.

Butcher, M. (2010). From 'fish out of water' to 'fitting in': The challenge of re-placing home in a mobile world. *Population, Space and Place*, 16, 23–36.

Büscher, M. and Urry, J. (2009). Mobile methods and the empirical. *European Journal of Social Theory*, 12(1), 99–116.

Büscher, M. and Urry, J., and Witchger, K. (Eds) (2011). *Mobile Methods*. London: Routledge.

Byrne, D. (2005). *Social Exclusion* (2nd ed.). Maidenhead: Open University Press.

Calhoun, C. (2002). The class consciousness of frequent travelers: Toward a critique of actually existing eosmopolitanism. *The South Atlantic Quarterly*, 101(4), 869–97.

Callegari, L. and Cintra, L.A. (2012, February 16–22). Mieux vaut être salarié au Brésil que chômeur en Europe. *Courrier international*, 1111, 16–17.

Callinicos, A. (1985). Anthony Giddens: A contemporary critique. *Theory and Society*, 14(2), 133–66.

Caner, D. (2002). *Wandering, Begging Monks: Spiritual Authority and the Promotion of Monasticism in Late Antiquity*. Berkeley: University of California Press.

Carmon, Z., Wertenbroch, K., and Zeelenberg, M. (2003). Option attachment: When deliberating makes choosing feel like losing. *Journal of Consumer Research*, 30(1), 15–29.

Casado-Díaz, M.A. (2009). Social capital in the sun: Bonding and bridging social capital among British retirees. In M. Benson and K. O'Reilly (Eds), *Lifestyle Migration: Expectations, Aspirations and Experiences* (pp. 87–102). Farnham: Ashgate.

Casado-Díaz, M.A., Kaiser, C., and Warnes, A.M. (2004). Northern European retired residents in nine southern European areas: Characteristics, motivations and adjustment. *Ageing & Society*, 24, 353–81.

Chambers, D. (2007). Interrogating the 'critical' in critical approaches to tourism research. In I. Ateljevic, A. Pritchard, and N. Morgan (Eds), *The Critical*

Turn in Tourism Studies: Innovative Research Methodologies (pp. 105–19). Oxford: Elsevier.

Chan, T.W. and Goldthorpe, J.H. (2007). Class and status: The conceptual distinction and its empirical relevance. *American Sociological Review*, 72, 512–32.

———— (2010). Introduction: Social status and cultural consumption. In T.W. Chan and J.H. Goldthorpe (Eds), *Social Status and Cultural Consumption* (pp. 1–27). Cambridge: Cambridge University Press.

Chernoff, A. (2011, September 15). The jobless in New Jersey find refuge in tent city. *CNN*. Retrieved from: http://edition.cnn.com/2011/US/09/15/tent.city. new.jersey/index.html [Accessed 15 July 2015].

Chopra-Gant, M. (2006). *Hollywood Genres and Postwar America: Masculinity, Family and Nation in Popular Movies and Film Noir*. London: I.B. Tauris Publishers.

Clarke, J., Hall, S., Jefferson, T., and Roberts, B. (2006). Subcultures, cultures and class. In S. Hall and T. Jefferson (Eds), *Resistance through Rituals: Youth Subcultures in Post-War Britain* (2nd ed.) (pp. 3–59). London: Routledge (Original work published 1993).

Clifford, J. (1992). *Traveling Cultures*. In L. Grossberg, C. Nelson, and P.A. Treichler (Eds), *Cultural Studies* (pp. 96–112). New York: Routledge.

Cloke, P., May, J., and Johnsen, S. (2010). *Swept Up Lives? Re-envisioning the Homeless city*. Malden, MA: Blackwell Publishing.

Cohen, E. (1972). Towards a sociology of international tourism. *Social Research*, 39(1), 164–82.

———— (1973). Nomads from affluence: Notes on the phenomenon of drifter-tourism. *International Journal of Comparative Sociology*, 14(1–2), 89–103.

———— (1979). A phenomenology of tourist experiences. *Sociology*, 13, 179–201.

———— (1982). Marginal paradises: Bungalow tourism on the islands of southern Thailand. *Annals of Tourism Research*, 9, 189–228.

———— (2004). Backpacking: Diversity and change. In G. Richards and J. Wilson (Eds), *The Global Nomad: Backpacker travel in theory and practice* (pp. 43–59). Clevedon: Channel View Publications.

———— (2009). Death in paradise: Tourist fatalities in the tsunami disaster in Thailand. *Current Issues in Tourism*, 12(2), 183–199.

Cohen, E. and Cohen, S. (2012). Current sociological theories and issues in tourism. *Annals of Tourism Research*, 39(4), 2,177–202.

Cohen, S.A. (2010a). Personal identity (de)formation among lifestyle travellers: A double-edged sword. *Leisure Studies*, 29(3), 289–301.

———— (2010b). Reconceptualising lifestyle travellers: Contemporary 'drifters'. K. Hannam and A. Diekmann (Eds), *Beyond Backpacker Tourism: Mobilities and Experiences* (pp. 64–84). Bristol, NY: Channel View Publications.

———— (2011). Lifestyle travellers: Backpacking as a way of life. *Annals of Tourism Research*, 38(4), 1,535–55.

Cohen, S.A., Duncan, T., and Thulemark, M. (2013). Introducing lifestyle mobilities. In S.A. Cohen, T. Duncan, and M. Thulemark (Eds), *Lifestyle Mobilities: Intersections of Travel, Leisure and Migration* (pp. 1–18). Farnham: Ashgate.

Cohen, S.A. and Gössling, S. (2015). A darker side of hypermobility. *Environment and Planning A* (In press).

Conradson, D. and McKay, D. (2007). Translocal subjectivities: Mobility, connection, emotion. *Mobilities*, 2(2), 167–74.

Corrigan, P. (1997). *The Sociology of Consumption: An introduction*. London: Sage.

Cresswell, T. (1999). Embodiment, power and the politics of mobility: The case of female tramps and hobos. *Transactions of the Institution of British Geographers*, 24, 175–92.

——— (2001). The production of mobilities. *New Formations*, 43, 11–25.

——— (2006). *On the Move: Mobility in the Modern Western World*. London: Routledge.

——— (2008a). *Constellations of Mobility: Towards Cultural Kinetics* [Online paper]. Retrieved from: http://www.dtesis.univr.it/documenti/Avviso/all/all181066.pdf [Accessed 15 July 2015].

——— (2008b). Place: Encountering geography as philosophy. *Geography*, 93(3), 132–40.

——— (2010). Mobilities I: Catching up. *Progress in Human Geography*, 35(4), 550–58.

——— (2011a). Mobilities II: Still. *Progress in Human Geography*, 36(5), 645–53.

——— (2011b). The vagrant/vagabond: The curious career of a mobile subject. In T. Cresswell and P. Merriman (Eds), *Geographies of Mobilities: Practices, Spaces, Subjects* (pp. 239–53). Farnham: Ashgate.

——— (2013). Citizenship in worlds of mobility. In O. Söderström, D. Ruedin, S. Randeria, G. D'Amato, and F. Panese (Eds), *Critical Mobilities* (pp. 105–24). London: Routledge.

——— (2014). Mobilities III: Moving on. *Progress in Human Geography*, 38(5), 712–21.

Cresswell, T. and Uteng, T.P. (2008). Gendered mobilities: Towards an holistic understanding. In T. Cresswell and T.P. Uteng (Eds), *Gendered Mobilities* (pp. 1–12). Farnham: Ashgate.

Crick, M. (1996). Sun, sex, sights, savings and servility. *Criticism, Heresy and Interpretation*, 1(1), 37–76.

Curran, D. (2013). Risk society and the distribution of bads: Theorizing class in the risk society. *The British Journal of Sociology*, 64(1), 44–62.

Cuthill, V. (2004). Little England's global conference centre: Harrogate. In J. Urry and M. Sheller (Eds), *Tourism Mobilities: Places to Play, Places in Play* (pp. 55–66). London: Routledge.

D'Andrea, A. (2006). *Global Nomads. Techno and New Age as Transnational Countercultures in Ibiza and Goa* [PDF version]. London: Routledge.

D'Andrea, A., Ciolfi, L., and Gray, B. (2011). Methodological challenges and innovations in mobilities research. *Mobilities*, 6(2), 149–60.

Dallmayr, F. (1982). Rejoinder to Giddens. In A. Giddens, *Profiles and Critiques in Social Theory* (p. 27). Berkeley: University of California Press.

Dann, G. (1999). Writing out the tourist in space and time. *Annals of Tourism Research*, 26(1), 159–87.

Davidson, R. (1980). *Tracks*. London: Picador.

de Botton, Alain (2002). *The Art of Travel*. New York: Pantheon.

de Laine, M. (2000). *Fieldwork, Participation and Practice: Ethics and Dilemmas in Qualitative Research*. London: Sage Publications.

de Saussure, F. (1990). *Cours de linguistique générale* [Published posthumously by C. Bally, A. Riedlinger, and A. Séchehaye]. Paris: Éditions Payot (Original work published 1916).

Deleuze, G. (2006). *Foucault* (S. Hand, Trans., Ed.). Minneapolis, MN: University of Minnesota Press (Original work published 1986).

Deleuze, G. and Guattari, F. (1987). *A Thousand Plateaus: Capitalism and Schizophrenia* (B. Massumi, Trans.). Minneapolis, MN: University of Minnesota Press (Original work published 1980).

Department for Work and Pensions (2014). Households Below Average Income. Retrieved from: https://www.gov.uk/government/uploads/system/uploads/attachment_data/file/325416/households-below-average-income-1994-1995-2012-2013.pdf [Accessed 15 July 2015].

DePastino, T. (2003). *The Citizen Hobo: How a Century of Homelessness Shaped America*. Chicago: The University of Chicago Press.

Derrida, J. (1982). *Margins of Philosophy* (A. Bass, Trans.). Brighton: The Harvester Press (Original work published 1972).

——— (1997). *Of Grammatology* (Rev. ed.) (G.C. Spivak, Trans.). Baltimore, MD: The Johns Hopkins University Press (Original work published 1967).

——— (2000). *Of Hospitality: Anne Dufourmantelle Invites Jacques Derrida to Respond* (R. Bowslby, Trans.). Stanford, CA: Stanford University Press (Original work published 1997).

Desforges, L. (2000). Traveling the world: Identity and travel biography. *Annals of Tourism Research*, 27(4), 926–45.

Dews, P. (1979). The Nouvelle Philosophie and Foucault. *Economy and Society*, 8(2), 127–71.

Dietz, M. (2005). *Wandering Monks, Virgins, and Pilgrims: Ascetic Travel in the Mediterranean World, AD 300–800*. Pennsylvania: The Pennsylvania State University.

Dordick, G.A. (1997). *Something Left to Lose: Personal Relations and Survival Among New York's Homeless*. Philadelphia: Temple University Press.

Douglas, M. and Isherwood, B. (2002). *The World of Goods: Towards an Anthropology of Consumption*. London: Routledge (Original work published 1979).

Dreyfus, H. and Rabinow, P. (1983). *Michel Foucault: Beyond Structuralism and Hermeneutics* (2nd ed.). Chicago: Chicago University Press (Original work published 1982).

du Bois-Reymond, M. (1998). I don't want to commit myself yet: Young people's life concepts. *Journal of Youth Studies*, 1(1), 63–79.

Dunn, R. (2008). *Identifying Consumption: Subjects and Objects in Consumer Society*. Philadelphia: Temple University Press.

Eagleton, T. (1991). *Ideology: An Introduction*. London: Verso.

Edensor, T. (2001). Performing tourism, staging tourism: (Re)producing tourist space and practice. *Tourist Studies*, 1(1), 59–81.

Elias, N. (2001). *Society of Individuals* (E. Jephcott, Trans., and M. Schroter, Ed.). New York: Continuum (Original work published 1987).

Elliott, A. (2002). Beck's sociology of risk: A critical assessment. *Sociology*, 36(2), 293–315.

Elliott, A. and Lemert, C. (2006). *The New Individualism: The Emotional Costs of Globalization*. London: Routledge.

Elsrud, T. (2001). Risk creation in traveling: Backpacker adventure narration. *Annals of Tourism Research*, 28(3), 597–617.

Enloe, C. (1990). *Bananas, Beaches and Bases: Making Feminist Sense of International Politics*. Berkeley: University of California Press.

Esping-Andersen, G. (Ed.) (1993a). *Changing Classes: Stratification and Mobility in Post-Industrial Societies*. London: Sage.

Esping-Andersen, G. (1993b). Mobility regimes and class formation. In G. Esping-Andersen (Ed.), *Changing Classes: Stratification and Mobility in Post-Industrial Societies* (pp. 225–41). London: Sage.

Euben, R.L. (2006). *Journeys to the Other Shore: Muslim and Western Travellers in Search of Knowledge*. Princeton: Princeton University Press.

Europe 2020 [website]. Retrieved from: http://ec.europa.eu/europe2020/index_en.htm [Accessed 15 July 2015].

European Commission (n.d.) Poverty and Social Exclusion. European Commission. Employment, Social Affairs and Inclusion. Retrieved from: http://ec.europa.eu/social/main.jsp?catId=751 [Accessed 15 July 2015].

Fairclough, N. (1989). *Language and Power*. Harlow: Addison Wesley Longman.

Falzon, Mark-Anthony (Ed.) (2009). *Multi-Sited Ethnography: Theory, Praxis and Locality in Contemporary Research*. Farnham: Ashgate.

Featherstone, M. (1987). Lifestyle and consumer culture. *Theory, Culture & Society*, 4, 55–70.

——— (2007). *Consumer Culture and Postmodernism* (2nd Ed.). London: Sage Publications (Original work published 1991).

Feldner, H. and Vighi, F. (2007). *Žižek: Beyond Foucault*. Hampshire: Palgrave Macmillan.

Fincham, B. (2008). Balance is everything: Bicycle messengers, work and leisure. *Sociology*, 42(4), 618–34.

Firat, A.F. and Venkatesh, A. (1995). Liberatory postmodernism and the reenchantment of consumption. *Journal of Consumer Research*, 22, 239–67.

Foucault, M. (1969). *L'archéologie du savoir*. Paris: Gallimard.

—— (1978). *The History of Sexuality: An Introduction* (Vol. 1) (R. Hurley, Trans.). New York: Pantheon Books (Original work published 1976).

—— (1981). The order of discourse: Inaugural lecture at the Collège de France. In R. Young (Ed.), *Untying the Text: A Post-Structuralist Reader* (pp. 48–79). London: Routledge and Kegan Paul (Original work published 1970).

—— (1983). Preface. In G. Deleuze and F. Guattari, *Anti-Oedipus: Capitalism and Schizophrenia* (R. Hurley, M. Seem and H.R. Lane, Trans.) (pp. xi–xiv). Minneapolis: University of Minnesota Press.

—— (1988). Power and sex. In M. Foucault, *Politics, Philosophy, Culture: Interviews and Other Writings 1977–1984* (A. Sheridan et al., Trans., L.D. Kritzman, Ed.). New York: Routledge (Original work published 1977).

—— (1990). *History of Sexuality: The Use of Pleasure* (Vol. 2) (R. Hurley, Trans.). New York: Vintage Books (Original work published 1984).

—— (1991a). *Discipline and Punish*. London: Penguin (Original work published 1975).

—— (1991b). Governmentality. In G. Burchell, C. Gordon, and P. Miller (Eds), *The Foucault Effect: Studies in Governmentality* (P. Pasquino, Trans.) (pp. 87–104). Chicago: The University of Chicago Press (Original work published 1978).

—— (1997a). Michel Foucault: An interview by Stephen Riggins. In P. Rabinow (Ed.), *Ethics, Subjectivity and Truth: Essential Works of Foucault 1954–1984* (Vol. 1) (R. Hurley et al., Trans.) (pp. 121–33). New York: The New Press (Original work published in 1982).

—— (1997b). On the genealogy of ethics: An overview of work in progress. In P. Rabinow (Ed.), *Ethics, Subjectivity and Truth: Essential Works of Foucault 1954–1984* (Vol. 1) (R. Hurley et al., Trans.) (pp. 253–80). New York: The New Press (Original work published 1983).

—— (1997c). The ethics of the concern of the self as a practice of freedom. In P. Rabinow (Ed.), Ethics, Subjectivity and *Truth: Essential Works of Foucault 1954–1984* (Vol. 1) (R. Hurley et al., Trans.) (pp. 281–301). New York: The New Press. (Original work published 1984).

—— (1997d). Polemics, politics, and problematizations: An interview with Michel Foucault. In P. Rabinow (Ed.), *Ethics, Subjectivity and Truth: Essential Works of Foucault 1954–1984* (Vol. 1) (R. Hurley et al., Trans.) (pp. 111–119). New York: The New Press (Original work published 1984).

—— (1997e). The Hermeneutic of the subject. In P. Rabinow (Ed.), *Ethics, Subjectivity and Truth: Essential works of Foucault 1954–1984* (Vol. 1) (R. Hurley et al., Trans.) (pp. 93–106). New York: The New Press.

—— (1997f). What is enlightenment? In P. Rabinow (Ed.), *Ethics, Subjectivity and Truth: Essential works of Foucault 1954–1984* (Vol. 1) (R. Hurley et al., Trans.) (pp. 281–319). New York: The New Press (Original work published 1984).

—— (1998a). Different spaces. In J.D. Faubion (Ed.), *Aesthetics: Essential works of Foucault 1954–1984* (Vol. 2) (R. Hurley et al., Trans.) (pp. 175–85). London: Penguin (Original work published 1967).

———— (1998b). Nietzsche, genealogy, history. In J.D. Faubion (Ed.), *Aesthetics: Essential Works of Foucault 1954–1984* (Vol. 2) (R. Hurley et al., Trans.) (pp. 369–91). London: Penguin (Original work published 1971).

———— (1998c). Structuralism and post-structuralism. In J.D. Faubion (Ed.), *Aesthetics: Essential Works of Foucault 1954–1984* (Vol. 2) (R. Hurley et al., Trans.) (pp. 433–58). London: Penguin (Original work published 1983).

———— (2002a). The subject and power. In J.D. Faubion, (Ed.), *Power: Essential Works of Foucault 1954–1984* (Vol. 3) (R. Hurley et al., Trans.) (pp. 326–49). London: Penguin (Original work published 1982).

———— (2002b). The political technology of individuals. In J.D. Faubion, (Ed.), *Power: Essential Works of Foucault 1954–1984* (Vol. 3) (R. Hurley et al., Trans.) (pp. 403–17). London: Penguin (Original work published 1988).

———— (2002c). The subject and power. In J.D. Faubion, (Ed.), *Power: Essential works of Foucault 1954–1984* (Vol. 3) (R. Hurley et al., Trans.) (pp. 326–49). London: Penguin (Original work published 1982).

———— (2002d). Truth and juridical forms [Two lectures]. In J.D. Faubion, (Ed.), *Power: Essential Works of Foucault 1954–1984* (Vol. 3) (R. Hurley et al., Trans.) (pp. 1–89). London: Penguin (Lectures were delivered 1979).

———— (2002e). Truth and power. In J.D. Faubion, (Ed.), *Power: Essential works of Foucault 1954–1984* (Vol. 3) (R. Hurley et al., Trans.) (pp. 111–33). London: Penguin (Original work published 1977).

———— (2005). *The Order of Things* [PDF version]. London: Routledge (Original work published 1966).

———— (2007). What is critique? In M. Foucault, *The Politics of Truth* (L. Hochroth and C. Porter, Trans., S. Lotringer, Ed.) (pp. 41–81), Los Angeles: Semiotext(e) (Original lecture delivered 1978).

Franklin, A. (2003). The tourist syndrome: An interview with Zygmunt Bauman. *Tourist Studies*, 3(2), 205–17.

———— (2007). The problem with tourism theory. In I. Ateljevic, A. Pritchard, and N. Morgan (Eds), *The Critical Turn in Tourism Studies: Innovative Research Methodologies* (pp. 131–48). Oxford: Elsevier.

Franklin, A. and Crang, M. (2001). The trouble with tourism and travel theory? *Tourist Studies*, 1(1), 5–22.

Franquesa, J. (2011). 'We've lost our bearings': Place, tourism, and the limits of the 'mobility turn'. *Antipode*, 43(4), 1,012–33.

Freeland, C. (2012). *Plutocrats: The Rise of the New Global Super-Rich and the Fall of Everyone Else*. New York: Penguin Press.

Frello, B. (2008). Towards a discursive analytics of movement: On the making and unmaking of movement as an object of knowledge. *Mobilities*, 3(1), 25–50.

Fussell, P. (1980). *Abroad: British Literary Travelling Between the Wars*. Oxford: Oxford University Press.

Galani-Moutafi, V. (2000). The self and the Other: Traveler, ethnographer, tourist. *Annals of Tourism Research*, 27(1), 203–24.

Gangl, M. (2002). Changing labour markets and early career outcomes: Labour market entry in Europe over the past decade. *Work, Employment and Society*, 16(1), 67–90.

Geertz, C. (1984). Distinguished Lecture: Anti anti-relativism. *American Anthropologist*, New Series, 86(2), 263–78.

Gelder, K. (2006). *Subcultures: Cultural Histories and Social Practice* [PDF version]. Retrieved from http://www.amazon.com/Subcultures-Cultural-Histories-Social-Practice/dp/0415379520 [Accessed 15 July 2015].

Geoffroy, C. (2007). 'Mobile' contexts/'immobile' cultures. *Language and Intercultural Communication*, 7(4), 279–90.

Gershuny, J. and Fisher, K. (2014). Post-industrious society: Why work time will not disappear for our grandchildren [working paper]. Retrieved from: http://www.sociology.ox.ac.uk/materials/papers/wp20143.pdf [Accessed 15 July 2015].

Giddens, A. (1979). *Central Problems in Social Theory: Action, Structure and Contradiction in Social Analysis*. Berkeley: University of California Press.

——— (1981). *A Contemporary Critique of Historical Materialism: Power, Property and the State*. Berkeley: University of California Press.

———(1984). *The Constitution of Society: Outline of the Theory of Structuration*. Berkeley, CA: University of California Press.

——— (1985). *The Nation-State and Violence*. Cambridge: Polity Press.

——— (1989). A reply to my critics. In D. Held and J.B. Thompson (Eds), *Social Theory of Modern Societies: Anthony Giddens and His Critics* (pp. 249–305). Cambridge: Cambridge University Press.

——— (1990). *The Consequences of Modernity*. Cambridge: Polity Press.

——— (1991). *Modernity and Self-identity: Self and Society in the Late Modern Age*. Cambridge: Polity Press.

——— (1993). *New Rules of Sociological Method: a Positive Critique of Interpretative Sociologies* (2nd ed.). Stanford, CA: Stanford University Press (Original work published 1976).

——— (2003). The globalizing modernity. In D. Held and A. McGrew (Eds), *The Global Transformations Reader: An Introduction to the Globalization Debate* (2nd ed.) (pp. 60–66). Cambridge: Polity Press (Original work published 2000).

Goldthorpe, J.H. (1996). Class analysis and the reorientation of class theory: The case of persisting differentials in educational attainment. *The British Journal of Sociology*, 47(3), 481–505.

———(2002). Globalisation and social class. *West European Politics*, 25(3), 1–28.

Goldthorpe, J.H. and Marshall, G. (1992). The promising future of class analysis: A response to recent critiques. *Sociology*, 26(3), 381–400.

Grant, R. (2003). *Ghost Riders: Travels with American Nomads*. London: Abacus.

Greenblatt, E. (2002). Work/life balance: Wisdom or whining. *Organizational Dynamics*, 31(2), 177–93.

Greenwald, G., McAskill, E., Poitras, L., Ackerman, S. and Rushe, D. (2013, July 12). How Microsoft handed the NSA access to encrypted messages. *The Guardian*.

Retrieved from: http://www.guardian.co.uk/world/2013/jul./11/microsoft-nsa-collaboration-user-data [Accessed 15 July 2015].

Gregory, D. (1989). Presences and absences: time-space relations and structuration theory. In D. Held and J.B. Thompson (Eds), *Social Theory of Modern Societies: Anthony Giddens and his critics* (pp. 185–214). Cambridge: Cambridge University Press.

Gregson, Nicky (1989). On the (ir)relevance of structuration theory to empirical research. In D. Held and J.B. Thompson (Eds), *Social Theory of Modern Societies: Anthony Giddens and his critics* (pp. 235–48). Cambridge: Cambridge University Press.

Grossberg, L. (1996). Identity and cultural studies: Is that all there is? In S. Hall and P. du Gay (Eds), *Questions of Cultural Identity* (pp. 87–107). London: Sage Publications.

Habermas, J. (1987). *The Philosophical Discourse of Modernity: Twelve Lectures* (F. Lawrence, Trans.). Cambridge: Polity Press (Original work published 1985).

Hall, S. (1990). Cultural Identity and Diaspora. In J. Rutherford (Ed.), *Identity, Community, Culture, Difference* (pp. 222–37). London: Lawrence and Wishart.

——— (1992). The west and the rest: Discourse and power. In S. Hall and B. Gieben (Eds), *Formations of Modernity* (pp. 275–320). Cambridge: Polity Press and Blackwell Publishers.

——— (1996). Who needs 'identity?' In S. Hall and P. du Gay (Eds), *Questions of Cultural Identity* (pp. 1–17). London: Sage Publications.

Hall, S. and Jefferson, T. (Eds). (2006). *Resistance through Rituals: Youth Subcultures in Post-War Britain* (2nd ed.). London: Routledge (Original work published 1993).

Hamilton, C. (2003). *Growth Fetish*. Crows Nest, NSW: Allen and Unwin.

Hannam, K. and Ateljevic, I. (Eds) (2008). *Backpacker Tourism: Concepts and Profiles*. Clevedon: Channel View Publications.

Hannam, K. and Knox, D. (2010). *Understanding Tourism*. London: Sage Publications.

Hannam, K., Sheller, M., and Urry, J. (2006). Mobilities, immobilities and moorings [Editorial]. *Mobilities*, 1(1), 1–22.

Hannerz, U. (1990). Cosmopolitans and locals in world culture. In M. Featherstone (Ed.), *Global Culture: Nationalism, Globalization and Modernity* (pp. 237–51). London: Sage.

——— (1992). *Cultural Complexity: Studies in the Social Organization of Meaning*. New York: Columbia University Press.

——— (1996). *Transnational Connections: Culture, People, Places*. London: Routledge.

Harvey, D. (1993). From space to place and back again: Reflections on the condition of postmodernity. In J. Bird, B. Curtis, T. Putnam, G. Robertson, and L. Tickner (Eds), *Mapping the Futures: Local cultures, Global Change* (pp. 2–28). London: Routledge.

Heaphy, B. (2007). *Late Modernity and Social Change: Reconstructing Social and Personal Life* [PDF version]. Oxfordshire: Routledge.

Hebdige, D. (1979). *Subculture: The Meaning of Style*. London: Routledge.

Held, D. (1989). Citizenship and autonomy. In D. Held and J.B. Thompson (Eds), *Social Theory of Modern Societies: Anthony Giddens and His Critics* (pp. 162–84). Cambridge: Cambridge University Press.

———— (Ed.) (2004). *A Globalizing World? Culture, Economics, Politics*. London: Routledge.

———— (2005). Principles of cosmopolitan order. In G. Brock and H. Brighouse (Eds), *The Political Philosophy of Cosmopolitanism* (pp. 10–27). Cambridge: Cambridge University Press.

Held, D. and McGrew, A. (2003). The great globalization debate. In D. Held and A. McGrew (Eds), *The Global Transformations Reader: An Introduction to the Globalization Debate* (2nd ed.) (pp. 1–50). Cambridge: Polity Press (Original work published 2000).

Hine, C.M. (2000). *Virtual Ethnography*. London: Sage Publications.

Hirsch, F. (2005). *Social Limits to Growth*. London: Routledge (Original work published 1977).

Hobsbawm, E. (2000). *Nations and Nationalism since 1780: Programme, Myth, Reality* (2nd ed.). Cambridge: Cambridge University Press (Original work published 1990).

Hoey, B. (2009). Pursuing the good life: American narratives of travel and a search for refuge. In M. Benson and K. O'Reilly (Eds), *Lifestyle Migration: Expectations, Aspirations and Experiences* (pp. 31–50). Farnham: Ashgate.

———— (2010). Place for personhood: Individual and local character in lifestyle migration. *City & Society*, 22(2), 237–61.

Hoffmann, M. (2013, March 31). Life is too short for an undesirable satori. *The Japan Times*. Retrieved from: http://www.japantimes.co.jp/news/2013/03/31/national/media-national/life-is-too-short-for-an-undesirable-satori/ [Accessed 15 July 2015].

Holston, J. and Appadurai, A. (1999). Cities and citizenship. In J. Holston (Ed.), *Cities and Citizenship* (pp. 1–18). Durham: Duke University Press.

Holt, D.B. (2002). Why do brands cause trouble? A dialectical theory of consumer culture and branding. *Journal of Consumer Research*, 29, 70–90.

Hottola, P. (2004). Culture confusion: Intercultural adaptation in tourism. *Annals of Tourism Research*, 31(2), 447–66.

———— (2005). The metaspatialities of control management in tourism: Backpacking in India. *Tourism Geographies*, 7(1), 1–22.

———— (2008). The social psychological interface of tourism and independent travel. In K. Hannam and I. Ateljevic (Eds), *Backpacker Tourism: Concepts and Profiles* (pp. 26–37). Clevedon: Channel View Publications.

Huggan, G. (2001). *The Postcolonial Exotic: Marketing the Margins*. London: Routledge.

Hulme, P. and Youngs, T. (2002). Introduction. In P. Hulme (Ed.), *The Cambridge Companion to Travel Writing* (pp. 1–13). Cambridge: Cambridge University Press.

Iso-Ahola, S. (1982). Toward a social psychological theory of tourism motivation: A rejoinder. *Annals of Tourism Research*, 9(2), 256–62.

Israel, M. and Hay, I. (2006). *Research Ethics for Social Scientists: Between Ethical Conduct and Regulatory Compliance*. London: Sage Publications.

Iyengar, S. and Lepper, M. (2000). When choice is demotivating: Can one desire too much of a good thing? *Journal of Personality and Social Psychology*, 79, 995–1,006.

Jarvis, J. and Peel, V. (2010). Flashpacking in Fiji: Reframing the 'global nomad' in a developing destination. In K. Hannam and A. Diekmann (Eds), *Beyond Backpacker Tourism: Mobilities and Experiences* (pp. 21–39). Bristol: Channel View Publications.

Jessop, B. (1989). Capitalism, nation-states and surveillance. In D. Held and J.B. Thompson (Eds), *Social Theory of Modern Societies: Anthony Giddens and His Critics* (pp. 103–28). Cambridge: Cambridge University Press.

Kalir, B. (2013). Moving subjects, stagnant paradigms: Can the 'mobilities paradigm' transcend methodological nationalism? *Journal of Ethnic and Migration Studies*, 39(2), 311–27.

Kaplan, C. (1996). *Questions of Travel: Postmodern Discourses of Displacement*. Durham, NC: Duke University Press.

Kelts, R. (2014, May 7). The satori generation: A new breed of young people have outdone the tricksters of advertising. *Adbusters*. Retrieved from: https://www.adbusters.org/magazine/113/satori-generation.html [Accessed 15 July 2015].

Keynes, J.M. (1963). Economic possibilities for our grandchildren. In J.M. Keynes, *Essays in Persuasion* (pp. 358–73). New York: W.W. Norton & Company (Original work published 1930).

Khazanov, A.M. (1994). *Nomads and the Outside World* (2nd ed.) (J. Crookenden, Trans.). Wisconsin: The University of Wisconsin Press (Original work published 1983).

Kibicho, W. (2009). *Sex Tourism in Africa: Kenya's Booming Industry*. Farnham: Ashgate.

Korpela, M. (2009). *More Vibes in India: Westerners in Search of a Better Life in Varanasi*. Tampere: Tampere University Press.

Kozinets, R. (2002), Can consumers escape the market? Emancipatory illuminations from Burning Man. *Journal of Consumer Research*, 29, 20–38.

Laing, R.D. (1967). *The Politics of Experience*. New York: Ballantine Books.

Langan, C. (1995). *Romantic Vagrancy: Wordsworth and the Simulation of Freedom*. Cambridge: Cambridge University Press.

Larsen, J. and Urry, J. (2008). Networking in mobile societies. In J.O. Bærenholdt and G. Brynhild (Eds), *Mobility and Place: Enacting Northern European Peripheries* (pp. 89–101). Aldershot: Ashgate.

Lash, S. (1993). Reflexive modernization: The aesthetic dimension. *Theory, Culture & Society*, 10(1), 1–23.

Lash, S. and Urry, J. (1994). *Economies of Signs and Space*. London: Routledge.

Latour, B. (2003). Is re-modernization occurring – and if so, how to prove it? A commentary on Ulrich Beck. *Theory, Culture & Society*, 20(2), 35–48.

Law, J. and Urry, J. (2003). *Enacting the Social* [Online paper]. Retrieved from: http://www.lancs.ac.uk/fass/sociology/papers/law-urry-enacting-the-social.pdf [Accessed 15 July 2015].

Le Grand, J. (2003). Individual choice and social exclusion [case paper]. London: Centre for Analysis of Social Exclusion. Retrieved from: http://eprints.lse.ac.uk/4645/1/Individual_Choice_and_Social_Exclusion.pdf [Accessed 15 July 2015].

Lea, J. (1998). *Tourism and Development in the Third World*. London: Routledge (Original work published 1988).

Levine, R. (2006). *A Geography of Time: The Temporal Misadventures of a Social Psychologist, or How Every Culture Keeps Time Just a Little Bit Differently*. Oxford: Oneworldpublications.

Lisle, D. (2006). *The Global Politics of Contemporary Travel Writing*. Cambridge: Cambridge University Press.

London, J. (2006). *The Road*. New Brunswick, NJ: Rutgers University Press (Original work published 1907).

MacBeth, J. (2000). Utopian Tourists: Cruising is not just about sailing. *Current Issues in Tourism*, 3(1), 20–34.

McCabe, S. (2005). Who is a tourist: A critical review. *Tourist Studies*, 5(1), 85–106.

MacCannell, D. (1999). *The Tourist: A New Theory of the Leisure Class* (3rd ed.). Berkeley, CA: University of California Press (Original work published 1976).

Macdonell, D. (1986). *Theories of Discourse*. Oxford: Blackwell.

Maffesoli, M. (1996). *The Time of the Tribes: The Decline of Individualism in Mass Society* (D. Smith, Trans.). London: Sage (Original work published 1988).

McIntyre, N. (2013). Mobilities, lifestyles and imagined worlds: Exploring the terrain of lifestyle migration. In S.A. Cohen, T. Duncan, and M. Thulemark (Eds), *Lifestyle Mobilities: Intersections of Travel, Leisure and Migration* (pp. 193–207). Farnham: Ashgate.

McLennan, G. (1984). Critical or positive theory? A comment on the status of Anthony Giddens' social theory. *Theory, Culture & Society*, 2(2), 123–9.

McNaughton, D. (2006). The 'host' as uninvited 'guest': Hospitality, violence and tourism. *Annals of Tourism Research*, 33(3), 645–65.

Malkki, L. (1992). National Geographic: The rooting of peoples and the territorialization of national identity among scholars and refugees. *Cultural Anthropology*, 7(1), 24–44.

Malmberg, I. (2011). Suomalaispariskunta hyppäsi oravanpyörästä ja lähti ikuiselle matkalle. *Helsingin Sanomien Kuukausiliite*, 11. Discussion related to the article is available from: http://www.hs.fi/kotimaa/Suomalaispariskunta

+hypp%C3%A4si+oravanpy%C3%B6r%C3%A4st%C3%A4+ja+l%C3%A4
hti+ikuiselle+matkalle/a1305548184920 [Accessed 15 July 2015].

Manson, M. (2012, December 27). No office, no boss, no boundaries – Rise of the nomadic rich. *CNN*. Retrieved from: http://travel.cnn.com/new-nomads-814536 [Accessed 15 July 2015].

Maoz, D. (2006). The mutual gaze. *Annals of Tourism Research*, 33(1), 221–39.

Marcus, G.E. (1995). Ethnography in/of the world System: The emergence of multi-sited ethnography. *Annual Review of Anthropology*, 24, 95–117.

Massey, D. (1993). Power-geometry and a progressive sense of place. In J. Bird, B. Curtis, T. Putnam, G. Robertson, and L. Tickner (Eds), *Mapping the Futures: Local Cultures, Global Change* (pp. 60–70). London: Routledge.

———— (1994). *Space, Place, and Gender*. Minneapolis: University of Minnesota Press.

Meštrović, S.G. (1998). *Anthony Giddens: The Last Modernist*. London: Routledge.

Mick. D.G., Broniarczyk, S.M., and Haidt, J. (2004). Choose, choose, choose, choose, choose, choose, choose: Emerging and prospective research on the deleterious effects of living in consumer hyperchoice. *Journal of Business Ethics*, 52, 207–211.

Mills, S. (2001). *Discourse* [PDF version]. London: Routledge (Original work published 1997).

Molz, J.G. (2007). Cosmopolitans on the couch: Mobile hospitality and the internet. In J.G. Molz and S. Gibson (Eds), *Mobilizing Hospitality: The Ethics of Social Relations in a Mobile World* (pp. 65–80). Aldershot: Ashgate.

———— (2009). Representing pace in tourism mobilities: Staycations, slow travel and the amazing race. *Journal of Tourism and Cultural Change*, 7(4), 270–86.

———— (2010). Performing global geographies: Time, space, place and pace in narratives of round-the-world travel. *Tourism Geographies: An International Journal of Tourism Space, Place and Environment*, 12(3), 329–48.

Molz, J.G. and Gibson, S. (2007). Introduction: Mobilizing and mooring hospitality. In J.G. Molz and S. Gibson (Eds), *Mobilizing Hospitality: The Ethics of Social Relations in a Mobile World* (pp. 1–25). Aldershot: Ashgate.

Moufakkir, O. and Reisinger, Y. (Eds) (2012). *The Host Gaze in Global Tourism*. Oxfordshire: CABI.

Mowforth, M. and Munt, I. (2009). *Tourism and Sustainability: Development Globalisation and New Tourism in the Third World* (3rd ed.). London: Routledge.

Munt, I. (1994). The 'Other' postmodern tourism: Culture, travel and the new middle classes. *Theory, Culture & Society*, 11, 101–23.

Mythen, G. (2005). Employment, individualization and insecurity: Rethinking the risk society perspective. *The Sociological Review*, 53(1), 129–49.

Noy, C. (2004). This trip really changed me. *Annals of Tourism Research*, 31(1), 78–102.

Nudrali, O. and O'Reilly, K. (2009). Taking the risk: The British in Didim, Turkey. In M. Benson and K. O'Reilly (Eds), *Lifestyle Migration: Expectations, Aspirations and Experiences* (pp. 137–52). Farnham: Ashgate.

Ong, A. (2006). Mutations in citizenship. *Theory, Culture & Society*, 23(2–3), 499–531.

Online Etymology Dictionary (2010). Adventure. *Online Etymology Dictionary*. Retrieved from: http://www.etymonline.com/index. php?term=adventure&allowed_in_frame=0 [Accessed 15 July 2015].

O'Regan, M. (2008). Hypermobility in backpacker lifestyles: the emergence of the internet café. In P.M. Burns and M. Novelli (Eds), *Tourism and Mobilities: Local–Global Connections* (pp. 109–32). Oxfordshire: CABI.

———— (2013). Others have the clock but we have time: Alternative lifestyle mobilities and the resurgence of hitchhiking. In S.A. Cohen, T. Duncan, and M. Thulemark (Eds), *Lifestyle Mobilities: Intersections of Travel, Leisure and Migration* (pp. 35–50). Farnham: Ashgate.

O'Reilly, C.C. (2006). From drifter to gap year tourist: Mainstreaming backpacker travel. *Annals of Tourism Research*, 33(4), 998–1,017.

O'Reilly, K. (2000). *The British on the Costa del Sol*. London: Routledge.

———— (2002). Britain in Europe/The British in Spain: Exploring Britain's changing relationship to the Other through the attitudes of its emigrants. *Nations and Nationalisms*, 8(2), 179–93.

———— (2003). When is a tourist? The articulation of tourism and migration in Spain's Costa del Sol. *Tourist Studies*, 3(3), 301–17.

———— (2007). Intra-European migration and the mobility – Enclosure dialectic. *Sociology*, 41(2), 277–293.

Pakulski, J, and Waters, M. (1996). The reshaping and dissolution of social class in advanced society. *Theory and Society*, 25(5), 667–91.

Papastergiadis, N. (2000). *The Turbulence of Migration: Globalization, Deterritorialization and Hybridity*. Cambridge: Polity Press.

Pearce, P. and Lee, U-Il (2005). Developing the travel career approach to tourist motivation. *Journal of Travel Research*, 43, 226–37.

Pereiro, X. (2010). Ethnographic research on cultural tourism: An anthropological view. In G. Richards and W. Munsters (Eds), *Cultural Tourism Research Methods* (pp. 173–87). Oxfordshire: CABI.

Piketty, T. (2014). *Capital in the Twenty-First Century* (A. Goldhammer, Trans.). Cambridge: Harvard University Press.

Pocock, J.G.A. (1985). *Virtue, Commerce, and History: Essays on Political Thought and History, Chiefly in the Eighteenth Century*. Cambridge: Cambridge University Press.

Pocock, N.J. and McIntosh, A.J. (2011). The return from travel: A new beginning? *Current Issues in Tourism*, 14(7), 631–49.

Poulantzas, N. (2000). *State, Power, Socialism* (P. Cauriller, Trans.). London: Verso (Original work published 1978).

Pratt, M.L. (1992). *Imperial Eyes: Travel Writing and Transculturation*. London: Routledge.

Prozorov, S. (2007). *Foucault, Freedom and Sovereignty*. Aldershot: Ashgate.

Rasmussen, E.D. (2004). Liberation hurts: An interview with Slavoj Žižek. *Electronic Book Review*. Retrieved from: http://www.electronicbookreview. com/thread/endconstruction/desublimation [Accessed 15 July 2015].

Ravenscroft, N. and Gilchrist, P (2009). The emergent working society of leisure. *Journal of Leisure Research*, 41(1), 23–39.

Reid, A. (1990). *Whereabouts: Notes on Being a Foreigner*. Buffalo, NY: White Pine Press.

Reid, D.G. (2003). *Tourism, Globalization and Development: Responsible Tourism Planning*. London: Pluto Press.

Richards, G. (2011). Creativity and tourism: The state of the art. *Annals of Tourism Research*, 38(4), 1,225–53.

Richards, G. and Wilson, J. (2004). Drifting towards the global nomad. In G. Richards and J. Wilson (Eds), *The Global Nomad: Backpacker Travel in Theory and Practice* (pp. 3–13). Clevedon: Channel View Publications.

———— (Eds) (2004b). *The Global Nomad: Backpacker Travel in Theory and Practice*. Clevedon: Channel View Publications.

———— (2004c). The Global Nomad: Motivations and behaviour of independent travellers worldwide. In G. Richards and J. Wilson (Eds), *The Global Nomad: Backpacker Travel in Theory and Practice* (pp. 14–39). Clevedon: Channel View Publications.

Rickly-Boyd, J.M. (2013). 'Dirtbags': Mobility, community and rock climbing as performative of identity. In S.A. Cohen, T. Duncan, and M. Thulemark (Eds), *Lifestyle Mobilities: Intersections of Travel, Leisure and Migration* (pp. 51–64). Farnham: Ashgate.

Ricoeur, P. (1992). *Oneself as Another* (K. Blamey, Trans.). Chicago: The University of Chicago Press.

Riiali, M. (2014). Ikuisesti häämatkalla. *Hyvä terveys*, 9, 49–53.

Riley, P. (1988). Road culture of international long-term budget travelers. *Annals of Tourism Research*, 15, 313–28.

Rojek, C. (2005). *Leisure Theory: Principles and Practices*. Hampshire: Palgrave MacMillan.

———— (2010). *Labour of Leisure: The Culture of Free Time*. London: Sage Publications.

Rojek, C. and Urry, J. (1997). Transformations of travel and theory. In C. Rojek and J. Urry (Eds), *Touring Cultures: Transformations of Travel and Theory* (pp. 1–19) [PDF version]. London: Routledge (Original work published 1997).

Rosanvallon, P. (2008). *Counter-Democracy: Politics in an Age of Distrust* (A. Goldhammer, Trans.). Cambridge: Cambridge University Press.

Ross, A. (2009). *Nice Work If You Can Get It: Life and Labor in Precarious Times*. New York: New York University Press.

Roszak, T. (1969). *The Making of a Counter Culture: Reflections on the Technocratic Society and Its Youthful Opposition*. New York: Doubleday & Co.

Rousseau, J.-J. (2002). *The Social Contract and the First and Second Discourses* (S. Dunn, Ed.). New Haven, CT: Yale University Press.

Rushe, D. (2013, August 14) Google: Don't expect privacy when sending to gmail. *The Guardian*. Retrieved from: http://www.theguardian.com/technology/2013/aug/14/google-gmail-users-privacy-email-lawsuit [Accessed 15 July 2015].

Ryan, C. and Hall, M.C. (2001). *Sex Tourism: Marginal People and Liminalities*. London: Routledge.

Saldanha, A. (2007). *Psychedelic White: Goa Trance and the Viscosity of Race*. Minneapolis: University of Minnesota Press.

Sarcina, G. (2012, February 16–22). Comme un vol de cols blancs … *Courrier international*, 1111, 12–13.

Sassen, S. (2005). The repositioning of citizenship and alienage: Emergent subjects and spaces for politics. *Globalizations*, 2(1), 79–94.

———— (2008). *Territory, Authority, Rights: From Medieval to Global Assemblages* (Rev. ed.). Princeton: Princeton University Press (Original work published 2006).

Savage, M. (2014). Piketty's challenge for sociology. *The British Journal of Sociology*, 65 (4), 591–606.

Schlichter, D.S. (2014). *Paper Money Collapse: The Folly of Elastic Money and the Coming Monetary Breakdown* (2nd ed.). Hoboken, NJ: John Wiley & Sons (Original work published 2011).

Schwartz, B., Ward, A., Monterosso, J., Lyubomirsky, S. White, K., and Lehman, D.R. (2002). Maximizing versus satisficing: Happiness is a matter of choice. *Journal of Personality and Social Psychology*, 83(5), 1,178–97.

Shankar, A., Cherrier, H., and Canniford, R. (2006). Consumer empowerment: a Foucauldian interpretation. *European Journal of Marketing*, 40(9/10), 1,013–30.

Sheller, M. (2004). Demobilizing and remobilizing Caribbean paradise. In J. Urry and M. Sheller (Eds), *Tourism Mobilities: Places to Play, Places in Play* (pp. 13–21). London: Routledge.

———— (2011). Mobilities. *Sociopedia.isa*. Retrieved from: http://www.sagepub.net/isa/resources/pdf/Mobility.pdf [Accessed 15 July 2015].

Sherlock, K. (2001). Revisiting the concept of hosts and guests. *Tourist Studies*, 1(3), 271–95.

Shields, R. (Ed.) (1992). *Lifestyle Shopping: The Subject of Consumption*. London: Routledge.

Simmel, G. (2004). *The Philosophy of Money* (3rd enlarged ed.) (D. Frisby, Ed., K. Mengelberg, D. Frisby, and T. Bottomore, Trans.). London: Routledge (Original work published 1900).

Simons, J. (1995). *Foucault and the Political*. London: Routledge.

Skrbis, Z., Kendall, G., and Woodward, I. (2004). Locating cosmopolitanism between humanist ideal and grounded social category. *Theory, Culture & Society*, 21(6), 115–36.

Smart, B. (1982). Foucault, sociology, and the problem of human agency. *Theory and Society*, 11(2), 121–41.

Smith, V. (Ed.) (1989). *Hosts and Guests: The Anthropology of Tourism* (2nd ed.). Philadelphia: University of Pennsylvania Press (Original work published 1977).

Snedden, M. (2013, August 30). When work is a non-stop vacation. *BBC*. Retrieved from: http://www.bbc.com/capital/story/20130829-when-work-is-a-nonstop-vacation [Accessed 15 July 2015].

Söderström, O., Randería, S., Ruedin, S., D'Amato, D.G., and Panese, F. (2013). Of mobilities and moorings: Critical perspectives. In O. Söderström, S. Randería, D. Ruedin, D.G. D'Amato, and F. Panese (Eds), *Critical Mobilities* (pp. 1–21). Lausanne: EPFL.

Sørensen, A. (2003). Backpacker ethnography. *Annals of Tourism Research*, 30(4), 847–67.

Speed, C. (2008). Are backpackers ethical tourists? In K. Hannam and I. Ateljevic (Eds), *Backpacker Tourism: Concepts and Profiles* (pp. 54–81). Clevedon: Channel View Publications.

Spivak, G. (1990). *The Post-Colonial Critic: Interviews, Strategies, Dialogues*. London: Routledge.

Standing, G. (2011). *The Precariat: The New Dangerous Class*. London: Bloomsbury.

Taylor, C. (1984). Foucault on freedom and truth. *Political Theory*, 12(2), 152–83.

The World Bank (2006). Poverty Overview. The World Bank. Retrieved from: http://www.worldbank.org/en/topic/poverty/overview [Accessed 15 July 2015].

Thompson, C.S. (2007). *The Suffering Traveller and the Romantic Imagination*. Oxford: Clarendon Press.

Thompson, J.B. (1989). The theory of structuration. In D. Held and J.B. Thompson (Eds), *Social Theory of Modern Societies: Anthony Giddens and His Critics* (pp. 56–76). Cambridge: Cambridge University Press.

Torkington, K. (2012). Place and lifestyle migration: The discursive construction of 'glocal' place-identity. *Mobilities*, 7(1), 71–92.

Torpey, J, (2000). *The Invention of the Passport: Surveillance, Citizenship and the State*. Cambridge: Cambridge University Press.

Travel Club [website] (2013). Retrieved from: http://www.thetravelclub.org [Accessed 15 July 2015].

UN Millennium Project (2006). Fast Facts: The Faces of Poverty. Retrieved from: http://www.unmillenniumproject.org/resources/fastfacts_e.htm [Accessed 15 July 2015].

United Nations (2013) 232 Million International Migrants Living Abroad Worldwide – New UN Global Migration Statistics Reveal. Department of Economic and Social Affairs. Retrieved from: http://esa.un.org/unmigration/wallchart2013.htm [Accessed 15 July 2015].

Uriely, N. (2001). 'Travelling workers' and 'working tourists': Variations across the interaction between work and tourism. *International Journal of Tourism Research*, 3, 1–8.

Urry, J. (1982). Duality of structure: Some critical issues. *Theory, Culture & Society*, 1, 100–106.

——— (2001). *Sociology beyond Societies: Mobilities for the Twenty-First Century* [PDF version]. London: Routledge (Original work published 2000).

———— (2002a). Mobility and proximity. *Sociology*, 36(2), 255–74.

———— (2002b). *The Tourist Gaze: Leisure and Travel in Contemporary Societies* (2nd ed.). London: Sage Publications (Original work published 1990).

———— (2003). *Global Complexity*. Cambridge: Polity Press.

———— (2007). *Mobilities*. Cambridge: Polity Press.

Urry, J. and Sheller, M. (2004). Places to play, places in play. In J. Urry and M. Sheller (Eds), *Tourism Mobilities: Places to Play, Places in Play* (pp. 1–10). London: Routledge.

Van Den Abbeele, G. (1992). *Travel as Metaphor: From Montaigne to Rousseau*. Minneapolis: University of Minnesota Press.

van Dijk, J.A.G.M. (2006). *The Network Society: Social Aspects of New Media* (2nd ed.). London: Sage Publications (Original work published 1999).

van Dijk, T.A. (2006). Discourse and manipulation. *Discourse Society*, 17, 359–88.

———— (2008). *Discourse and Context: A Sociocognitive Approach*. Cambridge: Cambridge University Press.

Veal, A.J. (2001). Leisure, culture and lifestyle. *Society and Leisure*, 24(2), 359–76.

Veblen, T. (2014). *The Theory of the Leisure Class: An Economic Study of Institutions* [PDF format]. Retrieved from: http://oll.libertyfund.org/titles/1657 [Accessed 15 July 2015] (Originally published 1899).

Vogt, J.W. (1976). Wandering: Youth and travel behaviour. *Annals of Tourism Research*, 4(1), 25–41.

Vollmann, W.T. (2009). *Riding Toward Everywhere*. New York: HarperCollins.

Walters, W. (2004). Secure borders, safe haven, domopolitics. *Citizenship Studies*, 8(3), 237–60.

Walzer, M. (1986). The politics of Michel Foucault. In Hoy, D.C. (Ed.), *Foucault: A Critical Reader*. Oxford: Basil Blackwell (Original work published 1982).

Warnes, A.M., Friedrich, K., Kellaher, L., and Torres, S. (2004). The diversity and welfare of older migrants in Europe. *Ageing and Society*, 24(3), 307–26.

Warnes, A.M., King, R., Williams, A., and Patterson, G. (1999). The well-being of British expatriate retirees in southern Europe. *Ageing and Society*, 19(6), 717–40.

Warnes, A.M. and Williams, A. (2006). Older migrants in Europe: A new focus for migration studies. *Journal of Ethnic and Migration Studies*, 32(8), 1,257–81.

Wearing, S., Stevenson, D., and Young, T. (2010). *Tourist Cultures: Identity, Place and the Traveller*. London: Sage Publications.

Weber, Max (1978). *Economy and Society: An Outline of Interpretive Sociology* (G. Roth and C. Wittich, Eds). Berkeley: University of California Press (Original work published 1922).

———— (2005). *The Protestant Ethic and the Spirit of Capitalism* [PDF version]. London: Routledge (Original work published 1905).

Weber, Marten (2013, February 27). The modern nomad. *The Huffington Post*. Retrieved from: http://www.huffingtonpost.com/marten-weber/the-modern-nomad_b_2715483.html [Accessed 15 July 2015].

Welk, P. (2004). The beaten track: Anti-tourism as an element of backpacker identity construction. In G. Richards and J. Wilson (Eds), *The Global Nomad:*

Backpacker Travel in Theory and Practice (pp. 77–91). Clevedon: Channel View Publications.

Western (s.v.). In *Encyclopædia Britannica* online. Retrieved from: http://www. britannica.com/EBchecked/topic/640481/western [Accessed 15 July 2015].

White, N.R. and White, P.B. (2007). Home and away: Tourists in a connected world. *Annals of Tourism Research*, 34(1), 88–104.

White, T. (2008). Sex workers and tourism: A case study of Kovalam beach, India. In J. Cochrane (Ed.), *Asian Tourism: Growth and Change* (pp. 285–97). Amsterdam: Elsevier.

Williams, A. and Baláž, V. (2015). Tourism risk and uncertainty: theoretical reflections. *Journal of Travel Research*, 54(3), 271–87.

Williams, A. and Hall, M. (2000). Tourism and migration: New relationships between production and consumption. *Tourism Geographies: An International Journal of Tourism Space, Place and Environment*, 2(1), 5–27.

Williams, R. (1977). *Marxism and Literature*. Oxford: Oxford University Press.

Wilson, J., Fisher, D., and Moore, K. (2009). The OE goes 'home': Cultural aspects of a working holiday experience. *Tourist Studies*, 9(1), 3–21.

Wolff, J. (1996). *An Introduction to Political Philosophy*. Oxford: Oxford University Press.

Worsley, P. (1990). Theory, culture and post-industrialist society. In M. Featherstone (Ed.), *Global Culture: Nationalism, Globalization and Modernity* (pp. 83–95). London: Sage Publications.

Wright, E.O. (1989). Models of historical trajectory: An assessment of Giddens's critique of Marxism. In D. Held and J.B. Thompson (Eds), *Social Theory of Modern Societies: Anthony Giddens and His Critics* (pp. 77–102). Cambridge: Cambridge University Press.

WYSE Travel Confederation (2013). New Horizons III: A global study of the youth and student traveller 2012 [Executive summary]. Retrieved from: http://www.slideshare.net/WYSETravelConfederation/new-horizonsiii-v7execsummaryv4s [Accessed 15 July 2015].

Žižek, S. (2000). *The Ticklish Subject: The Absent Centre of Political Ontology*. London: Verso.

Index

For Product Safety Concerns and Information please contact our EU
representative GPSR@taylorandfrancis.com
Taylor & Francis Verlag GmbH, Kaufingerstraße 24, 80331 München, Germany

www.ingramcontent.com/pod-product-compliance
Ingram Content Group UK Ltd.
Pitfield, Milton Keynes, MK11 3LW, UK
UKHW020948180425
457613UK00019B/579